Danny Morrison

HUNGER STRIKE – STAIL OCRAIS

1974 & 1976
Sasana/England

Michael Gaughan
died 3 June 1974
Parkhurst Prison

Frank Stagg
died 12 February 1976
Wakefield Prison

1981
Éirinn/Ireland

Bobby Sands
died 5 May 1981

Francis Hughes
died 12 May 1981

Raymond McCreesh
died 21 May 1981

Patsy O'Hara
died 21 May 1981

Joe McDonnell
died 8 July 1981

Martin Hurson
died 13 July 1981

Kevin Lynch
died 1 August 1981

Kieran Doherty
died 2 August 1981

Thomas McElwee
died 8 August 1981

Micky Devine
died 20 August 1981

Dedication

To the families of Irish republican prisoners who died on
hunger strike, 1974–1976–1981

Michael Gaughan
Frank Stagg
Bobby Sands MP
Francis Hughes
Patsy O'Hara
Raymond McCreesh
Joe McDonnell
Martin Hurson
Kevin Lynch
Kieran Doherty TD
Thomas McElwee
Micky Devine

EDITED BY DANNY MORRISON

HUNGER
STRIKE

Reflections

Elsinor

First published in 2006 by Brandon

This edition 2019
by
Elsinor Verlag (Elsinor Press), Coesfeld, Germany
Email: info@elsinor.de

Photographs reproduced by permission of *An Phoblacht/Republican News*

Cover design by Seán Mistéil
Printed in Germany
ISBN 978-3-939483-54-0

Contents

INTRODUCTION
Danny Morrison

MANY YEARS AFTER THE ENDING OF THE HUNGER STRIKES AND BLANKET PROTEST a prison officer said:

> "At first we thought they were dirty animals. The stench was incredible. Our stomachs turned when we went near the cells and we couldn't understand how anyone could live in such filth. But eventually there was some grudging respect for those on the protest. They were incredibly determined. I didn't agree with what they were doing but you had to admire them for sticking it out. At first I thought it would only last a few days, or a week or two at the most, but they kept going for years and then queued up to give their lives. I don't think I would have been able to do it, no matter what the cause."*

The blanket protest lasted for five years; the no-wash/no slop-out or 'dirty' protest for three years; the first hunger strike for 53 days; and the second hunger strike, when ten prisoners died, an incredible seven months.

Kieran Nugent, from Belfast, was the first republican prisoner sentenced and sent to the new H-Blocks. He was stripped naked, refused to put on the uniform and was beaten. His mattress and bedding were removed. The only thing in the cell was a blanket which he draped over his shoulder and thus began the blanket protest. On one occasion, the governor came into his cell and said, "We are going to break you."

Nugent recalled: "He stood there shouting at me. Gave me a slap in the face and then he stood back and watched the other warders beat me up."

---

*[pp 256-257, Inside The Maze – The Untold Story of the Northern Ireland Prison Service by Chris Ryder. Methuen 2000. ISBN 0 413 75240 2]

Over the years Nugent was joined by hundreds of others. In 1978 the prisoners began the no-wash/no slop-out protest which was to last until 1 March 1981, the day that Bobby Sands began his hunger strike.

Throughout the protest the prisoners suffered a variety of beatings, brutal anal searches whilst forced to squat over a mirror, solitary confinement, periods on a 'Number 1' bread and water diet (ruled to be illegal by the European Court of Human Rights) and loss of remission for each day on protest. Punishments also included loss of visits, letters, parcels, exercise, association and recreation, access to newspapers, magazines, books and radios. Each cell was supplied with The Bible. In the cold weather the prisoners stood on it to insulate their feet from the bare floor. They also wrote communications (known as 'comms'), and Bobby Sands some of his poetry, on the margins of the Bibles' fine Indian paper and on rice (cigarette) paper which folded small and was ideal for smuggling. Sometimes they smoked leaves from the Bible when they had no papers in which to roll their contraband tobacco. The prisoners defied the authorities and secreted pens, papers, tobacco and even small crystal set radios, inside their own bodies.

The first major breakthrough in highlighting the conditions came after Archbishop Tomás Ó Fiaich's visit in August 1978. He said he was shocked by "the inhuman conditions" and continued:

> one would hardly allow an animal to remain in such conditions, let alone a human being. The nearest approach to it that I have seen was the spectacle of hundreds of homeless people living in sewer-pipes in the slums of Calcutta… From talking to them it is evident that they intend to continue their protest indefinitely and it seems they prefer to face death rather than submit to being classed as criminals. Anyone with the least knowledge of Irish history knows how deeply rooted this attitude is in our country's past.

The British were unmoved and condemned Ó Fiaich's comments.

Few in public life in Ireland, few journalists, artists, writers or poets, could claim ignorance of the H-Blocks after Archbishop Ó Fiaich's visit to the jail.

Yet, little or no investigative journalism about developments in the northern prisons came out of the state broadcasting organisation, RTE. Proposed inquiries were throttled at birth and the rigid application of state censorship under which republicans were banned from radio and television was policed by a powerful clique of revisionists, associated with the almost now defunct Workers Party. There was literally such a climate of intimidation that few journalists dissented from the orthodoxy: 'IRA evil/Brits good/unionists misunderstood'.

Within the British media a few conscientious journalists, to their credit, probed the abuses in the interrogation centres; made programmes about the H-Blocks; the RUC's shoot-to-kill policy; challenged Thatcher's (1988) broadcasting ban; and eventually examined collusion between British forces in the North and their surrogates in loyalist paramilitary organisations.

What was the response of Irish artists, writers and poets (Shelley's 'unacknowledged legislators of the world') to the imagery of "people living in sewer-pipes in the slums of Calcutta"?

By and large, a deafening silence, a blank canvas.

In *Warrenpoint*, the critic Denis Donoghue satirically notes: "Nationalism is a fine flower, so long as it grows in Israel, Tibet, Poland and Lithuania."

His observation was a censure of the revisionists and those whose passion for human rights or national liberation is in direct proportion to the distance oppression is from home, the farther the revolutionary struggle is from Ireland.

Bobby Sands in his poems was even more critical, asking where were those in society who were meant to uphold or express in culture some defence of the oppressed? Many of them were more than eloquent when it came to condemning the IRA. But somehow they lost their voices when it came to condemning British violence and the brutality within the interrogation centres which were the first part of the conveyor belt, leading to the Diplock Courts and then the H-Blocks. He wrote:

> The Men of Art have lost their heart,
> They dream within their dreams.
> Their magic sold for price of gold
> Amidst a people's screams.

They sketch the moon and capture bloom
With genius, so they say.
But n'er they sketch the quaking wretch
Who lies in Castlereagh.
The poet's word is sweet as bird,
Romantic's tale and prose.
Of stars above and gentle love
And fragrant breeze that blows.
But write they not a single jot
Of beauty tortured sore.
Don't wonder why such men can lie,
For poets are no more.

They simply sat on the fence or sniped from it while throwing their hands up in theatrical despair at the 'intransigence' of all sides. This was disingenuous: it was the prisoners who were defenceless and had their backs to the wall – not Thatcher.

Thus it was an honourable minority of artists, writers and poets that bore witness.

Musicians like Christy Moore, Donal Lunny, the band Moving Hearts, balladeers like the Wolfe Tones, artists like Bobby Ballagh, actors like Stephen Rea, and a small number of other musicians, poets and writers were there 'before' and 'after'. Ballagh's 1980 image of, prophetically, a dead blanket man on a mortuary slab (on our cover) was first used on the cover of Tim Pat Coogan's book, *On The Blanket*, which was itself an important contribution to raising public awareness about the protest.

There were, of course, mainstream works written during or informed by this grim period, and published later.

A discussion of sorts about the role or responsibility of the poet in a conflict situation arises in Seamus Heaney's *Station Island* (1984) when the poet self-consciously struggles with a sense of guilt. It is a narrative about a pilgrimage to Lough Derg – St Patrick's Purgatory – where the poet fasts (a metaphor for hunger-striking) and meditates.

Like Dante's wanderings through Hell and Purgatory, disparate souls address the poet.

The resonances are actually quite powerful because in *The Divine Comedy* one of those to address Dante is the spirit of Count Ugolino, who had fought for the sovereignty of Pisa. In 1289, in the month of March, which also happens to be the month when Bobby Sands began his hunger strike, Ugolino was arrested and thrown into prison along with his two sons and grandsons. The door was sealed; they were deprived of food and starved to death.

In *Station Island* the ghost of a friend of the poet, a shopkeeper (presumably, William Strathearn) who was assassinated by loyalists, addresses him. A dead hunger striker (presumably, Francis Hughes) also makes an apparition, as does that famous but unnamed self-exile James Joyce.

To Strathearn, the poet apologises:

> "Forgive the way I have lived indifferent –
> forgive my timid circumspect involvement."

He is told there is nothing to forgive – which must be very reassuring.

Francis Hughes describes his slow death, how his blanket protest is like a transcendental ambush. But Heaney associates his death with decay; there is nothing life-affirming about his sacrifice. Those responsible for Hughes' predicament, and the objective of Hughes' hunger strike (which can be depoliticised into a demand for dignity), are not referred to. Instead, the poet thrashes out:

> "I hate how quick I was to know my place.
> I hate where I was born, hate everything
> That made me biddable and unforthcoming".

Like Dante's *ascent* from Hell, Heaney is slowly rising… to an important conclusion. Joyce tells him:

> "Your obligation
> is not discharged by any common rite.
> What you must do must be done on your own
> …

"let others wear the sackcloth and the ashes...
"'That subject people stuff is a cod's game,
infantile, like your peasant pilgrimage."

Shriven and advised by Joyce the poet breathes a sigh of relief. But back in that real, other world from which Heaney hailed, Ian Paisley, twenty five years later, was still demanding that republicans be forced to wear sackcloth and ashes in public (that is, that they publicly 'repent' – a reference from the Old Testament).

Remarkably, in May 2007, Ian Paisley, to universal surprise, entered into the northern executive in a power-sharing arrangement with Sinn Féin's Martin McGuinness.

The protests which began in the H-Blocks and Armagh Women's Prison in the autumn of 1976 were caused by the British government reneging on an agreement it had made in 1972 about the status of prisoners convicted in relation to the conflict.

Republicans were in jail was because of the armed struggle in the North. It had grown out of the failure of the civil rights movement, and as a reaction to both the violence of the unionist government and British rule in support of the union. The objective of republicans was Irish independence and they viewed their struggle as a continuation of the fight for freedom which had been subverted by the partition of Ireland in 1921.

The vast majority of the prisoners were young, in their late teens and mid-twenties; were Volunteers of the Irish Republican Army (IRA), sympathisers or supporters of the IRA; while others belonged to the Irish National Liberation Army (INLA).

After the conflict broke out in the North in the early 1970s, arrests and prosecutions led to an exponential growth in the number of convicted republicans held in Belfast Prison (Crumlin Road Jail). When these arrests failed to stem the IRA campaign the British government in August 1971 introduced internment without trial, exclusively against the nationalist community, despite violence from loyalists. Hundreds of republican suspects were imprisoned in various jails. These included a former RAF base called The Long Kesh, eight miles from Belfast; a converted ship, the Maidstone, anchored in Belfast Lough; Armagh Jail; another prison camp at Magilligan, County Derry; and Crumlin Road Jail.

The internees were not required to do menial prison work or wear prison garb – grey denim trousers and jacket, black boots, blue and white striped shirt. They were not regimented by the prison authorities, nor obeyed commands according to a prison number, but organised and supervised their own daily regime. They had more rights than sentenced prisoners but they had no release dates and were subjected to regular aggressive military searches. They slept on bunk beds in Nissen huts, situated in barbed-wire enclosed cages (which the authorities called 'compounds'). In fact, they had something equivalent to prisoner-of-war or political status.

Using the leverage of this anomaly – two sets of republican prisoners being treated in different ways – the sentenced republican prisoners in Crumlin Road went on hunger strike in May 1972 demanding political status.

Thirty-five days into the strike and before there were any deaths, the British conceded 'special category status', which was political status in all but name. The republican prisoners, numbering around eighty, including those in Armagh Women's Prison, and about forty convicted loyalists who also benefited, were allowed to organise themselves in the same way as the internees. The sentenced prisoners in Crumlin Road Jail were eventually moved to their own cages in a section of Long Kesh Camp, where their numbers swelled to several hundred over the years.

The British army was responsible for the security around the outside of Long Kesh. Soldiers and guard dogs patrolled the perimeter of the cages and soldiers in watch towers monitored the activities of the prisoners. There were also regular searches by prison staff, supported by the military, for tunnels and tools of escape. The huts within each cage were locked by prison staff at night and unlocked each morning. Magilligan Prison Camp had a similar lay-out and regime. Female internees and sentenced prisoners in Armagh Jail had political status but were held in traditional cell blocks. Within the jails the republican prisoners, who considered themselves as revolutionaries and part of a guerrilla army, used their time to educate themselves and studied history, politics, literature and languages.

In the Twenty-Six-Counties the Offences Against The State Act, authorising the use of non-jury courts, was re-enacted in 1972 as part of the crackdown on the IRA and its supporters. Those convicted once again organised republican structures within the jails, planned escapes, and organised education classes. One IRA prisoner, Tom Smith, was shot dead attempting to escape from Portlaoise Prison in 1975. Often, there were confrontations between inmates and the authorities over prison conditions. However, successive governments never attempted to criminalise the prisoners in the way, for example, it had been tried in the 1940s when prisoners resisted and died on hunger and thirst strike. Republican prisoners were not required to wear a prison uniform and could associate with each other as a defined group.

Within Britain itself – where there was no internment – republican prisoners were initially small in number, were badly mistreated and often the victims of racist beatings and intimidation. Later, when they were better organised and relatively stronger in number they were segregated from the general prison population in special control units. But in those early days there were several hunger strikes, mostly around the demand for repatriation to a prison closer to home. Two republican prisoners were to die on hunger strike: Michael Gaughan in June 1974 and Frank Stagg (on his fourth hunger strike) in February 1976.

This new, 2019 edition opens with a powerful account by Frank's brother George Stagg of Michael and Frank's hunger strikes, their deaths and the disgraceful hijacking of Frank's body and burial by the Dublin government under tonnes of concrete in Leigue Cemetery, Ballina.

By granting political status in 1972 the British government settled the prisons in the North for a while. However, the powerful image of Long Kesh as a POW camp irked British politicians and contradicted their government's propaganda. Ministers depicted the IRA's campaign as 'terrorism', which had no justification, no mandate and no support.

But to outside observers Britain was imprisoning captured enemy combatants with a status that suggested some legitimacy (and also occasionally engaged in secret contacts and explorative talks with the IRA and/or Sinn Féin). The observers also noted that British propaganda was no different from that used by British administrations dealing with national liberation organisations and insurgencies in colonial confrontations throughout the former empire. When it became expedient the renowned 'terrorist' leaders would, no doubt, be welcome in No 10 Downing Street as 'statesmen'.

In 1975/76 the British government launched a major three-pronged offensive.

Under 'Ulsterisation' it began scaling down the numbers of British troops deployed in the North. Fewer troops in the firing line meant fewer British army fatalities which in turn helped stem any domestic, anti-war or troops out sentiment (which the IRA had hoped its campaign would generate). Troops were replaced by members of the local Royal Ulster Constabulary (RUC) and the Ulster Defence Regiment (UDR). Predictably, increased casualties among the RUC and UDR, whose members were overwhelmingly drawn from the unionist community, allowed Britain to depict the conflict as sectarian, the 'Catholic IRA' killing the 'Protestant RUC' with Britain as 'honest broker' acting to keep apart the two 'warring, religious communities'.

Under 'Normalisation' the RUC was to be delegated primacy in security matters. In other words, the situation was to be presented as a difficult 'policing' problem. Simultaneously, the British pushed for increased talks between the constitutional political parties to agree upon that elusive objective – devolution and an 'internal solution'.

In preparation for the third prong of this offensive, 'Criminalisation', British ministers began to claim that the nature of the conflict had changed. 'Godfathers of violence' were now 'lining their own pockets' and the IRA was 'masterminding a criminal conspiracy'.

Editorial and feature writers, particularly in the North, took the cue – and took sides. Without question they adopted and echoed the rhetoric uttered by direct rule ministers.

The Emergency Provisions Act, which allowed for non-jury, single-judge Diplock Court trials, became central to the new offensive. The burden of proof was now shifted to the accused who had to prove his or her innocence, and statements (most of which were obtained by ill-treatment) became admissible as evidence. Most of these statements were taken in special interrogation centres by a select group of eighty RUC detectives. Indeed, up to 80% of all convictions were subsequently based on self-incriminating statements made by prisoners, many of whom were beaten during interrogation. It was years before campaigns by human rights organisations successfully highlighted and exposed these abuses.

In 1975, Long Kesh (which the British had earlier renamed 'The Maze' in an attempt to escape the obloquy and connotations of brutality associated with the prison) was expanded, with a wall dividing the old from the new. Eight new prison blocks designed in the shape of an 'H', with four wings containing up to 26 cells in each and an administrative area connecting them, were built.

The government announced that anyone arrested for a scheduled offence (a wide range of defined activities related to subversion) from 1 March 1976 would be considered a criminal and would be sent to the new regime in the H-Blocks or to Armagh Women's Prison without political status.

There was a major contradiction in the British position in that Section 31 of the Emergency Provisions Act (and, later, the Prevention of Terrorism Act) defined scheduled offences and 'terrorism' as "the use of violence for *political* ends" (my italics).

Having been arrested under special laws, been questioned in special interrogation centres, been tried in special courts with special rules of evidence, the prisoners were told when they arrived at the specially-built H-Blocks there was nothing 'special' about them.

Even *with* political status life in prison was harsh. At times of major tension in the jail or after specific confrontations the IRA and loyalist paramilitaries threatened some prison officers and carried out some attacks. But up until 1976 no prison officer had been killed as a result of working in the prisons. In the main, prison officers were not singled out by the IRA for attack. In 1974, after the cages of Long Kesh were burned down by republican prisoners, the British army shot dead an internee, Hugh Coney, who was trying to escape. And other prisoners died through medical neglect as a result of prison staff not responding to emergency calls.

But it was not until April 1976 – a month after the withdrawal of political status – that the first prison officer, Patrick Dillon, died at the hands of the IRA. During the protest one third of the prison officers who worked in the H-Blocks had been brought in from Britain on special bounties, and most of them were former servicemen.

Although Britain was to eventually fail in its objective of forcing the prisoners to accept criminal status, it was not before a heavy price was paid. Those who suffered were the prisoners, their families, protestors and civilians on the outside (including children and a mother killed by plastic bullets, and a milkman and his son whose vehicle crashed into a lamppost during a nationalist riot), and prison officers and their families. All of them were caught up in a clash of wills which one governor was later to describe as "a battle for the false aim of criminalisation that was always going to fail."

Even the IRA's chief opponents within the British army privately rejected the notion that the IRA was 'a criminal conspiracy', or a movement without support. Writing a secret assessment of the IRA in 1978 Brigadier James Glover, the most senior army officer on the Defence Intelligence Staff, stated that the IRA was representative of the nationalist working class, "of which they [Volunteers] form a substantial part [and] do not fit the stereotype of criminality which the authorities have from time to time attempted to attach to them."

A few months after the blanket protest began their families formed Relatives Action Committees (which Mary Nelis describes). Later, a National H-Block/Armagh solidarity committee rallied in support of political status. Leading members of this committee were assassinated by loyalists, more than likely in collusion with British forces, given what we know now.

The prisoners set out five demands. These were:

The right to wear their own clothes.
The right to abstain from penal labour.
The right to free association.
The right to educational and recreational facilities.
Restoration of lost remission as a result of the protest.

The Labour government, which had introduced criminalisation, was replaced by the Conservatives under their leader, the implacable Margaret Thatcher, in 1979.

In 1980, the IRA publicly called a halt to its reprisals against prison officers to facilitate mediation attempts by the all-Ireland primate, Cardinal Ó Fiaich. However, after several months of talks the British government refused to budge and thus began the 1980 hunger strike by seven prisoners.

It lasted 53 days. During it, there was a marked increase in the mobilisation of public support. Thousands demonstrated throughout Ireland. Many public figures were forced to respond. Some, including the Irish government, adopted the stance that it was difficult if not impossible for Thatcher to act under pressure. If only the prisoners would end their fast the government would put pressure on the British to change its policy.

The hunger strike, led by Brendan Hughes, ended dramatically on 18 December. It was called off by Brendan Hughes to save the life of Sean McKenna who was close to death, at a time when the British became involved in secret contacts with the republican leadership. The British stated that they sought a resolution, but the hunger strike was called off while a paper containing proposals was in transit, and before it reached the prisoners. (This subsequent realisation by the Northern Ireland Office and the prison administration could only have intensified their intransigence and informed their view that no offer need have been made.) A British representative (code named 'Mountain Climber') supplied a document outlining the proposals to Fr Brendan Meagher (code named 'the Angel') at a meeting in Belfast's International Airport (which Meagher describes here).

The British side had been promising to progressively introduce a liberal prison regime. However, as soon as the hunger strike ended, they reneged and the 'concerned' politicians and prelates all but disappeared, some, no doubt, smug with the impression that the morale of the protestors and the back of the protest had been broken: a 'defeat' for the Republican Movement. The administration dug in its heels, insisted that the prisoners must wear prison-issue clothing, and made it impossible for the prison leader Bobby Sands to work out a compromise.

Mary Doyle, herself a hunger striker in 1980, writes about the anger and frustration the prisoners felt.

And so, the prisoners announced a second hunger strike, led by Bobby Sands.

In the political literature of the period and in media references Bobby Sands' name tends to overshadow his nine comrades. (Some of the writers in this book refer to Bobby Sands' name being raised by a prisoner facing a death sentence in the Philippines, by a PLO teenager on the streets of West Beirut, and by a Russian at the grave of Ezra Pound in Venice. ANC prisoners on Robben Island when planning a hunger strike used the expression "doing a Sands.")

Bobby's name is highlighted for many reasons. He was a jail veteran, already a well-established leader and prison spokesperson. He was a writer and a poet. He devised the strategy of the staggered hunger strike. He became MP for Fermanagh and South Tyrone in that extraordinary by-election. He was the first to die at a time when the international coverage was at its height, and his iconic image, that smile, that long flowing hair, became instantly recognisable, like Ché Guevara's.

But in the counties, the local areas, the home places, the townlands and streets of the other hunger strikers, each local hunger striker – Francis, Raymond, Patsy, Joe, Martin, Kevin, Kieran, Tom and Micky – is immortalised on the lips of old and young alike, and a fierce pride in the memory of each man and the detail of each man's life is passed down the generations. Similarly in Mayo where the names Michael Gaughan and Frank Stagg are remembered with pride and awe.

During the hunger strike there were many attempts at mediation, including one by the Irish Commission for Justice and Peace in July 1981. This occurred at a time when the British were again in touch with the Republican Movement through 'a back channel'. While the British representative suggested there could be a settlement those responsible for prisons refused to put the details of the offer formally to the prisoners and in a way that was verifiable. No deal thus emerged.

The hunger strike continued but as a weapon was neutered by relatives of the strikers who increasingly began authorising medical intervention once the prisoners lapsed into a coma. Terry George, who made the film *Some Mother's Son* on this sensitive subject, describes what influenced him and how he brought his work to the screen.

The prisoners ended the hunger strike on 3 October 1981. Within two weeks the British conceded their right to wear their own clothes. The prisoners were united and organised and fought on for the rest of their demands through sabotaging the workshops and using their numbers to establish segregation.

Within two years the prisoners had political status and the IRA command structure within the jail was recognised by the administration. In the words of a former governor, they (the prison authorities) "learned at a terrible price that you could only run a prison like the Maze with prisoners like that with their consent."

The final admission of the political nature of the prisoners was the repatriation of all republican prisoners in English jails back to Ireland (the demand of Michael Gaughan and Frank Stagg in 1974 and 1976) and their early release, along with the political prisoners North and South, under the 1998 Belfast Agreement.

Almost forty years after the deaths of the ten H-Block prisoners, their sacrifice and that of their comrades, continue to have an impact in Ireland and further afield.

Certainly the hunger strike's most initial tangible effects were to re-energise and increase support for the Republican Movement, and inspire many people to join the IRA and Sinn Féin. The stupidity of British Prime Minister Margaret Thatcher's depiction of the hunger strike as "the IRA's last card" was there for the world to see, though not understood by her herself.

Until 1981 republicans were highly suspicious of electoral politics, with good reason given the history of splits on the issue, particularly on the subject of abstentionism. Electoral politics, they felt, were synonymous with constitutional politics. Were it not for the elections of Bobby Sands to Westminster and Kieran Doherty and Paddy Agnew to Leinster House it is doubtful if Sinn Féin could have made its transition to embracing electoralism so smoothly. The election of Kieran Doherty and Paddy Agnew broke single party dominance of Leinster House by a Fianna Fáil government and ushered in the era of coalition governments.

For northern nationalists, 1981 set in train a growing confidence which had been absent before that period. Today, nationalist morale is buoyant despite the protracted nature of the peace process and many disappointments.

Former prisoners, blanket men, surviving hunger strikers and escapees went on to become Sinn Féin negotiators and in impressive numbers were elected to office at council level, to the northern Assembly, the Dáil and Westminster. In May 2019, Martina Anderson, who spent over thirteen years in prison, mostly served in England, was, again, elected to the European parliament, having outpolled her DUP rival in first preferences, in an election dominated by the issue of Brexit and the threat it poses to the Irish peace process and the Irish economy.

For many, the 1981 hunger strike is the historic event of the North since the foundation of the state in 1921. Indeed, many republicans refer to the hunger strike as their '1916'.

The hunger strike remains of enduring interest to Irish people, historians, political analysts and students. Several books about the period have been published, including a biography on Bobby Sands by Denis O'Hearn, *Nothing But An Unfinished Song*, and, of course, *Ten Men Dead* by the late David Beresford, first published over thirty years ago, continues to sell and has never been out of print. Here, Beresford tells of how he came to write that book which has been described as the definitive account of the hunger strikes. On film, Steve McQueen's *Hunger*, with Michael Fassbinder as Bobby Sands, won the prestigious Caméra d'Or at the 2008 Cannes Film Festival, and a host of international awards. In 2016 Brendan Byrne's documentary, *66 Days*, was broadcast on Netflix to major critical acclaim.

The first edition of this book was published by the Bobby Sands Trust on the twenty-fifth anniversary of the hunger strike in 2006 and included the views and reminiscences of a variety of writers, poets, journalists, musicians, activists, critics, filmmakers, playwrights, and broadcasters. All contributors gave their services for free. Some were/are activists. Some, like the writer Eugene McCabe, are pacifists. Bill Brown gives a perspective from the unionist community, Pedram Moallemian as a teenager in Tehran watching events unfold in Belfast.

I look back at 1981 with extreme sadness but with astonishment at the epic nature of that prison struggle and at the courage of those men and women.

The British government, the RUC, the courts, the prison administration thought it could criminalise my generation of republican patriots by breaking the prisoners.

They took away their freedom, then their clothes, shoes and socks and locked them up for twenty-three hours a day. Then they took away the walk around the prison yard in fresh air, under blue skies. They took away their smokes – that small precious allowance of tobacco which in every prison steadies and calms nerves and makes the day endurable. They took away their beds. When this didn't break them they took away the light that streamed through the window. They took away the space under the door. They took away the sound of music, poetry books and literature, photographs of loved ones, letters home, their visits… their very lives.

Leaving them with nothing.

Or so they thought.

Danny Morrison, Belfast, 5 May 2019

'FOR YOU, FRANK'

George Stagg

FRANK STAGG DIED ON HUNGER STRIKE IN AN ENGLISH JAIL IN FEBRUARY 1976, less than twenty months after the death on hunger strike of his fellow Mayo man and comrade, Michael Gaughan. Frank's brother, George, tells the incredible story of how Frank's body was hijacked on the orders of a Fine Gael/Labour coalition government and entombed beneath four tonnes of concrete in an unmarked grave, all to deny him his dying wish to be buried beside Michael Gaughan

My father had been in the old IRA and had been arrested in the Tan War and the Civil War. In fact, as a young girl my mother saw him being arrested by the Tans and being marched over to the barracks in Hollymount and that's when she first took a shine to him! Frank was the seventh of thirteen children. He had a confident air about himself and would protect us younger ones in school or in football games etc., against any bullying, or the like. He was a very honest man, wouldn't tell you a lie. I looked up to him and I'd have followed him anywhere – which in the end, I had to.

He was a good singer and some of the songs he sang included ones about the characters in Hollymount, and the Toormakeady ambush. He was also an outstanding handballer at which he won Mayo and Connaught championships. He was a top class club footballer as well.

The land around Robeen, the home place, was not bad, but the holdings were very small, about fifteen to thirty acres per family. Many people were forced to emigrate and so Frank left for England in 1960 when he was eighteen. He worked as a construction worker, then on the buses in Coventry and later married a fellow Mayo woman, Bridie Armstrong.

When the troubles broke out in the Six Counties Frank felt he had to do something for the nationalist people. He had become involved with

Sinn Féin, fund-raising, selling ballot tickets, and then he joined an IRA unit in Coventry. He and five others were arrested in a police swoop in 1973 and were charged with conspiracy to cause explosions. He was sentenced to ten years but for refusing to do penal work he spent many long periods in solitary confinement and was on hunger strike on several occasions with similar demands each time – he wanted to be treated as a political prisoner and repatriated to a prison in the Six Counties. He also demanded that his family not be strip-searched on visits. My mother, Mary, in her seventies, was frequently strip-searched and had to run the gauntlet of English National Front protestors outside the prison, screaming abuse into her face. I approached the Irish government to intervene with the British Home Secretary to provide my mother with some protection. I met Garret Fitzgerald. He was very arrogant and dismissive and wanted to lecture me about how Fine Gael dealt with hunger strikers themselves. I got up and said, "I don't want lectures, I want protection for my mother."

Two years before Frank's arrest, Michael Gaughan from Ballina, who was in the London IRA, had been sentenced to seven years for a bank raid. In prison he encountered the Kray twins, East End gangsters, who were bullying a number of Jamaican prisoners. Michael defended the Jamaicans, faced up to the Krays telling them that he had the IRA behind him. They soon backed off!

It was in Parkhurst Prison that Frank met Michael and they became close friends and comrades.

Another group of IRA prisoners from Belfast, including the Price sisters, Hugh Feeney and Gerry Kelly, had begun a hunger strike demanding that they be repatriated closer to home in Ireland to serve their sentences where prisoners had political status. Frank and Michael joined them on hunger strike.

The prisoners were force-fed, every three days over a period of more than two hundred days. Six or seven burly warders would move your bed into the middle of the cell, surround you, force your head back, clamp your mouth with a block of wood and force a tube down your throat and into your stomach. The night before Michael died in Parkhurst in June 1974 the warders had force-fed him, cutting his throat and loosening his teeth. He had no way of protesting or alerting them. Food, or gruel, had been lodged in his lungs. Frank went into see him and Michael said: "I'm dying. They've clogged my lungs."

When Michael's body was brought back to Dublin it lay in state in a Franciscan church where thousands filed past it. During the funeral procession from Dublin to Ballina thousands upon thousands of people lined the streets in all the towns to pay their respects. The Fine Gael/Labour coalition government was furious.

Michael was buried with full IRA military honours in Leigue Cemetery in Ballina.

The hunger strike ended two weeks later after assurances were given that the prisoners would be moved to jails in the Six Counties. But when the four Belfast prisoners were eventually transferred, Frank was not included. The authorities went back on their word. Instead, they moved him to another jail where he began his protest all over again. They said that Frank was not a native of the North but of the South of Ireland, so Frank went back on hunger strike again, his fourth in two years. This time he declared that he would not come off hunger strike until he had arrived at a prison in the North.

I visited him in Wakefield a number of times – one of those old, cold Victorian prisons. My sister, Martha, recalls Frank telling my mother that the warders were mocking him about a letter she (Martha) had written, begging him to come off and saying she didn't want him to die. She was very upset and apologised to Frank on the next visit. My mother told the family that the best way of dealing with differences of opinion is that we support Frank. We hadn't come through what he had suffered and was suffering.

Frank let it be known that in the event of his death he wanted to be buried with military honours and he wanted to be buried in the same grave as his comrade Michael Gaughan. He signed a codicil to his will to that effect a few days before he died. He had hoped that this would pressure the Dublin government – who didn't want another huge funeral like Michael's - to intervene with the British and get them to compromise. Instead, the Irish government asked the British government not to hand his body over to the Republican Movement.

I'm looking at the codicil which Frank wrote and signed:

> "I, Frank Stagg, give all authority to the Provisional Movement to make statements on my behalf. I make this request of my own free will.
> "Derek Highstead is to take full charge of my funeral arrangements.
> "I want full military honours.
> "I leave the route of the funeral to be arranged by the Republican Movement.
> "My demands are the same as always.
> "I request a visit from a doctor named by me.
> "F. Stagg. 7/2/1976. Wakefield Prison."

My mother and Bridie were with Frank in Wakefield Prison when he died in his cell at 6.20am, on 12th February, 1976. He had been sixty two days on hunger strike. He was thirty four. About eight o'clock in the morning I was in my car when I heard the news of his death on the radio. That's how I found out he was dead. I stopped the car, pulled in, and I just sat and thought about him for a while. He was at peace then, because he had gone through some torture.

Make no mistake, Frank did not want to die, he wanted to live. It was now our duty to honour his last wishes to the letter, and unite around him as Mam had said. But that is not how it turned out. Following the inquest and just before the release of his body we had a family meeting in my sister's house in Coventry to finalise arrangements for the removal of Frank's coffin to Ireland. Bridie, Frank's widow, was distraught but had been content that, as per Frank's final written wishes, Derek Highstead and myself would look after all the funeral arrangements. A relative of Bridie's, a priest, who had not supported Frank in any way or even, to my knowledge, up to that point had not shown or expressed any interest in Frank's welfare or situation, suddenly appeared on the scene for the first time since Frank's arrest and began to assert himself. He and my brother Emmet, who would later become a Labour Party TD, and who also had not been a supporter of Frank's republicanism, began to insist on a private funeral, which in reality, was the funeral best suited to the

Irish government but which also, knowingly, denied Frank's final wish. My mother and all the other siblings wanted to abide by Frank's will, that he be given the republican funeral his dying wish had requested and which he had arranged with his comrades.

It was a tense and extremely distressful time for us all - leading to bitterness and division which has only receded with the passage of time.

Meantime, the British police asked for a meeting with myself and Derek at which they insisted that the coffin could only be flown to Ireland in a cargo plane, instead of the hold of a passenger plane with all family mourners on board, as is normal procedure, and as Derek and myself had booked earlier. Now only one member of the family was to be allowed to accompany the coffin and, after consultation with Bridie and the family, it was agreed that was should be myself. There were only three seats at the back of the cargo plane, and when I boarded two of the seats were already occupied by two men. The middle seat was free and I sat in it. Nobody spoke. One of the men produced the Irish Independent from his pocket and proceeded to read it. Half-way through the flight he put the paper down and I asked him if I could have a read of it. I wanted to see what they were saying about Frank. When we landed and started taxiing towards the terminal I couldn't reconcile whereabouts we were in Dublin Airport. I said to one of the men, "What part of Dublin Airport is this?" "Dublin? This is Shannon." The other one stood up, produced a badge from his pocket and said, "Irish Special Branch. You are under arrest." "What did I do?" I asked. "I don't have to give you any more information, you are under arrest."

The pilot came down the plane and he looked at me with a sympathetic gaze. I later learnt that when the plane entered Irish airspace he was ordered by the government to divert to Shannon and refused the instruction. The Department of Justice was forced to hurriedly issue a National Security Alert with which the pilot had to comply.

I was bundled into a police car and taken to Ennis, about sixteen miles away, and was put in a cell. Then I was brought into another room and questioned about whether I had any involvement in "any oul organisation." Those were their actual words. I said, "No. But I'm a member of the Labour Party," which I was back then. After about an hour I was released without charge. A sympathetic taxi driver from Ennis drove me back to Shannon Airport mortuary but I was locked out by Gardaí. I was soon joined outside the morgue by that redoubtable local republican and Derry native, Brigid Makowski, who offered empathy, tea, sandwiches and, if needed, money. Brigid is since sadly deceased, RIP.

Meanwhile, my elderly mother and other members of our family were waiting anxiously at Dublin airport, awaiting our arrival, and didn't know what was going on. When they learnt that Frank's remains were in Shannon they immediately set out for there and brought down my car. Some of us kept vigil in my car outside the morgue from where we could see a small blurred image of the corner of the coffin through a frosted window. But at about three in the morning we were approached by a Garda superintendent who said, "We need that car to move away." I told him I wasn't moving. Next thing, about fifteen guards got around the car, lifted it off the ground and moved it back about twenty metres to a place from where we could no longer see the coffin. Shortly afterwards three figures in full-cover white boiler suits entered the morgue. They emerged about two hours later carrying several stainless steel type canisters and containers.

On Friday morning the mortuary was surrounded by armed troops. An Air Corps army helicopter landed and we saw Gardaí shoulder Frank's coffin to the helicopter. When we tried to follow them about a hundred guards blocked our way. We were shouting and screaming that we were prevented from seeing our brother. Everybody was in tears. I pointed my finger at a Superintendent and demanded to know where they were taking Frank. He refused to answer. I said: "I'm telling you now, I promise you. A day will come and I'll have him back. And I promise you that."

The helicopter was flown to our local church in Robeen which was surrounded by heavily armed troops and police and an armoured car. All roads to the church were blocked by checkpoints. Guards kept a watch on his coffin through the night and the church was lit up by arc lights from the road and fields.

Our distraught family was faced with a major dilemma. The state had possession of Frank's body. Do we take part in this 'state' operation, or not? Mam and the vast majority of us stayed away. Our Veronica, a true hard-nosed republican who supported Frank at all times, and who died herself shortly afterwards, went to the funeral. She told me some months after the funeral: "I just could not envisage a situation where Frank would be buried and I would not be there."

Looking back on it now, with all the tension and mixed emotions of that time, I'm completely at peace with the fact that every member of the family mourned Frank in their own way and in the way that they felt was right.

After Mass his coffin was placed in a hearse, followed by ten armoured cars, trucks and lorries and taken in haste to Ballina through backroads. Minister of Justice Patrick Cooney had ordered that Frank be buried about seventy yards from the Republican Plot in an empty part of Leigue Cemetery.

The following day the Republican Movement organised a march through Ballina. About twenty thousand people gathered. The Gardaí tried to stop us from getting into the cemetery but they relented under weight of numbers. When the IRA fired a volley of shots over the grave, the police and army attacked and scuffles broke out. Many people were injured in the baton charge and the discharge of rubber bullets by the army.

The Guards put on a 24-hour watch on the grave - five Gardaí in three cars and the Branch stationed in a builders hut, a few yards away. Anyone who visited the grave was photographed.

My mother had yet to visit the grave so I took her there the following week. Special Branch officers came out of the hut and took photographs of her as she knelt and prayed. I thought it was the most heartless thing I'd ever seen.

The caretaker of the cemetery was Gerry Ginty, who happened also to be a Sinn Féin councillor. His mother, Jane, also worked in admin, selling lots, etc. I asked Gerry one day, out of the blue, "By the way, who bought that grave, who paid for it?" He said, nobody. I asked could I buy it. I took out my chequebook to pay three pounds. "How much are you going to give me?" said Jane. I said, "Three pounds." "No," she said. "Give me a fiver. For a fiver you can get 'a double'. That grave and the one next to it." "Why?" I asked. And she said, "In case you ever have to dig down." So I bought both.

I got a headstone erected on the empty plot which read: "Here in a grave dug by government agents lies the body of Vol. Proinsias Stagg. His will required that he be buried in the Republican Plot alongside his comrade in the IRA Vol. M. Gaughan. Having died on hunger strike in an English jail his body was stolen and defiled by the pro British Dublin government of the day. The truth for which he lived will blossom when his remains are reburied with the Republicans of Mayo. Erected by his Comrades and family."

The Guards maintained a round-the-clock watch on the grave. But after about a year they realised that it was a waste of garda time and resources. So, instead of the vigil they poured concrete on top of the grave. We estimated that they must have used about four tonnes.

That summer, 1977, I got a call from Gerry Ginty, who had already been hatching a plan for the removal of Frank. He said, "We can do this!"

We didn't know if the concrete went down the sides also, entombing the coffin and making it virtually impossible to break into the grave from the side without using machinery, which would attract attention. We reckoned we needed six trustworthy people in total for the operation. Gerry and I made two. Gerry got one other, Con Ryan, and I got the other three – my brother-in-law Jimmy Doyle, Sean Cumiskey from Trim, and Paul Stanley from Kildare.

Gerry chose the night carefully, November 5th, a night when there was no moon, was very dark, but, unfortunately, a bitterly cold night, with continuous driving rain. We had two lookouts – one up the town, and the other down at the gates of the graveyard. Four of us would carry out the digging. Two on, two off. We made good progress but we were soon soaked through to the skin. There was hardly anyone out and about on a night like this but at one stage the blue light of a garda patrol car was flashing down near the gates and we thought we were gone. We later learnt that the driver stopped to offer a lift to a rain-drenched pedestrian. Once or twice headlights from cars leaving a nearby house swept across the cemetery and forced us to duck.

When we had dug about four foot down a massive rock materialised, about five foot in diameter and it must have weighed about a quarter of a ton. We thought: this is it, we're not going to be able to get this out. But Gerry said to keep trying. We sent for the lookout to give us a hand. Two men were down in the hole and we got a rope around it and rolled it up the bank, inch by inch. It was a miracle. After we removed it we stopped digging down and began to dig sidewise into Frank's grave. Then we discovered there was no concrete down the sides!

It wasn't long afterwards that we struck the wood of the coffin and thankfully it was in fairly good shape. We had quite a bit of trouble getting it to move because it was stuck there by suction. But, again, Gerry was very clever. He just dug little holes over the coffin and to the back of it, until we were able to put the ropes through and gently move it outwards.

I felt very proud. That I was fulfilling a great sense of duty. I was very mindful of the words I said to the superintendent at Shannon. "I'm telling you now, I promise you. A day will come and I'll have him back."

I placed my hands on the coffin and I whispered, "For you, Frank. We're doing this for you, Frank."

We placed the coffin on a sheet of plywood - which Gerry had 'carelessly' (!) left lying around a few days earlier after closing another grave - in case Frank's coffin would disintegrate while being moved. We carried it down to the Republican Plot and within a short time we had Frank's remains re-interred beside his comrade Michael Gaughan. We then said a prayer and then we saluted. We withdrew from the graveyard, it was not yet dawn, and each went his own way. I got in the car and headed back home.

Later, I rang my mother to tell her it was done, to listen out for the news, and she cried and she thanked me.

The RTE newsroom was tipped off and ran the story about the re-interment of Frank Stagg. Special Branch visited Gerry Ginty and asked him to accompany them to the cemetery. When they got there hundreds of people had gathered around the plot. One old man said: "Gerry, you did a great job last night." Even the detectives smiled at the jibe. No one was ever charged. Frank Stagg's dying wishes had been honoured.

I WILL SING

Christy Moore

O'HARA, HUGHES, MCCREESH AND SANDS, DOHERTY AND LYNCH,
McDonnell, Hurson, Elwee, Devine . . .

> The time has come to part, my love; I must go away.
> I leave you now, my darling girl, no longer can I stay.
> My heart, like yours, is breaking, together we'll prove
>   strong.
> The road I take will show the world the suffering that goes
>   on.
>
> The gentle clasp that holds my hand must loosen and let
>   go.
> Please help me through that door though instinct tells you
>   no.
> Our vow it is eternal and will bring you dreadful pain,
> But if our demands aren't recognised, don't call me back
>   again.
>
> How their sorrow touched us all in those final days.
> When it was time she held the door and touched his sallow
>   face.
> The flame he lit while leaving is still burning strong,
> By the light it's plain to see the struggle still goes on.
>
> – "The Time Has Come"

I will sing these simple lines as long as I can draw breath. The
men on hunger strike had their ideals, comradeship, beliefs and
military discipline to sustain them on to their final days.

Parents, wives and families had to play heartbreaking parts in this most awful drama without any such support systems. I glimpsed the pain caused by this awful dilemma in Bellaghy, the Bogside, Camlough and in West Belfast, and wrote this short song to try to honour all the sacrifice.

I will give it an airing each time I encounter those who seek to demean and trivialise the fallen men and their families. Those who seek to rewrite the story add steel to my determination to remember.

When I hear the revisionists and the downright liars, I will sing – for that is all that I can do. Detractors find this pathetic and facile, but their sneering matters not to me. My life's work has been endowed with songs of struggle. I sing these words to express the way I felt at the time of the hunger strike and in its aftermath.

> As their young lives ebbed away we helplessly looked on.
> In the month of May the black flags lay, in 1981.
> Deep mourning around Tamlaghtduff has turned to burn-
>   ing pride.
> Francis fought them every day he lived and fought them
>   as he died.
>
> "The Boy from Tamlaghtduff"

A SONG IN THEIR HONOUR
Frances Black, singer, Irish Senator

MY FIRST REAL EXPOSURE TO WHAT WAS GOING ON IN THE H-BLOCKS and Armagh Jail was when I was eighteen in 1979. I was walking into town with a friend and as we passed Trinity College there was a sign outside about a film that was going to be shown about 'the dirty protest'.

I honestly hadn't a clue what I was about to see. I hadn't been aware that three years earlier the British government had decided to phase out special category status for political prisoners as part of a bigger process known as 'criminalisation'. Both republican and loyalist prisoners, who had until then been granted special category status, were now to be treated as common criminals, whereas they saw themselves as political prisoners or POWs. They didn't have to wear prison uniforms or do prison work, were allowed extra visits and food parcels, and republican and loyalist groups were segregated from each other, in their own compounds or cages.

Kieran Nugent was the first IRA man to be convicted of an offence under the new policy. When he was handed his prison uniform he refused to wear it. He was given a blanket and was escorted to his cell. Other IRA and INLA prisoners followed his example, and in 1978 the mass, blanket protest turned into the dirty protest when republican prisoners refused to leave their cells. The prisoners' policy of non-cooperation meant that they were often confined for days on end in their tiny concrete cells with just a blanket. They had no choice but to empty their urine out over the floor and smear their excrement on the walls.

I was appalled and shocked by the conditions that the men were forced to live under and the fact that if they had been charged before 1st March 1976 they would have political status but after that date, convicted of the same charges they were to be treated as ordinary criminals.

This really opened my eyes to the injustice of the situation and both my friend and I decided that we had to do something to highlight their situation. So we joined up with many other young people who were as upset as we were at this terrible injustice. We started leafleting and went on protest marches. We wanted to highlight the lack of support for these men's reasonable demands.

In October 1980 when republican prisoners in Long Kesh began a hunger strike and were later joined by three women prisoners in Armagh Jail, we felt hopeful that their demands would be granted. We believed it wasn't much to ask. All they were looking for was five simple demands.

We were so disappointed when Margaret Thatcher refused to make any concessions.

When the next hunger strike started in March 1981 I think we all felt that this was really serious and could lead to the death of these men unless the southern government and the international community brought pressure to bear on the British. I was worried but I continued going to the marches and doing my best to highlight these issues.

The election of Bobby Sands gave great hope to the campaign. Everyone thought, surely they won't allow an MP to die. But that hope was short-lived as no concessions were forthcoming from the British government.

I will never forget the day that Bobby Sands died; it will stay with me forever. I remember standing in my mother's kitchen holding my six-months-old son when the news came on that Bobby Sands had died. I remember looking at my beautiful boy and thinking how Bobby Sands' mother must be feeling now, she must be heartbroken. Everyone I knew was saddened by his death, even people that didn't really take an interest in political issues: family, friends and so many people in my community. I couldn't believe that he had the courage to continue his hunger strike right till the end. I was struck by his unselfishness and how he was prepared to sacrifice himself for his principles.

As the hunger strikers died that summer the sense of despair and anger at the people who had the power to do something about their plight grew. I thought of all of the mothers and fathers who lost their sons. I thought of their families and all who loved them.

I still believe to this day that the fact that the demands were granted after ten men died is a shocking reflection on the callousness of the British government at that time.

This struggle had such an effect on me that I decided that if I ever recorded an album I would dedicate a song to these men.

So, in 1990 when I recorded an album with Kieran Goss, I included the song *The Time Has Come* in their honour. It was the least that I could do....

THE FEELINGS ARE STILL RAW

Mary Doyle, former hunger striker

I WAS BORN IN 1956 IN CATHERINE ROW, ONE OF THE FEW CATHOLIC streets in Greencastle, on the outskirts of North Belfast. I was the oldest in the family and had two brothers.

The Sands family lived nearby in Rathcoole. Bobby, Bernadette and Marcella, who's the same age as me, went to the same school as I did, Stella Maris. I remember Bobby hanging around Greencastle. Little did we know that years later we would be writing to each other from prison.

My mother came from Wicklow to Belfast when she was sixteen to her married sister's, and found work as a domestic servant. She met and married my father there. My parents had no republican background, but Daddy encouraged us to read, especially Irish history. History was hard to avoid, given what was happening on the streets. On Tuesday nights, we used to go to a wee disco up in the school, and there was always trouble outside. We would fight with the tartan gangs from Rathcoole, especially the KAI (Kill All Irish) gangs, even though we were outnumbered.

I became involved after internment. In fact, two days after Bloody Sunday, I had just turned sixteen and joined Cumann na mBan. I was arrested in March 1974 and charged with the attempted murder of two RUC men, but that was dropped. I was convicted instead of causing an explosion on a bridge over the M2 motorway and was sentenced to five years in Armagh Prison.

We had political status, and the administration recognised and worked with the IRA command structure in the jail through our OC, Eileen Hickey. In Armagh, there were remand and sentenced prisoners, internees until 1975, and then there were those

37

on protest after the withdrawal of political status in 1976. I had political status when Máiréad Farrell came into the jail in April 1976, and I was released in September just as Máiréad was going on protest after being sentenced.

At that time, there were over one hundred of us, and there was strength in numbers. For example, when the men burned down Long Kesh camp in 1974, we in Armagh took the governor hostage and barricaded the landing until we received reassurances that our comrades were safe.

One night in March 1975, my mammy and daddy went out for a drink in their local, Conway's Bar, which was mostly frequented by Catholics but had a few Protestant customers. My mammy was walking out into the hallway when she came across a number of gunmen. Two Catholics had been killed in the bar in a sectarian attack the year before. There was a scuffle as Mammy fought with one of the gunmen. Another threw a bomb into the hall.

My mammy was killed outright in the explosion, and two customers were badly maimed, with one man losing a leg. She was forty-one. Another dozen were injured, but Daddy, who was in the lounge at the back, was okay. The bombers were also hurt, and one of them, a man called Brown, later died from his injuries.

I was given twenty-four hours' parole, but because of Mammy's injuries, I wasn't allowed to see her. I just came home to a closed coffin. They showed me a box and said, "There's your mammy." For a long time, I couldn't accept her death. Years later, when Máiréad [Farrell] was shot dead in Gibraltar and her body was brought home, her coffin was sealed. But the family opened it for a couple of us, her former comrades, and we saw her for the last time. It is so important to be able to say goodbye to a loved one.

I reported back to the IRA after my release but was caught within twelve months, along with two others, in September 1977.

At my trial, I refused to recognise the court and was sentenced to eight years for possession of incendiary devices.

The governors and screws took great satisfaction in telling me I was now "a criminal". I joined Máiréad and the others, eventually numbering twenty, on the protest. Unlike the men in the H-Blocks, we were allowed to wear our own clothes, but for refusing to do menial prison work and take orders, we were confined to our cells and restricted to one visit a month. We lost parcels, letters and remission and our full entitlement to association. My father was in ill health, and it was my two brothers and my aunt who visited and looked after my needs as best they could.

The screws were abusive, particularly during cell searches. They seized all clothing coloured black – even though the clothes had come in through the censor – because we used to wear black tops and skirts to commemorate the dead on occasions such as Easter Sunday.

In February 1980, the screws escalated the protest by refusing to let us out of our cells to empty the chamber pots. There were two prisoners to a cell, and the pots were overflowing. When they opened the doors, we slopped it out onto the landing. They moved us to another wing and locked us up there. That's when the no-wash protest started in Armagh. Many of the screws were bad bastards, but there were some honest ones who would wonder how it had all come to this, though the answer was no mystery to us.

We had crystal sets to listen to the news, but the prisoners who still had political status would shout over to us. We also all met up at mass on Sundays, which was when we got supplied with tobacco and cigarette papers.

During the summer of 1980, the question was repeatedly asked: what's next? It was sort of inevitable that the only other avenue we had was to hunger strike. So we talked and talked about it. Máiréad, who was our OC, was in contact with the OC in the Blocks, and we knew they were talking about it as well.

The time came for people to volunteer. I thought long and hard about it but couldn't just think about myself. My father was sick and still hadn't got over losing my mammy. I had to think of my brothers. But I was very, very determined, and I wasn't expecting someone else to do what I wasn't prepared to do. So I put my name down. It wasn't done lightly – wasn't just a rash decision. I was almost twenty-five, so I think I was mature enough. I said to myself, *There's every possibility I will die.* It wasn't a case of, *Ach, we'll be on it a few weeks and Maggie Thatcher will give in.* I was never under that impression.

The leadership didn't want the hunger strike, and they sent in all this information about what it can do to you, your body and vital organs. They tried to deter us.

The men went on hunger strike on 27 October. Máiréad Farrell, Margaret (Máiréad) Nugent and I joined them on 1 December.

The morning we began, the screws put Máiréad, Margaret and myself in a double cell together. The cell was never without food. They took away breakfast and replaced it with lunch; took away lunch and replaced it with supper, etc. Jail food is notoriously rotten and cold – fat with a bit of meat through it – but all of a sudden the plates were overflowing with steaming hot chips that smelt so appetising.

A screw would say, "Those chips have been counted, so we'll know if you're eating."

They were taking blood samples every day and weighing us and would have known if we were eating. They were so petty.

We were advised to take salt diluted in the water and to drink about eight pints a day. That first night, I was as sick as a dog, throwing up.

We were still writing the letter campaign, calling for support, and had a good communications system. I remember someone in the remand wing shouting over to us that it was on the news that John Lennon had been shot dead. Here we were, sitting on hunger strike, and I'm shattered at the death of John Lennon! Máiréad was a fan of Paul McCartney – who went on to become "Sir" Paul! – but I loved John Lennon!

Going into the second week, they moved us to the so-called hospital wing and you had to have a bath. We hadn't washed in ten months. We were secretly looking forward to a hot bath, but the whole pleasure was taken out of it because we felt so weak and it drained us further.

Cardinal Ó Fiaich came in to see us and brought us cigarettes. Fr Murray was a brilliant chaplain, and there were times when I don't know what we would have done without him. He fought for us more so than most of the Catholic Church, who let us down very badly. Had they done more, the second hunger strike would never have taken place.

In mid-December, we knew that Seán McKenna, who was on hunger strike in the Blocks, was very ill. We were listening to the nine o'clock news one night and quickly looked at each other. Had we heard right? The hunger strike was over? We were glued, waiting for the ten o'clock news, and when it was confirmed we thought our demands had been met. We said, "Thank God, for the sake of Seán McKenna and his family that the Brits have seen sense and recognised us for what we are."

But then we were paranoid: what if they were just saying that on the radio? So, we decided to keep on the hunger strike. The next morning, the screws once again brought in breakfast, corn-flakes and mugs of tea, and told us the hunger strike was over. Máiréad said, "We're still on it."

The governor came in and said that if we were calling it off, "not to be eating that food", meaning the breakfast but to wait for guidance from the doctor. Máiréad came back from a visit and confirmed the news, and so we ended our hunger strike after nineteen days. A few days later, we were sent back to the wing to join the rest of the comrades.

My daddy had been 110 per cent behind me, but he couldn't come up during the hunger strike – it was too much for him. He came up when it was over, and you should have seen the relief on his face. He was the happiest man on earth.

As the days went on, it was such a kick in the stomach when we realised that the Brits had reneged on their promises. We were angry. Then there was talk of a second hunger strike. We discussed it, and Máiréad and I decided to put our names forward again.

Then I began to think about it more and more. You don't realise what you're putting your family through, and I decided I couldn't put my family through it again. So I withdrew my name, and then Máiréad said that she had also reconsidered and would not be taking part. Some of the other prisoners – some serving short sentences – volunteered, but in the end, there was to be no second hunger strike in Armagh. We didn't have large numbers to draw from, like in the Blocks.

For both of us, it was an agonising decision, because the women were always a part of the prison struggle. We weren't just "wee girls", the way some referred to us. I had been writing to Bobby Sands regularly, and I remember getting a comm from him. He said that when he heard there wasn't going to be a hunger strike in Armagh, he was the happiest man in Long Kesh. He didn't mean it chauvinistically, but comradely, affectionately.

Along with the men, we simultaneously ended the no-wash/no-slop out protest. We were still locked up all day but were allowed out at night and were able to watch the news on television.

When Bobby went on hunger strike, we had mixed emotions: pride, terror, but, above all, a sense of helplessness. We intensified the writing campaign, lobbying across the world. His election victory gave us a real buzz. We convinced ourselves that this would lead to talks and a resolution of the protest, but it didn't.

In the last days of his hunger strike, you were trying to stay continually awake, as if you were on watch. That Monday night, I was exhausted and fell asleep. The screws quietly opened the doors at 7.30 the next morning. There was an eerie silence throughout the wing. I went to slop out in the toilets, and Brenda Murphy came in and said, "Did you hear?"

I knew by the expression on her face.

"Bobby died this morning . . ."

I went back to my cell and just broke my heart. Even though we were expecting it from the reports of how he was deteriorating, it was still unreal. That night, we saw the scenes on the news, his poor mother and father. It was so sad, but we were so angry that it made us more determined, even though we were totally frustrated at having no means to express our anger.

Dolores O'Neill, who was on protest, was engaged to blanket man Tom McElwee from South Derry, who was serving twenty years. They had been arrested on the same IRA operation. Tom went on hunger strike after his cousin, Francis Hughes, died, a week after Bobby. Dolores got a visit with Tom before he died. I'll never forget the look on her face coming back from that visit. It was heartbreaking.

It never got easier, after each hunger striker died. It tore you apart.

It was a Saturday and I was just called for a visit when I learnt that the hunger strike was over. After seven long months, it was over. We all cried. I was relieved that no more comrades would be dying. I was relieved for their families. But I thought of the families of the ten men who had died and how they must be feeling.

It might be twenty-five years ago, but it's like yesterday. The feelings are still raw. And then, after it ended, we got our demands, slowly but surely.

Unless you have been in jail, you cannot understand the bond between comrades. I don't mean that we were anything special. It's just hard to explain that we were all there for one another. I had my down days, especially after my mammy was murdered. My comrades helped me through, and I would have been lost without them. I never had sisters, but there are some of those women to whom, even if I had had a sister, I couldn't have been closer.

FOR THE SOAP ON THE ROPE
A poem for Ireland
Denis Kevans

For the soap on the rope,
For the blood-glued strands of the passionate "cat"
For the screws' boots on the *Al Rawdah*
For the travelling triangles
For Lord Norbury's bad breath,
For the pocked walls in Kilmainham,

For the soap on the rope
We will forgive, we won't forget,
It's time to go.

For the orphans exported in chains of tears,
For the harpists' hands thrown in the snow,
For the harp strings severed by the battle-axe,
For the baby's mouth plucked from his mother's breast,
For the fishing trawlers dragged down by NATO submarines,
For Sellafield nuclear discharges in the Irish Sea,

For the soap on the rope,
We will forgive, we won't forget,
It's time to go.

For the gold of treachery, and the treachery of gold,
For the numbness in a woman's heart,
For the green skin of poverty,
For the sound of singing in sinking coffin ships,
For the chalice of love packed with ice,
For the glacier that fathered you,
For the lips in the gold ingots that whisper of love,
For the foul language you brought to the Isle of Song,
For the children forbidden to play,
For the Irish names on British military gravestones all round the world,

For the soap on the rope,
We will forgive, we won't forget,
It's time to go.

For the bards' heads on the spikes talking better than ever,
For the edible rocks we discovered everywhere,
For the song that was a vein of fire under the earth,
And thrived on the bed-sweat and spit of Kings and Emperors,
For the whip that spoke in the voice of a battered woman,
For the first lash of "a thousand",

For the soap on the rope,
We will forgive, we won't forget,
It's time to go.

For the hood of the torture victim,
For the whirr of the helicopter propeller,
For your infra-red night vision,
For Anne Devlin's legs,
For the body searches in Maghaberry,
For the child's fingers creeping the thick wire mesh
Of the gaol interview window,
And your dog bark dog bark bark "You must not touch the child."

For the soap on the rope,
We will forgive, we won't forget,
It's time to go.

For your victims in unnumbered graves,
For the blood money that walks at night,
For the phenol and the wire brushes in the H-Blocks,
For your predetermined corruption of children's minds
With bigotry and hatred,

For the soap on the rope,
We will forgive, we won't forget,
It's time to go.

For your corruption of the meaning of work,
For your new gaols, your newer gaols, your special gaols,
Your secure gaols, your old gaols, your masterpieces of gaols,
For O'Leary's dining table, for the Silent System,

For the lost songs,
For the unfilled womb,
For the lost seed,
For the sobbing prayers of helplessness,
For the key of the door of the Irish House of Parliament
Cast into a barrel of trinkets in the Flea Market,
For Her Majesty's Pleasure,
For the Master of Lunacy,
For the lies you tell, you told, you did tell,
You have to tell, you do tell, you shall tell,
You always tell, you have told, and you will tell,
You cannot help telling, and you practise telling,
For your sick evil souls shrivelled like peanuts in your heart,

For the croppy's acre,
For the tumbled houses,
For the soap on the rope,
For the success of the Famine,
For the soap on the rope,

We will forgive, we won't forget,
It's time to go,
For the soap on the rope,
We will forgive, we won't forget,
It's time to go.

NOTES

"cat" – cat -o'-nine-tails.
Al Rawdah – prison ship, 1948, moored on Strangford Lough, County Down Anne
Devlin – lover of Robert Emmett, 1803. Tortured by British military Maghaberry –
Women's Prison, County Antrim
O'Leary – legendary Fenian, sentenced to twenty years' imprisonment
croppy – Irish republican patriots of 1798 who wore their hair cropped short in the
          fashion of the French revolutionaries
Irish Parliament – closed down under the Act of Union which brought Ireland
          under direct rule from Westminster, 1800
Lord Norbury – a hanging judge in Ireland who, in 1803, sentenced Robert Emmet
          to be hanged, drawn and quartered.
Kilmainham – Dublin gaol where James Connolly and other leaders of the 1916
          Rising were executed by the British army

THE ANGEL

Brendan Meagher, Redemptorist, mediator during the hunger strikes

I am the Angel. I appear and disappear.

In April 1978, my Master called and said, "Do you remember what your colleagues sang way back there when Jesus was born?"

"Sure I do," I answered, and in a loud and somewhat raucous voice, I launched into, "Glooo. . . . o. .o. .o. .o. .oh. .o. .o. .o. .o. . oh . . . o. .o. .o. .o. .oh . . . ria," and was about to continue when the Master cried, "Enough!" and, taking his hands from his ears, intervened: "Okay, let's leave the singing." And he continued in an even voice.

"'Glory to God in the highest and Peace on Earth to all men and women of good will.' Well," he said, "I'm not seeing too much of that, neither the GLORY to God nor the PEACE among my friends in Northern Ireland these days. We really do need to bring our sisters and brothers together so that they can sing and be happy living together in a glorious peace. Go to everyone – the Protestant, the Catholic, the prisoner, the wounded, the blind, the lame, the oppressed – and make them free. Take the chains from their hearts. There is something of a lull in the conflict at the moment, so you and your companion, Aelred, get moving. Get those good people to sit down and talk, to iron out their differences, to dispel their fears. Make the lion to lie down with the lamb, and," he added a little wickedly, "they like marching. Get them to march together. That is what I want and it is your mission, and remember," he warned, "it is, in fact, the only way forward: people talking to each other, walking or maybe . . .," and here he winked, "marching together." Turning on his heel, he left.

So Aelred and the Angel set to it. With no fixed agenda, other than "getting to know you", they went everywhere, inviting people to put aside their fears and to come together and talk. Boy, but it was a topsy-turvy ride, the two angels appearing and disappearing all over the place. Nights were absorbed into days and back into nights, a kaleidoscopic mixture of black and white, moments of hope when a light appeared, only to flicker and fade into nothingness. But the angels kept on through thick and thin with only one objective, "the mission" – get them to sit down and talk and see what happens.

At first, through 1978 and into 1979, the response was mostly very positive, with those who would be considered the more extreme elements displaying even a certain enthusiasm for the talks. There was nothing else happening just then in any event, and sure, weren't they all people of good will! Certainly they would sit down together and dialogue. Of course, there was no agenda and that made it easy to say, "Yes, we'll talk."

The Angel was a very happy little man. He is said to have appeared in Belfast, in Dublin, in Portlaoise, in Dundalk. People were talking all over the place. The SDLP talked to Sinn Féin; the UDA came to Dublin and talked with an Taoiseach Charlie Haughey, in Government Buildings. That was a tricky one for Charlie, politically speaking, and the Angel well remembers Charlie's words of warning a couple of days prior to the meeting: "If this ever gets out, I will deny it ever took place."

After the meeting, the Angel enjoyed a terrific lunch with the hard men of the UDA – Barr, McMichael, Lyttle, Trainor – in the Hibernian Hotel and at someone else's expense. Incidentally, Dick Walsh had a reference to the meeting in *The Irish Times* a day or two later, but there was no furore.

Still, the Angel wondered why it was possible, though delicately so, to meet the UDA but impossible to meet Sinn Féin. It wasn't really his business, so he kept his head down and his mouth shut.

It was all very wonderful, everyone talking to each other. Well, almost! But it was all rather lightweight stuff. There was no agenda, it was non-threatening and everything and nothing was on the table.

Everything was beautiful!

Except that dark clouds were gathering over Northern Ireland's prisons. The half-forgotten prison population, continuing with "blanket" and "no-wash" protests against the criminalisation policy, were now threatening a hunger strike, a threat that loomed larger and larger and finally engulfed the mission. Back to the drawing board, Angel!

Now there was a real agenda: the five demands of the republican prisoners in Long Kesh and Armagh. It was something of a shock. All the lazy, hazy days of summer were now gone, and the players faced into an autumn and winter of discontent.

The first hunger strike.

Very soon it was evident that Aelred, the elder of the angels, was not a well angel. He was, in fact, totally exhausted and needed time out to recuperate. The Angel was left alone. He blessed himself and went out into the cold night.

Act Two of the drama began in sombre mood. Nobody knew where events would take them or to what they might lead. The Angel's role toughened up considerably. He had seen how his companion's health had crumpled and realised that he would have to toughen up too. He witnessed growing violence and widespread animosity as the whole population took up positions, fragmenting along sectarian lines. He suffered to see so many good people swept along in a sea of confusion.

The mission was in tatters.

The lion and the lamb returned to their respective lairs and attitudes hardened.

Now was the hour to express your true allegiance, to show on whose side you really belonged. The one small step forward was now transformed into a giant leap backwards. The mission of peace and glory was about to be baptised in a harsh reality. It would be purified in the furnace of suffering and death.

Yes, the Angel would have to toughen up if he were to serve, if he were to survive. He would have to become a hard Angel, and he did.

In a climate of polarisation, he continued to appear and disappear, visiting the prisoners in the H-Blocks, the Northern Ireland Ofice, Sinn Féin, the Dublin government, and the women prisoners in Armagh Jail, among others. Now it was different and he was meeting people who were for and against. People on the "inside" and on the "outside".

Things were utterly bleak.

Then came a flicker of hope. The Mountain Climber was in contact. There would be a genuine response from the British government to the "five demands". On a bleak and bitterly cold winter's evening in a Smiley-type operation, the Angel picked up the British response in Aldergrove Airport and did as he was asked, delivering it to the friends of the strikers, who had gathered in a safe house in Belfast to consider the offer. The document was being analysed and was being highly criticised when the Angel took a phone call from the chaplain in Long Kesh, Fr Toner, who informed him that the hunger strike had ended.

Now the document was the only available exit from an embarrassing situation, and it would be submitted, though with misgivings, to the strikers and to the world as sufficient reason for the ending of a strike that had, in fact, already fragmented.

Later that night, the Angel watched silently in the dim light of the prison hospital cell as Bobby and the Dark, in a tangled discussion, considered the two-page "solution".

"It's full of holes; it won't work."

"Let's give it a run, and, if it fails, we will set out on a second hunger strike."

"Okay, let's give it a try."

And the Angel knew that death was in the air when he heard Bobby say, "They will never give in till coffins come out of here, and I will be in the first one."

So the first hunger strike ended and there came a short period of respite.

But not for the Angel. He was chosen as a "guarantor" in a step-by-step approach to the implementation of the British "solution" to the prisoners' demands. He was constantly in and out of the Kesh, meeting with Bobby, Bik, the governor, Hilditch, the Northern Ireland Office, and with the republican friends of the prisoners on the outside. The tension remained high, and the Angel remembers the beads of sweat on the foreheads of prison guards, the clammy handshakes, and he often wondered who were the real prisoners. The adherence to a step-by-step resolution of the demands was never going to happen once the implementation of the steps was left in the hands of the governor and the prison staff. The reconciliation process soon faltered and then stopped, and a second hunger strike was announced, to be led by Bobby Sands.

The tension grew and grew and was now electric.

As the strike took shape, the tempo increased, and the Angel went into overdrive. There were visits to the cardinal in Armagh, where he had a well-earned lunch, topped off with a few drops of Black Bush. Whiskey has no religious preference. He was well received in Kinsealy by Taoiseach Haughey in spite of conveying to the good man that, as far as republican prisoners were concerned, they thought he wasn't "worth a shite". Charlie didn't exactly savour the comment, but he was man enough to invite the Angel to have a drink, and indeed he mixed him a very good gin and tonic. The Angel remembers on another occasion, accompanying the Sands family to visit Mr Haughey in Dublin a short time before Bobby's death and, returning late – curfew time – climbing the railing to the monastery yard only to find that the front doorbell had been disconnected and there was no room at the inn. He went to Stormont and waited and waited, smoking cigarette after cigarette to steady the nerves, while Mr Atkins and his team discussed the hunger strike in a room a few metres away. Finally, he was conveyed the "good news" according to Downing Street.

"Let them die," she said. The lady was not for turning.

Nor was Bobby Sands for turning, nor was Francie Hughes, nor Patsy O'Hare, nor Raymond McCreesh, nor Joe McDonnell. They were not for turning. Nor was Martin Hurson, nor Kevin Lynch, nor Kieran Doherty, nor Tom McElwee, nor Micky Devine. They had set out on the road less travelled, the road to freedom and respect, and they would not be turned, even by the prospect of death. This is my body . . . The Angel understood.

The Angel helped carry Bobby's coffin out of the family home in Twinbrook, and he walked with Bernie and Dáithí and Gerry and a hundred thousand others to Milltown Cemetery, and there he recognised a friend, a holy man who had come from afar.

"What are you doing here?" the Angel asked him when the graveside ceremony had ended.

"I wouldn't have wanted to be anywhere else," he replied. "This is the blood given for all of us to light up our darkness and to take away our fear and our blindness, so that we may see and, seeing more clearly, we can live together in peace and harmony."

The Angel thanked him and said, "That seems about right."

David Beresford in his book, *Ten Men Dead*, writes: "It requires a historical perspective from a time far in the future to gauge with any certainty what they did achieve, or failed to achieve. But there is some evidence to suggest that one day the hunger strike may be seen as a watershed in the Anglo-Irish conflict."

That day has already come.

Oh yes, you've heard it said, "It should never have happened", and that is true. Preventive measures and the concessions granted by James Prior within days of the end of the strike could have been applied much earlier. But that would have been "giving in", a surrender, and that would be unacceptable. Why that should have been, the Angel is not so sure. Has it something to do with a lack of love?

But the hunger strikes did happen, and it is important to remember that because ten men had sacrificed everything, they provided the foundation on which hardline republicans were forced to build by taking their place in the political arena. No sugar-sweet, rational debate could have moved the hardliners . . . nothing less than ten men dead.

Personal legacy: the nice Angel, who had started out in 1978 with such high hopes, had over the years become an ice Angel. He realised that if he was to stay with the mission, he must adapt to it. He did adapt and closed the door on his emotions.

A small incident indicates the depth of the transformation.

In 1999, the Angel stopped at a traffic light in downtown Fortaleza, a large city in the north-east of Brazil. As he did so, he noticed a tall, skinny youth approach the car, hand outstretched as though begging for a few coppers. The Angel, lowering the window, turned to select a few coins, from those he kept for such a purpose. On turning to deliver the coins, he felt something hard contact his head, glimpsed the barrel of a revolver, and, at the same moment, heard the young man say, "*Carteira!*" Wallet.

With total composure, the Angel replaced the coins, and, looking straight ahead, he said, "Fuck you. You can shoot me if you like, but neither coins nor wallet will you get." With that, he

crashed the door open, and the young criminal, totally perplexed, withdrew his gun, turned and took to his heels with the
Angel giving chase until dissuaded by the shouts of onlookers. In
the circumstances, it was a crazy reaction, as everyone well knows,
but for the Angel it was automatic, totally cold and unemotional,
without fear. You see, almost twenty years after the hunger strikes,
he was still a hard Angel.

– Fortaleza, Ceara, Brazil, 1 March 2006

WHAT THE KID KNOWS NOW
Ronan Bennett, writer, former prisoner

BACK THEN WHEN HE FIRST WENT TO PRISON, HE WAS A KID. THE KID believed in God the Father, the Son and the Holy Ghost. He especially believed in God the Father, the Son and the Holy Ghost when he was in trouble. And he was in trouble now. He'd spent three days in a police station where a woman had picked him out on an ID parade. He didn't find out until the trial that the woman had a daughter who was mixed up with the UDA and had just got caught with guns. The police thought her daughter could do with some help. So did her mother. She picked out the kid. The cops hadn't put him through the mill or anything, but they'd tried a few tricks, and a slap here and there. One of their own was dead, and they didn't care for the piece of shit in front of them. He wasn't trembling with fear or anything, but he was wary. You'd be wary, too. He was wary in the back of the Land Rover on his way to Crumlin Road. Couple of Brits with moustaches and SLRs, and they didn't care for the piece of shit in front of them either. The kid prayed under his breath, but he moved his lips enough for the Brits to know what he was doing. That way, he thought, they'd understand the depth of resistance. He wasn't going to shout "God Save Ireland!" or "Brits Out!" – and *Tiocfaidh ár Lá* had not been invented – so he moved his lips in prayer and hoped they'd look at him and later they'd tell their families back in England that those republicans, they're unfathomable. They'll never be beaten, and we have no business being there.

It was a front because really he was very wary of what was waiting for him in jail. He'd never set foot in jail before. He'd heard lots about it. Not much that was encouraging.

It was a Saturday, late, and no one was in any hurry to decide where he should be sent, so he was rushed through to a cell in B-wing, on the "ones". Loyalist prisoners out in B-wing yard threw saved-up piss into the cell, drenching him and the bed and bedding, and that night they howled his name from the bars and swore revenge on him and his mother and his brother and his dog and his budgie. It was not an encouraging start. Sunday being Sunday, nothing happened except more of the same. And despairing thoughts about how if this were what the next week, month, twenty years were going to be like, then he was not going to make it. He was not a physically tough kid. He did not back down, had never backed down, but standing up required nerve and effort. The world of men was still something of a mystery to him. It wasn't just that he was young; he had been brought up by women, for certain reasons to do with family. Fighting was not part of that upbringing. But if people were going to empty piss pots through the bars into his cell, there was going to have to be fighting. Twenty years – that's what the cops said he would get – twenty years like this? Not possible. On the Monday, he went before the Assistant Governor (AG) and the AG sent him to Long Kesh. He'd heard a lot about Long Kesh, too. Not much that was encouraging. Twenty years? Not possible. Not possible.

It was late in the afternoon by the time he got there. The October light was already muddy, and the yellow and orange light from the sodium lights was furred. There were sheets and pillow cases hanging on the wire, rain-spotted and in shreds, flapping like old ghosts. There were seagulls wheeling above the bins filled with their soups of cold porridge and white bread and tea. The wind whipped his face when he stepped out of the van at the cage gate. This was Long Kesh. Welcome to Long Kesh.

Before he stepped inside the cage, he'd had only a theoretical idea of what it meant for people to stand up for each other. Solidarity, communality, struggling together – these were simply phrases he'd heard. The sentiment he knew was good, and he thought he understood what they meant, but the truth is, he had no idea. None. These are the things that make people human. Ordinary everyday kindness is a part of it. Consideration is a part of it. Giving a sick neighbour a lift to the doctor is a part of it. Doing the messages for an elderly relative is a part of it. Taking another parent's kid to school because they have too much on their plate with the other three is part of it. Lending money to your friend who lost all his at Barney Eastwood's – that's a part of it, too. Without it, we live like the kid lived that short time on the ones in B-wing.

Except that in jail, communality – solidarity, whatever you want to call it – it comes at a high price. The stakes are higher. They are – this is not an exaggeration – potentially lethal. There is no one in the world more vulnerable than the prisoner, except maybe a very sick prisoner and there were some of those, too, in Long Kesh. Or maybe children who have been orphaned or snatched away from their parents. And there were some of those, too, in Long Kesh at that time. If a soldier in Burma or Peru or Pakistan shoots a poor man or woman dead, it's still, even if only on some vague theoretical level, a crime. If he shoots a prisoner dead, nobody gives a damn. Ask Hugh Coney's family. They'll tell you. No one is more vulnerable.

The people who designed and built Long Kesh weren't after any design awards, though the kid thought the bleakness of the place, the rain and the lights and the low hills beyond, had their own strange, disturbing beauty. It was not envisaged that the men who ended up here should be comfortable. The opposite. It was cold and sterile, and it was certainly intended that it be as grim as Crumlin Road, or the Joy, or Armley or Brixton or Sing Sing. They're not interested in awards. They're interested in isolating the prisoner, in making him still more vulnerable, in degrading, dehumanising and very quickly in totally subduing him.

The kid had a sense of this from his day or two on the ones in B-wing. But here in Long Kesh, something was different. Here, at a glance, he saw it wasn't dog eat dog; it wasn't about prisoners picking on the weakest or the most scared or the smallest. It wasn't about who was top dog and who was part of the pack sniffing around him. It was solidarity. It was about men in a vulnerable position standing up for themselves and each other and, in doing so, making a human situation out of inhuman conditions. There were always squabbles; there were personality conflicts and political fallings-out. The kid didn't sentimentalise or idealise it. But this was it: proof of what people at the bottom could achieve if they stuck by each other. *Shit,* he thought. *When I get out, this is what I'm going to take with me. This simple principle: stand up, stand up. Stand up for yourself and each other and that way you'll win.* He could be a pious, high-minded little prig at times, even if he'd dropped the prayers by then.

The fire came. As far as the kid was concerned, that was the price you paid for solidarity. You burn a prison down and shiver all through the winter because that is what you have to do to let them know they can't beat you, they can't separate you, they can't divide you, they can't intimidate you. They can't pick one man off and beat the shit out of him, because the rest won't stand for it, even if it means that every one of them is going to get a beating just as bad as the first man.

After the fire, the people who designed and built Long Kesh had a better idea. They weren't going to win any awards for the H-Blocks, but they did have a very clever idea. They knew now what the kid knew. They knew what it meant to let the prisoners they were supposed to be controlling mix together. They didn't fight or stab each other like they do in the yard at San Quentin or Folsom. They stuck together and fought back. So let's not let them do that this time. Let's put them in cells, let's take away their political status, let's force them into uniforms, and then we'll make the fuckers do what they're told. And if they don't, we will beat the shit out of them.

The kid got out before the first H-Block was opened. The woman who picked him out on the ID – she gave her testimony at the trial but forgot to mention the thing about her daughter and the guns. The judge didn't mind. He handed down life and ten years. But the appeal court judges weren't so happy about it – not cricket. That and a few other little details, like the fact that the witness had changed her descriptions three times and the first two times were nothing like him, so the cops hid those and produced only the third one, which was very like him. Except the first two came out anyway and ended up in front of the appeal judges, and they didn't like it. No, definitely not cricket. So the kid was okay.

Back inside, back in the Kesh, the kids coming in now weren't going into the cages where there was solidarity and communality and men sticking up for each other. They were going into boxes where they were abused and humiliated and every sordid thing a human could think of to make those who come under his control do the things he wants them to do were thought up and done. The kid was back in jail then, during the dirty protest. In Armley and then Brixton. In Armley, he was on the yard with an Irish prisoner and he smuggled him out an apple. The prisoner gave him back the apple and showed him the hole in his mouth where his teeth had been before the screws had kicked them out. In Armley, where the favourite pastime seemed to be suicide, it was dog eat dog, and if you talked about solidarity, you could be sure a tout would report you as a trouble maker and you'd end up on the block. The kid was glad, though, he wasn't on the Blocks.

He was out by the time Bobby Sands died. He didn't know him and he had never to his knowledge seen him on the outside or in the Kesh. But he knew what Bobby Sands and the other hunger strikers were doing. Yes, it was about political status, and yes, their sacrifice gave Sinn Féin the kick-start that has propelled them onto the world stage. People write about that and remember it and talk about it, and rightly so. In historical terms, Bobby Sands and his comrades appeared at a critical moment in the struggle, one of those moments that comes along in different guises in every struggle, sometimes epic, sometimes personal and anguished: Castro's landing in Cuba; the Hollywood Ten when they said they'd go to jail rather than name names; Ali la Pointe's refusal to surrender in Algiers; Rosa Parkes when she wouldn't give up her seat on the bus; the Levellers' mutiny at Burford – the list is long. In those critical moments, a key individual or set of individuals appear, and they say, "We're not turning back." The historical legacy of the hunger strikers is acknowledged and secure.

But this is not the only reason the kid remembers them now. The stakes were high and the price was high, but no one who lives, however imperfectly, by the rule of solidarity has to think too long about the reason: what Bobby Sands and the hunger strikers did is what makes us human.

IF JESUS

Micky Devine (1954–1981), hunger striker

If Jesus Christ appeared tonight
With his body bruised and bare
And said he lived in H-Block
And asked you did you care,
If he asked you would you help him
Before he went insane
To help him bear his burden of suffering and pain,

I wonder would it stir you
To raise your voice and cry
To tell the world of torture
And all the reasons why?
But what about his children
Who suffer day and night,
Have you raised a hand to free them
From their lonely hell-like night?

For this day a broken body
Will live through trial and fear
And feel the pain of hunger
And shed a silent tear.
He'll take a look around him
And to Heaven make a plea:
"They crucified you, Jesus,
Now they're doing it to me."

But even through his anguish
When nothing seems worthwhile
The thought of home and family
Will always raise a smile.
The efforts of his loved ones,
His friends and comrades too,
They've tried their best to help him.
The question is – will you?

(Written by Micky Devine in H-Block 5 on the eve of his hunger strike)

ORDINARY PEOPLE

Mary Nelis, mother of two prisoners, activist

IT WAS THE NIGHT OF 17 DECEMBER 1980, THE FIFTY-SECOND DAY OF the hunger strike by seven prisoners in the infamous H-Blocks of Long Kesh. The Derry Relatives' Action Committee had organised a candlelit procession for that evening for we knew that one of the hunger strikers, Seán McKenna, was dying.

Earlier in the week, we had erected a huge Christmas tree at the roundabout outside St Mary's Church in Creggan. We cemented it into the ground to ensure that British soldiers or the RUC would not remove it. We had spent the week writing hundreds of names and details of each prisoner and prison on cards, which we then painted and sprayed with glitter. The plan was for relatives to hang the cards on the tree at the end of the evening's procession. A great deal of artistic thought had gone into the making of the cards in the hope that people would see and understand the gravity of the situation within the H-Blocks and the reasons why the prisoners had made the decision to go on hunger strike. We were also conscious that one of the hunger strikers, Raymond McCartney, was from our own city.

We set off that evening with our lighted candles from various areas of the city. The Creggan route took us around the main roads of the estate, and, as we reached Circular Road, we were met by a sudden winter storm with gale-force winds, thunder and lightning, hailstones and sleet. We were literally almost lashed off the street. When the bedraggled procession arrived at the roundabout, the Christmas tree that we had cemented into the ground was lying at a ninety-degree angle. There was no way that we could get it upright, let alone put our cards and decorations on its branches.

As we waited for the people to arrive from the other parts of the city, the hailstones continued to beat down mercilessly upon us. Someone had shut the gates of the church, so there was no place we could shelter. We stood with the water dripping out of us, in the dark, for our candles and the street lighting had gone out. A woman stepped out of the darkness and began to recite the rosary.

"Holy Mary, Mother of God . . ." rose in fervent prayer from the trembling, frozen people gathered around a Christmas tree that, like ourselves, could hardly remain upright.

Later on, as people gathered in our house, trying to dry off, the phone rang.

It was Fr Denis Faul to tell us that the hunger strike had ended.

The news was greeted with a mixture of relief and joy for the McCartney family and all the hunger strikers, but it was tempered with anxiety because it was not clear whether the five demands of the prisoners had been conceded by the British.

The following morning, I set off to visit Long Kesh, accompanied by a couple from the Connemara Gaeltacht who had asked some months before for a visit with a prisoner fluent in the Gaelic language. It was a dreadful morning, with snow and high winds making driving hazardous. The bus became stuck on the Glenshane Pass and a snowplough had to clear the way. We arrived at the prison later than usual to find the place in a state of confusion. Once inside, I discovered that the prisoners who had joined in the fast some weeks previously were still on hunger strike. There was no news of the four women who were on hunger strike in Armagh Prison.

Communication had obviously broken down, and it was some days before relatives got the real picture and we were able to organise a rally at the huge hunger-strike noticeboard at the corner of Rossville Street, which we had erected on the first day.

Christmas that year was made more bearable by the sense of relief that the fast had ended and the news that Seán McKenna was recovering.

I had a visit on Christmas Eve, a time that was always emotionally difficult for relatives and for prisoners. Although two of my sons were in Long Kesh, they were in different H-Blocks and were never allowed to see each other. I had to visit each one separately, which meant queuing, going through a search, which was little more than an indecent assault, and then waiting to be transported in a van to the visiting area. When that visit finished, I had to go out of the prison and start the process all over again.

On that Christmas Eve, I had secreted in my vagina a small quantity of tobacco and cigarette papers, as well as a Turkish Delight. It was their Christmas presents. The female searchers knew that relatives, especially mothers, were smuggling in all sorts of things as the prisoners were not permitted anything. They also knew that it was Christmas and none of us wanted to lose our visit.

When the searcher told me that they had brought in a doctor from Lisburn, who was going to give me an internal vaginal examination, I was sure that she was bluffing. It was not the first time that we women had to undergo such a degrading experience, but it never stopped us from doing what we considered was vital to the survival of the prisoners.

Aware that I had two "little presents", and scared to call their bluff, I decided to admit that I had "something on my person", using their terminology. The problem was that I could not remember which I had inserted first, the tobacco or the Turkish Delight. In any event, in a spark of Christmas goodwill, they allowed me the visit, but I had to retrieve the "little present" and hand it over. It was the tobacco. At least the Turkish Delight survived, but when I managed to slip it to my son, he remarked that it had changed its shape since he was outside. He would have preferred the delight of the tobacco.

Christmas in Long Kesh for those on protest was something most of us couldn't contemplate. The thought of those you loved lying on the floor in maggot-infested cells, with not even a vestige of comfort by way of books, papers, cigarettes or sweets, was nothing short of a nightmare. Families in our situation had long given up on the notion of festivity, and many of us spent Christmas Day on hunger strike in solidarity with the prisoners.

My Christmas present in 1980 was a wee comm (communication), smuggled out during the visit. The protesting prisoners were not permitted to write or receive letters, so the only means of communication, outside of a thirty-minute visit each month, was through comms, written on cigarette paper with the tip of a biro, all of which had been smuggled in. To receive a comm at Christmas was special, even though we needed magnifying glasses to read them.

My son told me that he had awakened one morning to find that he was frozen to the mattress, which was frozen to the urine on the floor of the cell. He saw a little robin perched on the bars of the cell window. It hopped down into the cell and began to eat the scraps of food on the floor. He said that it made a better job of eating than he did because his lips were stuck together with scabs. The deteriorating health of the prisoners was one of the factors that influenced the decision to hunger strike.

In the early weeks of 1981, word began to filter out from the Blocks that the British had gone back on their word to implement the changes they had promised in their December 1980 document. Nevertheless, we took up clothes when we went on the January visit. There was mayhem at the parcels office as angry relatives argued with screws, who told us that "them naked boys" were not getting clothes. We knew then that the prisoners had really been betrayed, and it was back to the streets again.

The Relatives' Action Committee disrupted the Derry City Council meeting, brandishing socks and men's underwear at the assembled councillors and accusing them of playing politics with the lives of the prisoners, for it seemed to us that the issue of the right of prisoners to wear their own clothes would cost lives.

The National H-Block/Armagh Committee began preparations for a series of national marches throughout Ireland. The prisoners started on a letter-writing campaign through the comms, which had to be smuggled out of the prison. The strip-searching of relatives made it difficult to get the comms out, so a smugglers' volunteer visiting rota was set up. The comms were typed up by the group and sent all over the world. As a result, news of the plight of the hunger strikers began appearing in the media in practically every corner of the globe, and British embassies were coming under increasing pressure, trying to defend what Fr Faul and Fr Murray described as their "leper status" among the nations of the world.

Some relatives were given the task of meeting various diplomats, and as a result of a meeting held in the Russian Embassy in Dublin, the Soviet state television service arrived in Derry and spent several days filming the campaign. Some time later, I met a man whose son was attached to the Irish Embassy in Moscow who told me that the film became the top news item on Russian television.

On 1 May, Cardinal Basil Hume, the Archbishop of Westminster, in a statement to *The Irish Times*, described the hunger strike as a suicide. His opinion was shared by a number of other leading Irish and English church leaders, as well as politicians and journalists. We knew then that Bobby Sands would die, just as we knew that the British and Irish establishments were closing ranks to protect their own class interests.

On 3 May, relatives received letters from the Northern Ireland Office to the effect that prisoners would now be permitted to receive one letter per month. And so I found myself writing the first sanctioned letter to my son in five years, which began,

"Dear son, I am afraid that this is Bobby Sands' last night on this earth . . ."

I was listening to the radio as I was writing, so I heard the announcement that Bobby had died. I was so overcome with grief that I could not even move to answer the ringing phone.

I could hear the sirens blaring outside and the shouting of my children as they ran past me on to the street. But I could not stop crying. Five long years of tears were running down my cheeks.

The ordinary people mourned Bobby Sands, and the ordinary people buried him.

His death shocked not only Ireland but people throughout the world. There were demonstrations in Dublin, Belfast, Derry, Cork, Paris, Lisbon, Brussels, Milan, Athens, Zurich, Rio de Janeiro and other cities throughout the world.

In Paris, where we mothers had stood in 1977 in blankets and bare feet outside the British Airways offices on the Champs Elysées, thousands of people demonstrated and thousands more lined the streets. There was widespread criticism of Britain by the press in India, Russia, France, Central America and the US.

The European Parliament, which we mothers visited in 1979 on the invitation of the late Neil Blaney, debated the tragedy of the death of Bobby Sands.

Francis Hughes died at 5.43 p.m. on 12 May 1981. His funeral, on a beautiful, sunny, typical day in May, had a surreal feeling. I remember thinking, this could not be happening, as thousands of us made our way across fields of buttercups and daisies to bury this handsome son of Ireland, because the Brits and the RUC had closed off all the roads. The chatter, the cups of water supplied by local kind residents, the sun, the gentle breeze and the smell of the grass gave it all an air of unreality. It was the kind of day that you remembered when you went on picnics. Yet here we were, tripping through the daisies to bury a man who had died an agonising death on hunger strike.

In Derry, we decided to organise an exhibition to try to raise the consciousness of those who had set their faces against the hunger strike. The Spirit of Freedom Exhibition was due to open in Pilots Row Community Centre on 12 June. We had six weeks to put together an exhibition around the H-Block protest and the conditions for Irish political prisoners in British jails. Artists, writers, painters, relatives and supporters worked day and night to get the exhibition ready. We worked out of the old Gasyard/Bogside Community Association building and it was a common sight to see people at 3 a.m. walking along the path at the flyover, trying to recover from the effects of spray paint, which left us as high as kites.

We invited Charlie Haughey, who was An Taoiseach at the time, to officially open the exhibition. He sent his apologies and a letter wishing us success, and his wife, Maureen, personally phoned to explain that he would be out of the country on the date.

We invited the literary people, the medical profession, priests and nuns, teachers, artists and all sorts of famous people from all over Ireland. Many of them accepted our invitation, but many did not.

It is to the shame of the Christian community that not one priest or nun in the city attended the exhibition. But we were delighted to welcome people like Professor Ivor Browne, Professor Seamus Deane, the late and great actress Siobhán McKenna and other equally famous people who nailed their colours to the mast in support of the hunger strikers and the prisoners' demands.

Two days before the opening, the Western Education and Library Board informed the manager of Pilots Row Community Centre that it would not permit the exhibition to be held there. We were in despair, but someone suggested the Guildhall, the seat of Derry City Council and a symbol of unionist power in

Derry. We paid our deposit, and two days later, the Spirit of Freedom Exhibition opened to huge crowds and media interest.

However, over the next three months, despite our efforts and the international condemnation of the British government, we walked behind the coffins of six more hunger strikers, as well as those killed on the streets by plastic bullets and by unionist death squads.

As I write this, I am in tears for all those who died, for the hunger strikers, for the prisoners who subsequently died as a result of the cruelty in the H-Blocks and not least for the members of the Relatives' Action Committees – those great women and men, most of whom had never been out of their homes – who took up the cause of justice on behalf of the prisoners.

It is twenty-five years since the broken bodies of prisoners faced down the attempts to criminalise the republican struggle, and it is twenty-five years since mothers, sisters and wives travelled all over the world to break down the wall of silence around the H-Blocks.

Greater love indeed had all those who laid down their lives for the generations yet unborn and who would some day live in a free Ireland.

A THOUSAND MARCHES AND PICKETS
Lily Fitzsimons, activist

IT'S HARD TO BELIEVE THAT IT'S BEEN OVER TWENTY-FIVE YEARS SINCE the first H-Block and Armagh hunger strikes began in October 1980. We have taken part in thousands of marches and pickets. Down through the years, republicans and their supporters have always shown their support for the Irish POWs, from internment in 1971 right up to the blanket and no-wash protests which ended with the hunger strikes.

Even at the height of the cruel beatings and inhumane treatment of the prisoners, we never imagined that we would be carrying the dead bodies of our loved ones out of the H-Blocks. I can still recall our anger and dismay in 1974 and again in 1976 when, because of British intransigence, first Michael Gaughan and then Frank Stagg died on hunger strike in jails in England. We thought then, because of the massive protests all over Ireland and the bad public image of the Brits abroad, that it could never happen again. How wrong we were.

From the start of the blanket protest in 1976, until the 1980 and 1981 hunger strikes, there was an ongoing campaign on the outside in support of the prisoners' five basic demands. It wasn't always easy, what with the pro-Brit media generating anti-Irish feelings for the prisoners and their families. While local pickets and protests were very important in building support within the republican and nationalist communities, we also knew we had to highlight the terrible treatment and conditions that the Irish POWs were forced to endure. We hoped that support from outside Ireland would help to force the British government to move from its inflexible position, and compromise.

For over five years, up until the 1981 hunger strike, I, along with other women, travelled to many places, including Britain and the United States. We lobbied and talked to anyone who would listen. Our objective was to inform them of what was really happening in Ireland. We took every opportunity to highlight what the prisoners were forced to endure. We met politicians, human rights groups, Irish-Americans, any one or group we thought could put pressure on the British. At times, we felt we were running against the clock, especially during the hunger strikes.

When word reached us that Seán McKenna's condition had deteriorated and he had been moved to the Royal Victoria Hospital, we quickly organised a picket outside the hospital on the Falls Road.

By this time, of the men and women on hunger strike, the men were in an advanced state of weakness. While support on the outside was of great importance, it was the prisoners themselves who forced the British government to move. The document they sent to the prisoners on 18 December 1980 seemed, at first, to offer a principled settlement to the protest. But by the middle of January 1981, we knew the Brits were reneging on their commitments. It was a frustrating time, and the sadness when the prisoners declared their intention to commence a second hunger strike is indescribable.

We were devastated when, on 5 May, the news came out of the prison hospital that Bobby had died. Surely, we thought, now the British government will have to give in to the prisoners' demands. But again we were terribly wrong. We underestimated the contempt that Maggie Thatcher and her government had for all things Irish and republican, including the right to be treated with humanity.

A lot has happened since the deaths of the ten men on hunger strike. Although the political prisoners have been released, the scars of their incarceration remain with them. Many of those who campaigned on the streets, familiar faces, have passed on. Twenty-five years later, the bravery and dedication of the hunger strikers stands, and we remember them with pride and honour.

SMUGGLING THE COMMS
Marie Moore, veteran republican

WHEN I WAS A CHILD, LIKE EVERYONE ELSE, I HAD NO IDEA OF WHAT LAY before. The community I was born into had suffered a grievous wrong through the crime of partition and was kept in place through sectarian discrimination and fear. Most nationalist people kept their heads down, suffered in silence and voted for political parties which had no power or influence. But a small minority within the nationalist community, the republicans, refused to be humiliated and passed down the torch of resistance from generation to generation. So, within the nationalist tradition, there were these two cultures, the political and the physical force, neither of which was strong enough to bring about change.

One thing that was constant was that there were always arrests being made and there were always people in prison for their views or activism.

My introduction to republicanism was a shocking experience. It was Easter 1942. I was four years of age and was with my granny and granda, Mary and Frank O'Brien. We were in the living room of their Cawnpore Street home in the Clonard area of Belfast when suddenly a group of men ran into the kitchen.

There was a lot of shouting and commotion. Then suddenly there were these loud bangs, more screams and shouting. Shots were being fired all around us, and I was terrified. My granda grabbed me in his arms. Then there was more shooting, more shouting. Men ran past us and ran up my granny's stairs. They were carrying someone who had been shot. He was covered in blood. Another man was lying on the ground in my granny's kitchen. He had also been shot.

Other men, wearing black uniforms and carrying guns – RUC men – were all around us.

The two men who were shot in my granny's house were Tom Williams and RUC Constable Patrick Murphy. Tom was badly injured but survived only to be hanged later for the killing of the RUC man. Joe Cahill was with Tom Williams and the others.

An RUC man grabbed me and my grandfather. He put a gun to our heads. He was screaming at the men upstairs to come down or he would shoot us. It seemed like forever, and then we were thrown out into the street. My granny and granda were arrested and I was taken to a neighbour's house.

Looking back on those years, I'm not surprised I became a republican activist. My grandparents were republicans. I knew as a girl growing up about discrimination by unionists. I knew that my mother and grandmother were denied their right to vote and that, more than likely, so would I be. My father and grandfather could vote because they were householders. Married and single women generally were not. I also experienced discrimination in employment. Despite being qualified, I was bypassed for jobs with the old Belfast Housing Corporation and the Electricity Office.

In 1968, I joined the Belfast branch of the Civil Rights Association and went to as many meetings and demonstrations as possible. I was married in 1969 and was living beside Bombay Street. On the afternoon of 15 August 1969, the day after the Falls had been attacked and burned by the RUC, B-Specials and loyalist paramilitaries, the priests in Clonard Monastery rang the bells, calling on the people of the area to come to their aid and protect the monastery after the British army had run away. Loyalists from the Shankill were trying to raze it to the ground. The people flocked in their hundreds, even though they were defenceless, apart from a few shotguns and air rifles. I helped evacuate people from their burning homes, carried screaming children and family possessions from blazing houses. Fifteen-year-old Gerard McAuley, who was in na Fianna Éireann, was shot dead defending the people.

After a short time, it was obvious that the British army had come in not to protect us but to defend unionist rule and the union with Britain. They quickly turned their guns on us for continuing to demand our rights.

I was shot by a British army raiding party in the early 1970s. I was with a group of women and teenage girls out on what we called "hen patrol", shadowing what were then called, "duck patrols" by the British army. We were banging bin lids and creating as much din as possible, alerting local people to their presence. They opened fire on us, and I was hit in the foot.

The strange thing about my being shot is that it happened in Cawnpore Street. And what is even stranger is that the house where I was taken to be given first aid was the home of the same woman, Eileen McNally, who had looked after me when my granny and granda had been arrested some thirty years previously.

At the time I was shot, I was a married mother with two children. I was taken first to Belfast's Mater Hospital but then quickly moved from there and brought to Monaghan Hospital, where I was kept for six weeks. The British army had issued a statement saying that they had shot an IRA gunman dressed in women's clothes. This was their excuse for opening fire on women and children. I'm sure I would have been arrested and charged had I not been moved. I was maimed for life by the shooting, and I have been left with a slight limp.

The next twenty years were an epic story of repression and resistance, suffering and defiance. The Brits introduced internment and tortured those they had arrested. They murdered those on Bloody Sunday who were on an anti-internment march.

When internment was coming to an end, the Brits were building the H-Blocks for the next phase of their assault on the struggle – the criminalisation of Irish republicanism and resistance to British rule.

In the early 1970s, I had joined and become prominent in Sinn Féin. We were targets of loyalists and targets of the RUC. In 1978, the entire officer board of Belfast Sinn Féin and the editorial staff of *Republican News* were arrested and charged with conspiracy to pervert the course of public justice: that is, "treason", which amazingly was still a capital offence on the statute books! I was among those charged and ended up in Armagh Jail where the women were on protest against the withdrawal of political status. The charges were dropped in early 1979.

I was, by then, also a member of the Relatives' Action Committee. I was never at home. I was away every weekend marching, but Jack, my husband, was very supportive, and he and my mother looked after the kids.

These were awful days. Hundreds of prisoners were on the blanket protest in the H-Blocks, and dozens of women in Armagh Jail were also held in appalling conditions. The prison authorities were obsessed with isolating the prisoners and preventing information from emerging about their living conditions.

I had visited Kieran Nugent when he started the blanket protest. Before the hunger strikes, I also visited Bobby Sands, Raymond McCreesh and Tom McElwee. Their families were very generous. They could see their son or daughter only once a month but gave their visits to us.

Later, I took over from Tom Hartley at the H-Block Information Centre, organising the communication system with the protesting prisoners. We needed information out of the prison, and the prisoners needed information from the leadership of the republican movement on the outside. It was all done through comms, tiny messages written usually on cigarette paper and waterproofed by being wrapped in cling film (which had to be smuggled in as well).

The warders were aware that messages were being smuggled in and out through visits and were on constant alert. It was a nerve-wracking experience. There was a very brave group of women based in Belfast attached to Sinn Féin's POW Department, among them Mary Hughes (now deceased), Síle McVeigh, Maggie McCullough and Andrea Leonard. They were the best smugglers I ever came across. For almost two years, they brought messages in and out on a daily basis. Sometimes several times a day.

It was gruelling for them. They were rigorously searched before meeting the prisoner. They were under constant scrutiny from warders while on the visit, and very often they were searched after the visit. On top of that, they had to deal with the emotion of the actual visit itself. I don't recall them losing one comm.

They also smuggled in tobacco, pens, cameras, little crystal-set radios which fitted inside plastic tablet cases, miniaturised copies of *Republican News* and other things on request from the prisoners.

I think this was the most difficult period in my life. Despite the effort we put into supporting the prisoners, we all felt powerless when they started to die on the second hunger strike.

The hunger strike and the deaths of the ten men certainly changed the politics of the struggle, and at a personal level it changed people like me who were close to events.

It opened up an electoral battle front, and I became part of this new front when I was elected to Belfast City Council, then was elected deputy mayor of Belfast. I was the first Sinn Féin woman deputy mayor and the first republican to hold an official position on Belfast City Council in its history. And, of course, in recent times, Sinn Féin has become the main party representing the nationalist people in the North. All from Fermanagh and South Tyrone in April 1981.

I am proud to have been close to the blanket men, the women in Armagh, the hunger strikers.

We lost ten brave men in '81. But the British lost the argument, and ultimately lost the conquest.

"THE H-BLOCK SONG"
Francie Brolly, Sinn Féin MLA

WHEN I FIRST ENCOUNTERED SERIOUS ENGLISH POETRY AND WAS obliged to learn wallops of it by heart, my teacher in St Columb's College was Fr Coulter, better known as Wee Bunkum. His father, who also taught English in St Columb's, was called Oul' Bunkum. The reason I tell you this is that Wee Bunkum asked us one day if we knew why Wordsworth and Shelley and all those famous English bards wrote poetry. A couple of the brighter, more confident students in the class suggested some very idealistic motives, which had a ring of reason about them, but Wee Bunkum debunked the lot.

"They wrote to make money," he said.

I have to admit that I was similarly motivated to write "The H-Block Song".

I was released from Long Kesh Internment Camp in March 1975 and, among other things, became involved with the Dungiven Prisoners' Relief Committee. Funds were low and we had exhausted all the usual sources. At a crisis meeting in our local GAA hall one night in 1979, I volunteered to write a song, have it recorded in some friendly studio, and use the proceeds, if there were any, to keep the wolf from the door for another while. As in the human condition generally, the conception was stirring, but the pregnancy and labour were difficult, and at times I thought that the song would never be born. Whatever about Wee Bunkum's theory, it took more than my commitment to the Prisoners' Relief Fund to put "The H-Block Song" together.

I have been asked if I was writing about my younger brother,

Eunan, who was a blanket man in Long Kesh at the time and had joined the dirty protest. My mother, God rest her, said that it would be no great hardship to him because he never kept himself too clean anyway. She was a strong republican and expected us to do our duty. No, it was not about him. I was writing about the Irish Republican Everyman, advised by own life experience.

> I am a proud young Irishman;
> In Ulster's hills my life began.
> A happy boy through green fields ran;
> I kept God's and Man's laws.
> But when my age was barely ten,
> My country's wrongs were told again
> By tens of thousands marching men
> And my heart stirred to the cause.

My age was not ten when the Civil Rights Movement took to the streets in 1968, but I borrowed H.G. Wells' time machine and flew forward twenty years from 1948, when I was ten years old and I had found a copy of Dan Breen's *My Fight for Irish Freedom* hidden in my parents' bedroom. A former RIC man called Brennan came to live in Dungiven at that time, and the word got around that Breen had grabbed him once and made him dig his own grave. We used to shout "Dan Breen!" at him. Be that as it may, the reading of that book inspired the romantic phase of my lifelong passion for the first pillar of republicanism: freedom from domination, *liberté*.

> I learned of centuries of strife,
> Of cruel laws, injustice rife,
> I saw now in my own young life
> The fruits of foreign sway.

By 1966, the fiftieth anniversary of the Easter Rising, I had left Dan Breen behind and had become more concerned with the humiliating consequences of colonisation. I wrote a song then, which I called "The Seven Men", in tribute to the signatories of the Proclamation. James Connolly got a verse to himself:

> Connolly saw oppression's twin,
> The curse of poverty,
> The ill-paid serf, the hungry child,
> Despair and misery.
> His vision was of better times
> For the likes of me and you,
> And for that cause he fought and died.
> What more could one man do?

Now my mind was dwelling more and more on every aspect of equality – *égalité* – because, without it, only some of us are free.

> Descended from proud Connacht clan,
> Concannon served cruel Britain's plan;
> Man's inhumanity to man
> Had spawned a trusty slave

Don Concannon, a former miner, was appointed Minister of State for Northern Ireland by Prime Minister James Callaghan – a bit of nepotism maybe between one Paddy and another – in 1976. Now largely a historical nonentity, he is remembered for proclaiming from the sanctuary of Parliament on polling day in 1981 that a vote for Bobby Sands meant "approval for the perpetrators of the Mountbatten and Warrenpoint murders". The relative popularity of Bobby Sands and Mountbatten was clearly reflected in the election result.

In a most despicable intervention, Concannon, uninvited, flew from London to Belfast to make an appearance in the cell of Bobby Sands on his deathbed. He told Bobby Sands that the Labour Party completely supported Thatcher in her stance. From 1976 until 1979, Concannon had been responsible for the administration of the H-Blocks and knew of the brutal beatings taking place. He then went into the cell of Francis Hughes and said, "You have no support; you are going to die." Hughes, a dying man, responded, "Close the door on your way out." Ó Concheanainn was the name of an important Galway clan and Edward McLysacht in his *Surnames of Ireland* quotes Woulfe's derivation: "fairheaded hound".

> No strangers are these bolts and locks,
> No new design these dark H-Blocks,
> Black Cromwell lives while Mason stalks,
> The bully taunts the brave.

Roy Mason was a former miner too. Now Lord Mason of Barnsley, he was appointed Secretary of State for the North in 1976. He surely did see himself as a reincarnation of Oliver Cromwell. Geoffrey Wheatcroft of the *Daily Telegraph* described him as "the best Secretary of State we ever had" and said that he was "remembered still with affection in Ulster", as is Cromwell. In fact, his undisguised hatred of Irish republicans and nationalists reinvigorated the campaign and reinforced the resolve of our people. The English, "the fools, the fools", have learned very little about the Irish in 800 years. Mason is still alive, and at eighty-two years of age is as much of a threat to us as he ever was. However, he himself still demands round-the-clock personal security.

Does Britain need a thousand years...

Reconciliation and the adoption by all our people of "the common name of Irishman" will, as someone once said about the impossible, take a little longer, but it will happen sooner if we are left alone. *Fraternité abú!*

"The man who writes his country's songs is more important than the man who writes his country's laws." The revolutionary songs of this nation have informed, comforted, encouraged, sustained and emboldened our people through the ages, in good times and bad times, in the face of "cruel laws, injustice rife". It was my privilege to fashion "The H-Block Song", to put into some kind of order the words already written in the hearts of the great patriots of this generation, men and women, who declared defiantly:

> I'll wear no convict's uniform
> Nor meekly serve my time
> That Britain might brand Ireland's fight
> Eight hundred years of crime.

1980. THE PASSER-BY
Sorj Chalandon, French journalist

IT WAS . . . I DON'T KNOW WHERE OR WHEN. SOME RAINY DAY IN
Belfast, in a small street, lined with brick houses and sadness.

Sheltering under dark umbrellas, a small crowd was celebrating a Catholic dead for the republic. A very small crowd: thirty, forty perhaps – a few people from the area gathering in silence to hear an activist speaking of a fallen comrade.

Tom, the friend who was with me, whispered in my ear: "Tomorrow you will be millions of miles and millions of years away from here." He said that without a trace of cruelty, or cynicism, or anger. Just matter of fact. He was reminding me that I was a passer-by. A mere passer-by. A passer-by passes by and tomorrow will return to his country, and this small crowd, these words, this rain, these bricks and this grief will seem so far away that they will taste like forgotten memories.

There I was, me the journalist. I was clutching my little notebook. I was scribbling notes: the crowd, red bricks, tired faces. I was scribbling, and the rain would blur the ink on my page, word after word. On the next day, back in Paris, all I could see was this small crowd of fighting people. I would see them in front of me at the street corners of my city at peace. I was refusing to let them go. I had taken them with me forever. And this was just what my friend Tom had hoped.

It was . . . I don't know where or when. What I do know is that it was the autumn of 1980 and that republican Ireland was suffering the martyrdom of the hunger strike. The passer-by had to learn new names, new faces. They were called Brendan Hughes, Leo Green, Tom McFeely, Tommy McKearney, Ray McCartney,

Seán McKenna, Mary Doyle, Máiréad Farrell, Máiréad (Margaret) Nugent. They were everywhere, haunting people's days and nights, their conversations. They were present on gable walls and in children's angry outbursts. They were present in daily riots: they haunted the passer-by.

Women and men would march clad in blankets at the front of demonstrations. The gardaí would scatter their anger with truncheons; the soldiers of the Crown with gunfire. The letter H was everywhere.

The passer-by had to learn Irish words like *troscadh* – (to fast against someone) and *céalacan* (to obtain justice by fasting).

He had to revisit medieval Ireland, Catholic tradition, legends.

He had to remember that St Patrick had fasted for forty-four days to attract God's attention, that Conall the Red, King of Connacht, and his wife, had fasted against the Devil because they could not have children.

He had to revisit Thomas Ashe, re-examine the death of Terence MacSwiney, and also hear the words of Joseph Murphy, Tony D'Arcy, Jack MacNeela, Dolours and Marion Price, Michael Gaughan and Frank Stagg.

It was . . . I don't know where or when. Some rainy day in Belfast, in a small street, lined with brick houses and sadness. I embraced Tom. We parted . . . just for a while, enough to gather my strength: he in his brick house, and I, back in this indifference called peace.

What I know is that all this was before the tragedy. Some time before it. An eternity before it. The passer-by had never heard tell of Bobby Sands. He never suspected that so much pain was still to come. He did not yet know the names of Francis, Ray, Patsy, Joe, Martin, Kevin, Kieran, Thomas and Michael.

Brendan's face was still on the brick walls. The storm was rumbling, but the passer-by knew none of it. Besides, he was no longer a passer-by; the name no longer fitted.

AN EVENT OF SUCH MAGNITUDE
Owen Carron, Bobby Sands' election agent

SO MANY MEMORIES, A HARD AND DIFFICULT TIME TO LOOK BACK ON, AN intensely emotional and painful time for the prisoners, their families and all closely involved with them. It's a time that never leaves you, a time of sorrow, a time of dying.

This is why I find it hard to talk or write about it because doing so always sharpens your sorrow. Now it is such a different time, almost hard to explain to new generations how such events would have happened, the hunger strike of 1981 was an event of such magnitude, probably the greatest in the history of the late twentieth century in Ireland, a profound occurrence that changed the political landscape in the North and has resonances for all Ireland far beyond that time.

Nothing will ever be the same again.

But it's the personal memories that are the hardest – standing at a young man's bedside knowing he is dying, remembering the faces of ten young men who would never grow grey, like I have, or live to see their children and grandchildren grow up – a whole generation who sacrificed themselves, who died for us. Even in the Bible Paul says that it takes "a really good man to die for someone". The Ten were very ordinary young men but they had this exceptional quality and for this they will be remembered forever.

The families too had exceptional courage, fortitude and dignity. The ordinary people who campaigned and walked the streets in support of the prisoners were magnificent, as were the 30,492 voters in Fermanagh and South Tyrone who against all the odds gave political status to the prisoners by electing Bobby Sands their MP on 9th April, 1981. In my head I can still hear Danny Morrison's cheer interrupt the Returning Officer Alastair Patterson as he called out Bobby's result and the victory for the prisoners.

I recall my own naivety of the time thinking that this result would save Bobby Sands' life - but how wrong I was. I recall the frantic efforts to save his life, the British authorities' attempts to break and isolate him. The Irish government under Haughey was weak and half-hearted. I remember at the end of April 1981, in snow showers, standing locked out at the gates of Long Kesh with Ramsey Clark, the former United States Attorney General, Fr. Daniel Berrigan, the anti-war activist and Christian pacifist, and Marcella Sands, Bobby's sister. A few politicians were sincere, and I remember on Monday, April 13th, going into Long Kesh with two TDs, Síle de Valera and Neil Blaney, and Dr John O'Connell, to visit Bobby. He was weak but coherent and explained all that the blanket men had endured and why they had been forced into the hunger strike.

Of all the politicians we dealt with at that time I always remember the sincerity of Neil Blaney.

Of course, I remember my last visit with Bobby on the Saturday before he died. It was an emotional and exceptionally sad experience to see him and to hear him whisper goodbye. He was unable to see us, and he knew that he was dying.

And the last day of July 1981 was also very intense and emotional for me as I accompanied Gerry Adams and Seamus Ruddy to a meeting with the hunger strikers and Bik McFarlane in the prison hospital. Tom McElwee and Micky Devine were present, along with Liam McCloskey and Paddy Quinn. Down the corridor Kevin Lynch was dying in his cell, with his family at his bedside. Kieran Doherty was in his cell, drifting in and out of consciousness. In the days that followed, Kevin, Kieran and Tom all died, and on the 20th August Micky Devine died, the same day I was elected to Bobby Sands' seat.

It was a harrowing time, a time of exceptional courage and unimaginable sorrow and supreme sacrifice that won for the prisoners a huge moral victory.

Bobby Sands and his nine comrades were known all over the world and Britain and Thatcher were in the dock. The hunger strikers with the sacrifices of their young lives had destroyed British policy in Ireland and had wrought change from British power. But the price of freedom is always high.

And, finally, I would like to remember a few people, all dead from my own part of the world who did their little parts and stood up when it was hard. Eamon Carey who signed Bobby Sands' nomination. Councillor Tommy Murray, expelled from the SDLP because he seconded Bobby's nomination.

Pat Cox, who, against all the odds, got us an election office in the parlour of Mary Drumm's house at 26 Water Street, Enniskillen, when no one would give us a room. Joe McConell, who sat up all night with hundreds of RUC men in the Count Centre, to guard the ballot boxes in Bobby's election. Paul Corrigan who weighed in and worked in Bobby's election office.

Seo iad an chosmhuintir a sheas leis na príosúnaigh.

Solas na bhFlaitheas orthu.

AN INSPIRATION TO US
Michelle Gildernew, political activist & MP

EVERY TIME I GO THROUGH THE TURNSTILES AT A GAA MATCH OR AT THE
House of Commons in London I am transported back to wintry days in
Long Kesh during the Seventies and Eighties. My memories of this time
are engrained in my mind, and the most insignificant things bring me
back.

I was an infant when I visited my father and uncles who had been
interned in Long Kesh. My mother, Geraldine, drove the bus down the
M1 every week with the mothers and fathers, the brothers and sisters,
and the friends and girlfriends of the prisoners. One of my earliest
memories is of a British army raid on our home in The Branny when my
Auntie Bernie had to take me and my brothers down to my parents'
bedroom as the Brits pulled our home apart and huge Alsatian dogs
dripped soaking wet onto us.

It was at St Joseph's Primary School in Caledon that I first heard the
name of Thatcher. Our school principal, Charles Cush, poured scorn on
her for the cuts she made as Education Minister, including the end of the
School Milk scheme.

I remember the first hunger strike in 1980 because a family friend,
Tommy McKearney, had been on that protest and I, along with other
members of my family, had attended candlelit vigils and prayer services
for Tommy and his comrades.

I was ten when Bobby Sands began his hunger strike, an event that
was to change my life. Frank Maguire had been our MP since he had
been elected as a Unity candidate in 1974. He was only fifty one when
he died of a heart attack on 5th March, five days after Bobby started his
hunger strike.

I'm not sure who first suggested putting Bobby forward as a candidate for the subsequent by-election, but it was both breathtakingly risky and courageous. The people of Fermanagh and South Tyrone, many of whom had little or no previous experience in elections, got stuck into the campaign. My uncle Tony was a member of the Relatives Action Committee and the H Block/Armagh Campaign and worked with many veteran republicans from the constituency, including Owen Carron, Francie Molloy, Bernard O'Connor and Pat Cox. A generation of young people also participated in the election and continue to be active in Sinn Féin to this day.

I remember asking my mother why this election was so important. She answered, 'If we win this election we can save Bobby's life.'

I believe that the people who participated in that election, locals and the hundreds of people from outside the constituency, including Jim Gibney, Lucilita Bhreatnach, Danny Morrison and others, thought that they could save Bobby's life, and the lives of those coming behind him. But as determined as they were, Maggie Thatcher was adamant that the political prisoners in Armagh and the H-Blocks should be criminalised.

Most of these men and women would never have seen the inside of a prison had we grown up without being politicised by the regime which presided over gerrymandering, official discrimination, brutality and cruelty.

Thatcher thought that the prisoners would be easily broken, but the resilience and strength they displayed still fills me with awe. Many of the prisoners were only seven or eight years older than me, but they demonstrated leadership and dedication far beyond their youth.

There was an overwhelming amount of support for those men and women, most of them strangers to us. The people who canvassed in the by-election, who attended polling stations, who transported people to the polling station to vote, the speakers at rallies, prayer vigils and after-Mass meetings across Fermanagh and South Tyrone and those who took people who had travelled from across Ireland to help into their homes, deserve our gratitude.

The ten men who died continue to be an inspiration to us. Their families who loved and supported them through these terrible times demonstrated a love and trust that is immeasurable.

Young Martin Hurson from a neighbouring parish, lost his life on 13th July 1981, but all those on the protest became household names. Martin Hurson had written in a letter to his girlfriend, Bernadette Donnelly, that, "if any man dies in the H-Blocks, the Brits will have murdered him," a view all republicans, and many nationalists held. Later, in another letter to Bernie, Martin said, "Bobby will never be forgotten by the Irish people. The people on the outside did all they could to save his life, they could do no more."

The people of Fermanagh and South Tyrone are immensely proud and honoured to have elected Bobby Sands as our MP. When Bobby died we felt that we had lost a family member. We grieved with and for his parents, his son, his sisters and brother. We cried for him and his comrades. We continue to visit his, and other graves, and to mourn their loss.

Every time I get angry or frustrated by the political process, media bias or our opponents' derision, I think of him, and the others who fought and died for Irish freedom.

I am humbled to hold the seat Bobby Sands MP once held. I cannot emulate this giant of a man, a poet and storyteller, a strategist and a soldier, but I can try to help achieve what he fought and died for, an Ireland of equals.

In his own words, "Our revenge will be in the laughter of our children."

Ar dheis Dé go raibh a n-anamacha.

LAYING THE FOUNDATIONS FOR PEACE
Paddy Logue, trade unionist

THE RELATIVES' ACTION COMMITTEE ORGANISED A PROTEST ABOUT prison conditions on St Patrick's Day, 1980. I arrived at the half-demolished row of buildings which was referred to as "the Creggan shops" to march to Free Derry Corner in the Bogside. As I counted the people there, including some who were more onlooker than protester, it couldn't get past ninety-eight. Not a hundred protesters could be found in Derry on the national holiday.

Several months later, on Wednesday afternoon, 12 November, a large crowd of demonstrators poured into and eventually filled the Guildhall Square. Their banners identified schools, local estates and communities, women's and youth groups and, despite the official trade union movement's condemnation of the action, numerous workplaces and trade unions. As I helped speaker Eamonn McCann up to join me on the platform, he remarked, "It's the biggest mobilisation since the civil rights movement."

What had changed between March and November? Seven men had gone on hunger strike on 27 October, not in pursuit of "political status" as such, but in support of five demands, the most significant of which was the right of prisoners to wear their own clothes. The ticking bomb of the hunger strike served to concentrate the minds of all involved in public life in Ireland and put the prison issue on the political agenda.

In addition, a new organisation had been formed to garner support for the five demands, specifically from individuals like myself and from sectors of public life located outside the prisoners' family networks and the narrow Sinn Féin base.

The National H-Block/Armagh Committee and local committees throughout Ireland pushed the argument that the prisoners
were entitled to special consideration because they were arrested
under special powers, interrogated in special centres, judged by
the special Diplock courts, sentenced under special rules and
detained in special prisons. This argument was taken into local
and district councils, churches, voluntary organisations, community groups, trade union branches and conferences, political parties, local newspapers and radio stations. Most organisations or
public bodies with a relevant local or national focus were offered
the opportunity to support the five demands. Many refused.

The list of refusals included all the main political parties in
Ireland, the Irish Congress of Trade Unions, the GAA and the
Catholic Church. Cardinal Hume of Westminster stated that
hunger striking to death was suicide, a mortal sin.

For those outside Sinn Féin who supported the campaign, the
persuasive points were the human rights aspects of the prisoners'
incarceration and ongoing conditions in jail; issues of poverty and
inequality; the civil rights denial and sectarian track record of the
state and its agents in Northern Ireland; and a deep hostility to
Margaret Thatcher and her policies. To support the campaign on
these grounds, many had to overcome scruples about the violent
struggle in which these prisoners had been engaged. Those who got
involved were of the left: H-Block demonstrations were not noted
for the attendance of the well-heeled and professional classes.

The hunger strike ended just before Christmas 1980 and was
followed by the Bobby Sands hunger strike on 1 March. Seven
months later – on 3 October 1981 – the prisoners called it off.
The National H-Block/Armagh Committee gathered in a hotel
in Dublin to break the news to the families of the dead hunger
strikers. I can still hear the howl uttered by Goretti McDonnell,
the wife of the only hunger striker in a working marriage. It was
a dark ending to a dark year.

Ten men had died in the prison. Many had died outside the prison as a direct result of the hunger-strike campaign, including two members of the National H-Block/Armagh Committee. Miriam Daly was killed at home in Andersonstown, West Belfast, in June 1980; and Noel Little was assassinated in Belfast in November 1980. Another member, Bernadette McAliskey, was shot along with her husband in Coalisland, they and their family narrowly surviving assassination in January 1981. At the end of 1981, the mood among supporters was one of exhaustion, despair and a need to rethink. The seed of a strange thought took early and strong root in this garden of reflection. . . although it took some time to bloom. The "long war strategy" was not a strategy for victory: it was, in fact, the absence of a strategy.

The public organisations which had succeeded in avoiding or ignoring the issue for a full year managed to push their heads even further into the sand. But no experience as searing as the hunger strikes could fail to throw up lessons for the serious minded. These were learned differently by different people and over different periods of time.

Sinn Féin was the first to draw conclusions. It learned that electoral success, if managed strategically, could be a powerful tactic. It was slower to learn that political and military campaigns sat uneasily with each other and that the latter set an insurmountable barrier to the progress of the former. The confused "ballot box and Armalite" slogan delayed, but ultimately could not prevent, that lesson from being learnt. It was the big lesson of 1981.

The British and Irish governments learned that they needed a partnership to sustain their policies in Northern Ireland, a central plank of which would be, in Garret FitzGerald's words, "to shore up the SDLP against Sinn Féin". This was the second lesson of 1981. It wasn't until 15 November 1985 that the unionists got this message when the Anglo–Irish Agreement was enacted.

What of the people of the left who got involved in the campaign? Could they point to any improvement in the economic and social conditions of the communities who had supported the hunger strikers' campaign? Was there any noticeable advance in the equality agenda? Could they claim any reduction in sectarianism or increase in human rights consciousness or practice? Was the voice of the left heard in the post-1981 rethink?

The fact is that the hunger-strike campaign destroyed the independent left in the 1980s. Many left-wing activists desperately seeking social and economic solutions, were swept up into the roller-coaster electoral campaign of Sinn Féin. Others reverted to organisations which were content with mediocrity and irrelevance, happy for labour to wait . . . again.

The hunger-strike campaign first imagined and then helped to create a credible Sinn Féin and, in doing so, laid the foundations for a peace process. History will judge whether the one we have got is an appropriate tribute to the hunger strikers and their supporters of 1981.

WHEN ALL THOUGHT FAILS
Nell McCafferty, writer, activist

THE THREE OF US, FRIENDS FOR DECADES, FELL IN NATURALLY TOGETHER, amid a crowd of thousands. Though we all knew some members of the IRA, we were not IRA supporters. We had no time at all for the INLA. Yet, there we were, the three of us, grim-faced and marching to the Long Tower chapel for the funeral obsequies of twenty-three-year-old Patsy O'Hara of the INLA. It was the month of May.

Mary Holland, forty-seven, had just bought a house in Dublin, to which she was moving from London. She had been sacked from her beloved *Observer* newspaper by the newly appointed editor, Conor Cruise O'Brien. He did not like a profile she had written on Mary Nelis, who had gone round Europe, clad in a blanket, to raise awareness of the dirty strike in which her IRA son had been engaged for years in Long Kesh. Nelis of Sinn Féin had once been an SDLP supporter. Holland had traced, with sympathy and understanding, the change wrought in her political beliefs.

Michael, then forty-five, was, and is, an SDLP supporter. An architect with the Housing Executive, he had marched on Bloody Sunday against internment, and refused next day, along with thousands of civil servants, to engage in further work with the British army. Later, he refused to sign off on contracts for some of the many housing estates then being built, because of lax financial controls. The estates were a welcome response to civil rights demands.

Michael was sacked, reinstated after colleagues downed tools, and his action vindicated after an inquiry that lasted years. His career never again reached the heights predicted for him. He kept the day job but poured his considerable energy and skills into the Inner City Trust, run by Paddy "Bogside" Doherty, which was responsible for preserving listed buildings within Derry's walls. (Doherty had been sacked from a building firm after chairing the Citizens' Defence Committee during the Battle of the Bogside, 1969.)

I was by then a thirty-seven-year-old freelance journalist, *The Irish Times* having declined to reappoint me to a staff job which I'd resigned in 1978 to write the great failed novel. A weekly column which signalled my return to its pages in 1980 quickly collapsed when uproar within and without the paper greeted an article I had penned, suggesting that feminists had a moral obligation to support the demand for political status which underpinned the dirty strike of the Armagh women.

The three of us, each in our own way, had paid a personal and financial price for our engagement with the North.

We all had a glancing acquaintance with Peggy O'Hara, mother of the dead Patsy. Who didn't? She was glamorous and cheerful, with long, dark, curling hair and dangling earrings. Patsy looked like her. She ran the cleanest public toilets in Derry, in Waterloo city centre, in the days when public toilets were marble emporiums. If you ran in there during a riot, she would make you a cup of tea. The toilets are closed now and have been replaced by a group of statues, made by Eamonn O'Doherty, which commemorate the famine and emigration years.

I used to see Eamonn O'Doherty, who is from Derry, in a pub in the city of Dublin, to which he had gone for work, like myself, at the beginning of the 1970s. He is a friend of Michael's. In that pub one night, Patsy O'Hara's brother, Tony, was playing a guitar, as part of a folk group. He was on the run from the North. He was in good form.

I saw him in chapel, during the mass for Patsy. He had returned to the North, been convicted of a paramilitary offence, gone on the blanket protest and been released for the day on compassionate leave. He looked awful, sweaty and sallow, with wild eyes and a beard. He was shaking all over. I hadn't been into prison to see anyone since visiting the Armagh women in 1980. One year on, and the sight of this young man shook me. What was happening in the prisons?

My book, *The Armagh Women*, had come out before the hunger strikers started to die and was withdrawn after two weeks on foot of an uncontested libel suit by a former member of the Provisional IRA. The IRA had declined to intervene in the libel suit because, I was told, my book had not declared support for the Provisional IRA.

That's the way the propaganda war was fought in 1981. If you did not laud the "heroism" of the IRA, republicans held that you were against them. If you showed any understanding at all of why republicans fought, you were deemed by their opponents to be a supporter. So the book was pulped, a thing I always thought dreadful. (The man who sued me was looking to make a quick buck; he apologised to me in the year 2000.)

The thing I remember most about the march towards the chapel was the silence, the absence of humour, and the political incongruity of the huge gathering. There were no smiles, no bands, no loud hailer, no party political agreement. We were, if anything, puzzled, as we marched along, side by side. The simple solidarity of the civil rights movement had long since disappeared. We had wanted houses and votes way back then – such innocent stuff, it seemed in retrospect . The killing years had destroyed any illusion of innocence (though our ideal had always been the hard-nosed objective of destroying the unionist stranglehold on the North).

What were we doing then, marching in a show of solidarity with hunger strikers, all of whom were pledged to kill? Note that

I do not write "pledged to murder". That is because, early on in the war in the North, I made a clear distinction between killing and murder. It is the job of armies of the state to kill, if necessary – Hiroshima, for instance. It is the job of paramilitaries, sometimes, to kill: when the law is unjust, the place of every just person is outside that law.

Ah, enough of that.

We were silent on the day we marched behind Patsy O'Hara's funeral because we did not know what to say or what to do next. Horror silenced us. The one thing we were agreed on was that people like Patsy had not been born to kill or raised to kill. That much we knew about each other in Derry. We were marching to show the world that we did not consider ourselves different from Patsy O'Hara. Or, rather, to show the world that Patsy O'Hara was no different from us. He was just like us, one of us, in all essential regards. We considered ourselves a decent people. We were not just sending a message to the British. We were flagging our feelings to the South.

We were in despair. Those were days without hope. Our only hope was to stand together.

We were astonished. Where did Patsy O'Hara get the courage to face a surely certain terrible death? How did that come out of the INLA, which so few supported and most abhorred?

Of all the protests we had engaged in, his was the most peaceful of all. He had protested unto death with his body. Our puzzlement increased. We were marching in support of a man who had died for beliefs, objectives and paramilitary methods of attaining those objectives which we didn't support.

It made no sense at all.

The only thing that made sense was that he was from Derry, was from us and of us, and was just like us in his belief in civil rights. He had chosen a different means of pursuing them after the unionist and British response to 1968, and especialy after Bloody Sunday. Bloody Sunday had changed us all. Were we retracing our steps, back to Bloody Sunday?

That would be too coherent an answer. There was no coherence that day. The only answer that made sense was silence: the silence of agreement. We were agreed that Patsy O'Hara was not a criminal and should have been given political status. The election of Bobby Sands MP, just a month before, had seemed to us proof enough that nationalists believed that. The joyful shout of that vote had gone unheard, to our increasingly helpless disbelief.

I remember loads of silence during the days of the deaths of the ten hunger strikers. *Mayday, Mayday!* we were signalling during Patsy's funeral. The night Bobby Sands died, all you could hear as we walked in the dark was the sound of feet on the road in Derry. The afternoon that Francis Hughes died, I was in a car going through Leenane, County Galway, en route to Westport in Mayo. The sun was shining. A newsflash broke into music on the radio. The other passengers in the car were from the South. I wanted to break silence to relieve the tension; the others waited for me to say something that would allow normal life to resume. The music jarred on our nerves. When we got to Westport, I went off into a corner of the pub by myself, feeling conspicuous, a Northerner staying away from the feast. I did not know what else to do. Silence was best.

Politically, it was the loneliest time of my life. It took another seven years before I said publicly that I had come to the conclusion that the armed struggle was legitimate. Next day, the bomb went off at Enniskillen, and I was metaphorically covered in the blood of Protestant civilians. I was immediately banned from RTÉ, of course.

I sat alone in the house for a week after that.

I sat alone, again, the day the IRA destroyed its arsenal in 2004.

I am sixty-two now, and heartglad the war is over. I still don't understand Patsy O'Hara. I still don't know what to say about him. Thank Christ I walked behind his coffin. Silence is eloquent, when all thought fails.

HUNGER
Cyril Cusack (1910–1993), actor

Why did you haste away so soon, my love,
I left unwise with no regrets, my love,
for could the long way round be best, my love,
in childhood's wild and wasted wisdom – you –
to wait for baby buttercups, clover
and seaside heather, gliding waters over
sands and wind-whitening over all things true,
your frightening hunger and God's hunger too?
Now is the flying feathered curlew you,
the curling cloud rounding tall Errigal,
your Donegal and all your North your breath,
and shall I daring grudge you death, my love?

(*On the death of Joe McDonnell, 8 July 1981*)

MARCHING IN ENGLAND

Mary Pearson, secretary, Troops Out Movement

MANY OF US ACTIVE IN CALLING FOR BRITISH WITHDRAWAL FROM Ireland, who are based in England, Scotland and Wales, see the hunger strike of 1981 as the major turning point in people's awareness of the political situation in Ireland. People in Britain did not automatically support the hunger strikers, but many began to question the government's attitude towards Ireland and its people. The election of Bobby Sands was certainly a challenge to the Thatcherite view that "These people are just common criminals". This view was further challenged when 100,000 people attended the funeral of the said "common criminal". It was still in people's minds that 10,000 more people voted for Bobby than voted for Margaret Thatcher!

Activists in Ireland, particularly after the Birmingham pub bombings, had been caricatured in the media as supporters of terrorism. The same put-down is used today for people opposing the war in Iraq.

The hunger strike meant there was a far greater readiness to talk about the issues and less readiness to accept the government's line. Trade unions and Labour Party organisations who had previously steered clear of discussing Ireland were passing resolutions in support of the prisoners and for British withdrawal from Ireland. Individual councillors and trade union officers were putting their names to the petition for the five demands, as did twenty-seven Labour MPs and one Plaid Cymru MP. Unfortunately, this support was not reflected in the leadership of the trade unions or the Labour Party. On the contrary, the mainstream Labour politicians were desperate to be first in line to support the Tory government in "standing firm against terrorists".

The most awful and cruel spectacle came on 1 May 1981 (International Workers' Day!) when Labour spokesman on Northern Ireland, Don Concannon, MP for Mansfield, went in to see Bobby Sands, and told him that he was in total agreement with Thatcher's attitude and that he should call off his hunger strike immediately. This was in spite of a Marplan opinion poll in the *Guardian* in April, showing that 67 per cent of Labour voters wanted Britain out of Ireland.

Concannon's action, clearly supported by Labour leader Michael Foot, shocked and angered many, including people and organisations previously less vocal. Martin Flannery MP said it was, "totally insensitive and like sending a British tank to a Northern Ireland funeral". *The Irish Post* said, "with the exception of a handful of individual Labour MPs . . . I can't see any self-respecting Irish vote in the next general election or for many elections to come".

Many Irish people continued to vote Labour and still do, but there was some evidence of a protest vote at the time of the hunger strike. Steve Bundred, who was elected to the Greater London Council (GLC), wrote to Michael Foot calling for the withdrawal of British troops from Ireland and pointing out the number of ballot papers spoiled which were marked with the name of Bobby Sands or "H-Block".

In response to the Concannon malice, the fledgling Labour Committee on Ireland, a pressure group within the Labour Party, called a demonstration against Concannon in his own constituency of Mansfield on 4 July. It was widely supported by Troops Out Movement activists and radicals within the Labour Party. The demonstration was well attended and got good publicity as it was against a shadow spokesman on Northern Ireland.

We spent the morning picketing Concannon's surgery, which

was being held in the Town Hall. You'd have thought we were an invading army. The police were out in force, and all the buildings in the square had police on top of them with cameras filming and photographing everyone for at least two hours. People were joking that we should really be members of Equity (the actors' union), we were being filmed so much!

The march itself was delayed as the police initially refused to allow us to march because we were allegedly "causing offence" and likely to be attacked. There were a few men waving Union Jack/Red Hand of Ulster (with crown!) flags, shouting obscenities and being particularly insulting to women. They were screaming, "Look, it's spawned!" at me as I had my toddler daughter in her pushchair. The worrying thing about these people was the number wearing Labour Party ties.

Throughout the time of the hunger strike, there were a great many significant marches in London, Glasgow, Birmingham, Bradford, Leeds (held on the royal wedding day of Charles and Diana), Manchester, Staines and Cardiff, amongst many others. In addition to marches, there were other events, often getting just as much local publicity. There were pickets of Downing Street and government and council buildings, military establishments, Labour and trade union buildings and events; public meetings with speakers over from Ireland; film shows; and token fasts in solidarity.

Birmingham, my own city, probably didn't have the most or the biggest protests of the hunger strike but was significant because of its history. The Birmingham pub bombings of 1974 had left a vicious aftermath for Irish activists. Although the Troops Out Movement and others had made some progress within sections of the left and some labour movement organisations, street protest was rather hazardous. Prior to the hunger strike, I was physically attacked on three occasions: punched in the face whilst giving out leaflets entitled "To Stop the Bombing – Get the Troops Out"; was pushed onto the road into the path of an oncoming bus whilst giving out similar leaflets (my bag and hat ended up under the bus but, fortunately, not me); and was dragged from a "soap-box" by the hair across the Bull Ring, glimpsing a comrade being battered by an elderly lady with a red umbrella!

There was one incident following a picket of a British army display when, tragically, a child was killed by faulty wiring on the Irish Guards' stand. Several of our members were visited and questioned by the police. The army had suggested that we had tampered with their stand and that this had led to the child being electrocuted. An article appeared in the local paper saying exactly that. In fact, we had not even gone into the showground when the child was killed. We witnessed the ambulance going into and leaving the ground well before we went in to leaflet the army stands. This sort of harassment meant that supporters were often too timid to become overtly involved in protest. A week later, a tiny item in the paper stated that the army stand had faulty wiring.

Things began to change during the 1980 hunger strike. On the first day, Monday, 27 October, we held a torchlight procession. The police tried to make us assemble in a subway, but we refused as we had been threatened by the National Front (NF). We assembled in a nearby street, and strangely the police virtually disappeared. Within minutes, a crowd of National Front youth had gathered and started lobbing bricks and bottles at us. At first, they were falling short and hitting members of the press who were between our protest and the NF. When the missiles began to hit their target, our people began to retaliate and chase the fascists. Miraculously the police appeared just at that moment! In spite of this, we were still allowed to march, probably because it had all been witnessed by the press.

What surprised us most of all was that we had quite a good reception from people as we marched around the city centre.

Some looked very bemused, but the only barracking came from the organised fascists. This was a marked contrast to our previous experiences.

An interesting aside in relation to this is that all press photographs of the protest were embargoed by the police. We went a few days later to get photos from the local papers, which are normally available for sale to the public. At the *Birmingham Post & Mail* photo shop, a young woman on the desk let the cat out of the bag and said, "I'm very sorry, but the photos from that event are not available as they are subject to a police embargo." I asked to see the person in charge, who was quite clearly annoyed that we'd been told, but admitted, "It is out of our hands." Following a number of letters of complaint and our winning the support of the National Council for Civil Liberties, we were given permission to view the photos in the presence of the editor, but not to purchase them.

During the next few weeks, we managed to get support for the prisoners' demands from seven local councillors and over thirty significant local trade union and Labour Party officers, who put their names to a public letter. It may not sound like many, but it was a significant step forward. Then the same media, who had been quite open to us when they were being pelted with bricks and bottles, pilloried those who signed the letter, causing them to suffer harassment and even death threats from the National Front. So much so that by the time the 1981 hunger strike started, only two of the seven councillors were prepared to publicly support the prisoners' demands. However, the trade union support increased, and new supporters from student, community and black organisations, as well as some local doctors and people from the arts, put their names to the letter.

We collected signatures on the international petition for the prisoners' five demands, leafleted virtually every major trade union and Labour Party event, and, where we were allowed, giving out leaflets entitled "To Stop the Bombing – Get the Troops Out"; was pushed onto the road into the path of an oncoming bus whilst giving out similar leaflets (my bag and hat ended up under the bus but, fortunately, not me); and was dragged from a "soapbox" by the hair across the Bull Ring, glimpsing a comrade being battered by an elderly lady with a red umbrella!

There was one incident following a picket of a British army display when, tragically, a child was killed by faulty wiring on the Irish Guards' stand. Several of our members were visited and questioned by the police. The army had suggested that we had tampered with their stand and that this had led to the child being electrocuted. An article appeared in the local paper saying exactly that. In fact, we had not even gone into the showground when the child was killed. We witnessed the ambulance going into and leaving the ground well before we went in to leaflet the army stands. This sort of harassment meant that supporters were often too timid to become overtly involved in protest. A week later, a tiny item in the paper stated that the army stand had faulty wiring.

Things began to change during the 1980 hunger strike. On the first day, Monday, 27 October, we held a torchlight procession. The police tried to make us assemble in a subway, but we refused as we had been threatened by the National Front (NF). We assembled in a nearby street, and strangely the police virtually disappeared. Within minutes, a crowd of National Front youth had gathered and started lobbing bricks and bottles at us. At first, they were falling short and hitting members of the press who were between our protest and the NF. When the missiles began to hit their target, our people began to retaliate and chase the fascists. Miraculously the police appeared just at that moment! In spite of this, we were still allowed to march, probably because it had all been witnessed by the press.

What surprised us most of all was that we had quite a good reception from people as we marched around the city centre.

Some looked very bemused, but the only barracking came from the organised fascists. This was a marked contrast to our previous experiences.

An interesting aside in relation to this is that all press photographs of the protest were embargoed by the police. We went a few days later to get photos from the local papers, which are normally available for sale to the public. At the *Birmingham Post & Mail* photo shop, a young woman on the desk let the cat out of the bag and said, "I'm very sorry, but the photos from that event are not available as they are subject to a police embargo." I asked to see the person in charge, who was quite clearly annoyed that we'd been told, but admitted, "It is out of our hands." Following a number of letters of complaint and our winning the support of the National Council for Civil Liberties, we were given permission to view the photos in the presence of the editor, but not to purchase them.

During the next few weeks, we managed to get support for the prisoners' demands from seven local councillors and over thirty significant local trade union and Labour Party officers, who put their names to a public letter. It may not sound like many, but it was a significant step forward. Then the same media, who had been quite open to us when they were being pelted with bricks and bottles, pilloried those who signed the letter, causing them to suffer harassment and even death threats from the National Front. So much so that by the time the 1981 hunger strike started, only two of the seven councillors were prepared to publicly support the prisoners' demands. However, the trade union support increased, and new supporters from student, community and black organisations, as well as some local doctors and people from the arts, put their names to the letter.

We collected signatures on the international petition for the prisoners' five demands, leafleted virtually every major trade union and Labour Party event, and, where we were allowed,

CÁ BHFUIL AN GHRIAN?

Lucilita Bhreatnach, activist

CÁ BHFUIL AN GHRIAN, MAR NÍ FHACA MISE CEANN LE FICHE BLIAIN.

Tá amhrán ann a chum is a chanadh an banna úd *"Na Fíréin"*, is mé im' dhéagóir, ceann a bhíodh á sheinm againn ag Discó/Céilithe a d'eagraíodh na grúpaí Ógras (Óg-eagras Chonradh na Gaeilge) sna seachtóidí i ndeisceart Bhaile Átha Cliath.

'Cá bhfuil an ghrian?' a thugtaí air, amhrán mall, go h-iontach do na 'slow sets.' Ceann eile a chantaí faoin am sin ab ea "Tír na nÓg", amhrán rómánsúil faoi Niamh Chinn Óir is Oisín óg – "Is mheall sí é le póg." Agus cá raibh an ghrian?

Sin an ré a dhúisíonn mo smaointe faoin tráth sin, am na stailce ocrais. Ní raibh morán gréine ag soilsiú ar na máthaireacha, deirféaracha is mná céile a bhí "ar an bpluid", mar a deirtí, cosnochta ar mhórshiúl, sa bhfuacht faoin ngaoth aduaidh, ar thóir na poiblíochta ag lorg duine éigin le héisteacht lena dteachtaireacht. Tréimhse roimh na stailceanna ocrais a bhí ann, ó 1976 go 1980, nuair a bhí an "no-wash protest" tosaithe ag na cimí mar agóid, le haird a dhíriú ar an leatrom a rinne na Sasanaigh chun dheireadh a chur le stádas polaitiúil.

An bhliain sin, mí Iúil, 1980, a rugadh mo mhac Donnóg. Ag feitheamh ar an mbreith i gcúlgháirdín mo thuistí a bhíos, na crapaidh ag teacht is ag imeacht, go ceann cúpla uair an chloig is an ghrian ag scaladh anuas orm. Ar ball b'éigin dom dul go dtí an otharlann.

Faoin am sin bhí m'iníon Lucilita bliain go leith d'aois is bhí sí féin is a dearthair ins na *buggies* amuigh liom beagnach gach lá ag freastal ar chúraimí nó ag glacadh páirt san fheachtas faoin stádas polaitiúil a ghnóthú arís. Ar phicéid taobh amuigh de theach an Attaché Sasanach a raibh cónaí air gar dúinn a bhíodh muid, nó ag bailiú airgid sna tithe tabhairne is ar an tsráid nó ag tabhairt amach billeoga taobh amuigh de na séipéil is na hionaid siopadóireachta mar shampla. Nó ag caint trí "megaphone" ag míniú cad a bhí i gceist leis na cúig éilimh a bhí ag na cimí. Nó na "occupations" a dheineamar i nDún Laoghaire i siopa "Easons", san "Norwich Union" ag lorg poiblíochta os rud go raibh RTÉ, an príomh stáisiún teilifíse ag an am, ag clúdach aon rud faoin bhfeachtas a bhí ag tarlúint timpeall na tíre.

Bheidís breá teolaí te ina gcótaí is pluideanna sna *buggies* le clúdach plaisteach á gcosaint ón mbáisteach a thit go minic. Ach, níor chuir sé as do na páistí seo ná na céadta páistí eile a bhí lena dtuistí, ach go háirithe na máthaireacha a bhíodh chomh gnóthach sin ag cabhrú leis an bhfeachtas ó lá go lá.

Bhí cosaint is grá is spraoi ag na páistí óga sin a d'fhás ó shoin is atá cúig bliana is fiche agus beagnach ocht bliana is fiche d'aois anois, is i bhfad go maire siad! "Páistí ama na stailce ocrais" a déarfainn le daoine faoi ghasúir a bhíodh á dtúirlingt ó bhus go bus, ó shráid go sráid, ó chathair go cathair, am an dtaca sin. Naipcíní á n-athrú, bia á n-ullmhú dóibh agus neart grá is barróga á thabhairt againn dóibh.

Bhíodar in éindí linn ag léirsithe taobh amuigh de phríosún Ard Mhacha, ach níor ligeadh dúinn dul i ngiorracht áit ina raibh na banchimí (cé mhéid ? – ochtó) faoi ghlas. Is thosaigh na péas ag caitheamh piléir ruibéir linn, is scaipeamar i dtreo an bhus, ár bpáistí inár mbaclainn againn.

Cuirimís é sin i gcomparáid leis an bhfulaingt, an fuacht, an aistear ocrais, an fuath a bhí ag na húdaráis do na stailceoirí ocrais is a gcuid, a muintir, a ngrá geala, a bpáistí, a máthaireacha is athaireacha, deirféaracha is deartháireacha. Ní raibh aon chosaint acu ach iad féin, a ndígnit, a spiorad, a smaointe, a gcroí. An ceart acu féin ach formhór lucht cumhachta na hama go fíochmhar ina gcoinne.

Is tá páistí eile a rugadh ó shoin sa tír seo is thar lear, aineolach faoin dtréimhse seo i stair na hÉireann, tréimhse ghruama ina raibh an ghrian in easnamh, agus díreach 11 bliain ó cuireadh ar leath-taobh Alt 31, an t-Acht Cinnsireachta um Chraolacháin in éadan poblachtánaithe.

Daoine den aois chéanna formhór na stailceoirí ocrais, 23, 24, 25, 26, 27, fir is mná a bhí ar an bpluid i gCampa na Ceise Fada is i bpríosún Ard Mhacha.

Comóradh chúig bliain is scór atá romhainn i mbliana is beidh daoine den aois chéanna, 23, 24, 25, 26, 27, ag foghlaim faoi pholaitíocht na hama. Am inar sheas rialtas Fhianna Fáil *"who stood idly by"* (ar nós Thaoiseach Jack Lynch nuair a chuaigh arm Shasana isteach sna Sé Contae, mí Mheitheamh, 1969) gan seasamh dá laghad ar son chearta shaoránaigh na hÉireann.

Cár imigh an ghrian?

Blianta ina dhiaidh sin, am chuimhneacháin bháis Roibeard Ó Sandair i 2001 d'imigh an chéad ghrúpa de phoblachtánaithe ar ais ar chuairt go dtí na Campaí is na Blocanna H is Ospidéal an Phríosúin. Ba é sin an chéad chuairt mar é a bhí ann. Iarradh orm dul in éindí le Uachtarán Shinn Féin, Gearóid Mac Ádhaimh, Gearóid Ó Ceallaigh, Bic McFarlane, Ted Howell, an bheirt MP, Michelle Gildernew agus Pat Doherty, in éindí le Collete Adams is an duine ab óige, Drithle, a gar iníon, agus Risteard Mac Amhlaigh. Deichniúr a ceadaíodh isteach don chéad uair sin, is bhí foireann tiománaithe a thóg ann muid.

Lá tirim, an ghrian sa spéir ag soilsiú ar thalamh íseal Oirthear Aontroma. Shiúlamar ón mion-bhus is na caranna isteach in áit a raibh daoine ag iarraidh éalú uaidh i gcónaí. B'ait sin a shíleas. Ní raibh an rithim i gceart. Bhí torann na gcos, gan rithim, is sinne ag siúl isteach. Torann na gcos éagsúil leis na hamannta a bhíodh muid ag dul isteach chuig na "cainteanna" nó na comhráití. Bhí cuimhní cinn á scairteadh siar chughainn is ainmneacha daoine a bhíodh ann á bplé. Sin an balla agus sin imlíne an fhonsa áit a ndearnadh iarrachtaí é a ghearradh le heitilt ón áit, ach níor éirigh leo.

Scaipithe timpeall ar an bhfonsa tá salachar, bun toitíní, clocha beaga, poiteach, is ina measc rudaí dubha móra caite ar nós cuma liom. Cérbh iad sin, arsa mise liom féin. Rudaí fada dubha ar nós boid, seacht n-orlach nó mar sin ar fhaid is trí orlach ar leithead. Piléir rúibéir a bhí ionta, a lán lán díobh, iad fágtha ansin mar a thiteadar ó ghunnaí na saighdiúirí is na péas.

Isteach i gcúpla ceann de na botháin iarainn a chuaigh muid. Poill san iarann roctha is gaoth ghéar le cloisint ag séideadh. Ní dídean a bhí ann le teas ach miotal fuar a choimeád daoine istigh mar ainmhithe faoi ghlas. Seana phíosaí nuachtán i gcoirnéil, fliuch is scriosta, in éindí le cannaí stáin meirgeacha ón am a thugadar faoin mbáisteach fhliuch. Bhí leaba nó dhó ag seasamh in airde. I ndáiríre is spriongaí le fráma miotail agus poill a bhí iontu, sreanganna briste. Níor mhothaíos aon spiorad i ngiorracht dom a bhí fágtha nó a d'fhan ann nó a tháinig thar n-ais ar chuairt. Fiú is sinne ag bogadh timpeall in áit nach raibh éinne leis na blianta ba léir nar fhág aon duine a spiorad ann. Thógadar leo iad. Fágadh an áit gan anam, go marbhánta gan bheocht.

Bhí beirt ó na seirbhísí a chuir rialtas Bhlair, nó a rannóga speisialta, le muid a stiúradh, nó chun faire orainn. Isteach linn go dtí na Blocanna is an tOspidéal. Bhí sciathán amháin dúnta is níor fhéad muid dul síos ann, é faoi ghlas acu. Fiú anois, bhíodar ag imirt cluichí linn. Sciob duine éigin uainchlár a bhí ar chairtbhord ag deasc an bhairdéire ar an dtaobh thoir. Shiúlamar suas ar dheis, sa gcearnóg sul má chasann tú ar chlé, le dul isteach san áit ina raibh na buachaillí san ospidéal.

Ba é sin an uair deireannach a chonaic Breandán Mac Fairlin, Ceannfort na bPríosúnach iad, nuair a bhog is scar na húdaráis na stailceoirí óna gcomrádaithe, gan cead acu iad a fheiscint, dul ar chuairt chun nó labhairt leo riamh, riamh arís, is iad beo. Cén sórt daoine a dhéanann rudaí truamhéilleach mar sin? Scallfadh sé an croí ionat.

"Is a Dhómhnaill óg thóg tú an ghealach is an ghrian díom is . . . gur thóg tú Dia dhíom . . ."

Shiúlamar isteach i gceann de na cillíní. Bhí líne dhíreach ann ó sholas na gréine le roinnt deannaigh ag damhsa sa bhfrithchaitheamh ar úrlár a bhí go ró-shnasta, áit nach raibh éinne beo ann a thuilleadh. Dúnadh an doras mór trom iarainn ar mo chúl is mé ag breathnú amach an fhuinneog ar chomhaird mo chliabh. Dhún an doras le gleo, faoi ghlas. Chasas timpeall. Déanadh é seo d'aon ghnó chun go bhfeicfeadh muid conas mar a bhí acu tráth i gcillín bheag, áit ina raibh duine nó beirt amanna faoi ghlas ann ar feadh na scórtha is mílte laethanta. Bhreathnaíos amach an fhuinneoigín – fráma le barraí iarainn – ag smaoineamh faoin fhuiseoigín is an fiach dubh. Scríobh Roibeard Mac Sandair (Bobby Sands) faoin bhfuiseoig is ar shiombail na saoirse, is bhreac Piaras Béaslaí, príosúnach san naoú céad déag, faoin fhiach dubh a thiocfadh ar chuairt chuige ag an bpríosún freisin. Bhreathnódh an bheirt acu amach ar na héiníní is iad ag ceol is ag ardú na sciatháin go hard san aer le heitilt suas domhan mór.

Osclaíodh doras trom an chillín is amach linn ag siúl síos an pasáiste isteach i ngach cillín ina raibh na stailceoirí, is scairteadh amach a n-ainmneacha is smaoinigh muid orthu, is d'fhág roinnt againn slán leo ina n-aigne, ina gcroí, ina n-anam. Isteach go cillín Roibeaird Mac Sandair linn. Bhí Breandán Mac Fairlin in éindí liom, is bhí na cuimhní go láidir aige. Dúirt Gerry A, "Déan do shíochán leis, abair slán." Bhreathnaíos ar Bhreandán, "Ar mhaith leat a bheith leat féin?" a d'iarras air. "Níl sé sin uaim," a dúirt sé. Dúras, "Ar mhaith leat an t-amhrán a chum tú dó a chanadh?" *"It doesn't seem quite so long ago the last time that I saw you."* "Ba mhaith, ach ní féidir liom," a dúirt sé, is é ag slogadh siar ina scórnach. Sheasamar beirt ag machnamh is ag smaoineamh i lár an chillín. Chruinníomar uile le chéile ansin sa chillín, ag seasamh i gciorcal, bhí dhá nóiméad ciúnais againn le meas is in onóir agus i gcuimhne an deichniúr.

Amach linn is ansin a thárla sé: dhún an doras inár ndiaidh is ní raibh aon duine istigh ná éinne amuigh na éinne os ár gcomhair. "Cé rinne é sin?" a dúirt muid, scanradh an domhain orainn is sinne ag breathnú ar a chéile is thart timpeall ar an ngrúpa s'againn. D'oscail duine éigin an doras le breathnú cé bhí istigh ag magadh fúinn, ach ní raibh duine le feiceáil. Ní fhéadfadh muid ach breathnú ar a chéile, aghaidheanna liathbhán ag an bpointe sin, an eachtra á chasadh timpeall inár gcinn ag déanamh iarracht ar loighic a chur i bhfeidhm, rud éigin a ndearna muid dearmad air, sciob sceab gaoithe b'fhéidir. Ach, ní raibh aon leithscéal ann agus ní dúirt muid a thuilleadh. Ní dúirt éinne rud ar bith faoin eachtra, is ar aghaidh linn ag breathnú, ag mothú is ag glacadh pictiúirí lenár súile, clic, clic, clic, go mall réidh, fiú sórt cliniciúil á shú isteach, gach rud á shú isteach is na mothúcháin arda leis na céadfaí lán, ag ardú, ag comhoibriú lena chéile, go neamhspleách ar nós nach rabhadar ceangailte linn.

Nuair a d'fhilleas ar Bhaile Átha Cliath níos déanaí, im charr, ba léir nach aon ghnáth lá a bhí caite agam. Is muid ag fágáil, dúirt Gearóid Mac Ádhaimh liom, "Scríobhfaidh tú faoi seo uair éigin, i nGaeilge, nuair atá tú ullamh dó." Ag an am smaoinigh mé conas a fhéadfainn scríobh i slí a nochtódh an tráthnóna úd sa bhliain 2000, na tárlúintí is na mothúcháin a bhí nascaithe leo is sinne istigh i gCampa na Ceise Fada. Idir na smaointe pearsanta is na laethanta dubha . . .

Léiríonn an dareág focal seo an chaoi ina raibh an tréimhse sin ceithre bliana is fiche, cúig bliana is fiche ó shoin.

"Cá bhfuil an ghrian mar ní fhaca mise ceann le fiche bliain."

DEICH MBLÁTH
Lucilita Bhreatnach

"Rithim an ama" na Stailceoirí ocrais scaipithe
Ar nós síolta ár saoirse ag fás.

Daoine óga básaithe,
Is Rialtaisí shasanacha
Imithe

Ach, feicim bláth an streachailt ag bláthú
Is cloisim coiscéim na bpáistí ag súgradh
Is smaoiníom cad a dúirt Bobby Sands
'Sé gáire ár bpáistí ár ndíoltas

THOSE WONDERFUL HUMAN BEINGS
Anne Speed, activist

"The past is a foreign country; they do things differently there."
– L.P. Hartley

THERE WERE ASPECTS OF THE CAMPAIGN TO SUPPORT AND DEFEND THE hunger strikers that are both connected to and disconnected from political life today. The peace process is a product of the lessons learned, and the Ireland of today is different from the Ireland of that period. Yet, at the same time, it is similar. The protagonists are the same and the conflict is unresolved, but it has moved on. We learned lessons and we applied them.

In those days, the implications of political and personal decisions were immediate. The effectiveness of hunger strikes was measured by how long prisoners could survive without food, and by whether the concentration of minds and action would help save the prisoners' lives, or whether our political enemies could defeat the campaign that supported them.

During the hunger-strike period, our minds were concentrated on saving prisoners' lives by defeating the criminalisation policy of the British government. That was the import of the prisoners' five demands that would recognise that the prisoners in the H-Blocks and the women in Armagh were political prisoners. The British knew it, Dublin knew it, and that is why the stakes were so high.

That is why the British set about a sustained campaign to assassinate leading members of the campaign, through their agents, the UDA. The leader of the Irish Independence Party, John Turnley (a Protestant), and Queen's University historian,

Miriam Daly, were shot dead. The UDA made an attempt on the life of Bernadette McAliskey and her husband, Michael, in January 1981, severely wounding them both. Bernadette used to stay in my house in Dublin. Her life was in danger – so much so that the *Irish Press* asked me to contribute to an obituary. I remember visiting Bernadette in hospital after the near-fatal attack. As Bernadette struggled out of a coma, her disbelief in a creator was challenged by the apparition that appeared before her. Luckily it turned out to be nothing more than heavily bearded Belfast republican Tom Hartley, sitting at the end of the bed.

In order to win in the Twenty-Six Counties, the H-Block/Armagh campaign had to win the active support of public opinion. Sure, we had sympathetic support, but it was not organised or mobilised.

The right-wing 1973–77 Labour/Fine Gael government had been roundly trounced in the general election. Its Fianna Fáil replacement continued the see no evil, hear no evil strategy with regard to British policy, albeit without the hectoring anti-republican tones of Conor Cruise O'Brien, Paddy Cooney and Liam Cosgrave. The Section 31 censorship on Irish radio and TV that banned republicans from the airwaves was reinforced by an active left-wing sect in RTÉ, the Workers' Party. They benefited from and promoted anti-republican bias and censorship.

While Section 31 directly affected broadcasting, its effects dominated all mainstream media. The public was not getting the message about the Birmingham Six, the Castlereagh torture conveyor belt, collusion, sectarian killings and other aspects of Britain's iron-fist policy. How could they when the flagship current affairs programme on RTÉ, dominated by the Workers' Party and co-thinkers, portrayed even the SDLP as nationalist extremists?

Workers' Party spokespersons were regularly paraded in front of cameras to inform the audience that civil rights were old hat and that "bread and butter" issues were now the order of the day. They insisted that the "Provos" were "reactionary fascists", "mindless criminals", increasingly isolated and losing support to the new vanguard represented by the Workers' Party. Unionist sectarianism, the driving force of the northern state, never received a mention.

I had been in the US in 1977 with Bernadette McAliskey and Fergus O'Hare, on a speaking tour aimed at building solidarity. We found that Irish-Americans and left-wing activists were much more clued in to what was happening in the Six Counties. The activist audiences of trade unionists and students wanted to know about the prisons and the criminalisation policy. They asked how the brutal policy of Labour direct ruler Roy Mason was going to be defeated. That was the question of the hour. Bernadette, Fergus and I stressed that it could be defeated only through united action.

That policy was in reality a joint London–Dublin policy. The southern establishment, the silent partner, had a conservative anti-republican mentality. A defeat of the northern nationalist resistance was a very acceptable outcome if it could be done quietly and without too much public fuss that might arouse southern opinion.

We told audiences in several US cities about the huge anti-repression conference in Coalisland in 1977. This was when all the anti-unionist activists had come together to thrash out a proposal for a mass single-issue campaign on the prisoners. The strategy was beginning to gain support. It came into sharper focus in 1979 when Bernadette McAliskey ran in the European election that year. Sinn Féin still had a strategy of electoral boycott. I resigned from my job in Dublin to go and organise the campaign in Derry with Eamon McCann for six weeks. The outcome of that election campaign, and the public support that Bernadette received from the prisoners in response to her focus on the criminalisation policy, also sharpened our minds on the way forward. The traditional republican view that politics had to be subordinated to support for the armed struggle was increasingly recognised, by republicans, as self-defeating.

A short time later, the time was right for the National H-Block/Armagh campaign. The impetus was coming from the prisoners, from questioning republicans and from political activists. They wanted a focus on a mass campaign to restore political status for political prisoners and to restore credibility to the demand for Irish self-determination.

My own personal memories of the period are dominated by the four areas in which I was politically active: Derry, Belfast, Dublin and Wicklow.

At the time, I lived in Drumcondra on Dublin's north side, and I worked in Bray, County Wicklow, in the ITGWU branch office in the town. I travelled at weekends to Belfast to support the successful People's Democracy (the original PD) candidates, John McAnulty and Fergus O'Hare, in the 1981 local council elections. That was an eye-opener, particularly the systematic vote stealing by the Workers' Party. On polling day, the Workers' Party bus did a continuous revolving tour of the polling stations. They systematically tried to steal the votes of thousands of abstaining republicans. The small but significant size of the "Sticky" vote had been testament to how many times party members could vote in a day. The RUC tolerated it and the SDLP ignored it. It was not a threat to the status quo – quite the opposite, in fact.

This time, their role was challenged. Many republicans came out to vote for anti-H-Block/Armagh candidates, and activists tried to prevent Workers' Party personation. The result was that the Sticky vote collapsed. People's Democracy's aim, to "Dump Fitt" and to "Ditch Devlin" was successful. The anti-H-Block movement's most credible electoral spokespersons, Paddy Devlin and Gerry Fitt, suffered a bloody nose from which they would not recover. Politics was turning on its head.

When Bobby Sands defeated Harry West in the Fermanagh/ South Tyrone by-election, it opened even more eyes. The news that RTÉ current affairs head, Joe Mulholland, had reluctantly sent a camera crew to the count, on the basis that Sands had no chance, exposed a problem with the Sticky-Fine Gael-Labour view of the world – it was out of touch with reality.

The Drumcondra H-Block/Armagh Action Group met in my home in the evening. During the day, I supported the Bray H-Block/Armagh Action Group, using lunch hour to support campaign work. The Bray H-Block work was fascinating because it included ITGWU members who set up a sub-committee of the local branch of the union in support of the hunger strikers. The branch secretary, Bernard Connolly, a long-time Labour Party member, was sympathetic to the plight of the hunger strikers.

His stance was indicative of the support the hunger strikers were receiving on the ground from ordinary workers and among people generally. That was not reflected in the political structures of the state. The main political parties and the upper echelons of the trade unions were, by and large, H-Block-free zones. Those in the political and media establishment who were hostile presumed that the way to defeat the H-Block campaign was to ignore it, to pretend that it was not significant, to marginalise it.

If Sands' election defeated this cynical strategy, so too did the response to his funeral, when hundreds of thousands of people around Ireland took to the streets. In Bray, over 1,000 workers left their workplace, and walked to the Town Hall as a gesture of sympathy and to mark their disgust at Thatcher's policy. I can remember being so proud of the people of Bray and Wicklow that day and also of the work we had done to enable people to demonstrate their true feelings.

The campaign's biggest enemy was ignorance (and ignorance's best friend, prejudice). We had to connect the experience of the nationalists in the North (the "nationalist nightmare") with the consciousness of the people of the South. The relentless schedule of tours by mothers and sisters of prisoners around the Twenty-Six Counties helped. When they wore only a blanket at pickets and public demonstrations, it had an immediate and human impact.

The campaign to support the prisoners helped to connect 1971, when southern opposition to British policy (such as internment) was a powerful political force, to 1981, after years of repression. It helped wipe away the years of fear, engendered by the Garda heavy gang, the miscarriages of justice, the sinister police intimidation of parents that discouraged political involvement among the young, and visits to employers that lost people their jobs in a period of recession. Young people increasingly were no longer afraid.

In Bray, we learned the value of mass political action. We learned how to generate political interest, how to connect local with national support and how to challenge the political establishment. We could not go round those elected as political leaders. We learned not to place reliance on them, but to rely on our own capacity for political action. We challenged politicians directly to respond to the groundswell of public support for the prisoners.

The Fianna Fáil government of Charlie Haughey had a "republican" image. It was a mirage, but one many could not see through. Fianna Fáil representatives, high and low, expressed support in private to H-Block supporters and increasingly concerned members of the public. They said and did effectively nothing in public.

This hypocrisy was evident as Bobby Sands neared death. The family demanded and was allowed meetings with An Taoiseach, Mr Haughey. Having listened sympathetically to the Sands family, Haughey put his arm around Bobby Sands' mother and said, looking her straight in the eye, *"I will not let your son die."* All that deeper understanding of our own economic and political exclusion. I can recall one particularly effective protest when Charlie Haughey spoke at a meeting on a UN programme for women's rights in Dublin. Women unfurled a banner supporting the Armagh women and held it unfurled under the platform during the entirety of his speech. It was actions such as this, one of many thousands, which helped to break the silence.

The campaign and our efforts to build it were inspired by those wonderful human beings who, in losing their lives, gave new life to a years-old struggle for justice and equality.

I feel privileged that I had an opportunity to participate in history.

STILL LIVES ON IN MINDS AND HEARTS
Seán Kelleher, republican, former teacher

IT IS HARD TO BELIEVE THAT ALMOST TWENTY-FIVE YEARS HAVE PASSED since ten young men died in the H-Blocks of Long Kesh in what many of us in the south of Ireland refer to as the Six Counties. A person would need to be in his or her mid-thirties now in 2006, or older, to have any memory or understanding of what that traumatic period was all about. A generation has grown up that relies mainly on parents, other people and media accounts to get a feel for how such events impacted on Irish lives and drew the attention of the media and people worldwide.

As those of us who lived in the Ireland of 1981 know, the IRA and the British army were involved in an intense and often bitter struggle. The latter's objective was to defeat the IRA and maintain British rule in the North. The former wanted the British government to disengage from the North, so that an independent republic could be established, embracing the whole island of Ireland. However, republicans knew that Irish unity could not be achieved overnight or in the short term. The immediate aim of IRA prisoners was to be granted political status and not be classified as criminals.

Here in West Cork, where I still reside, people were asking what could be done to alleviate the worsening situation in the North, and Long Kesh in particular. It gives me a sense of pride and satisfaction that community leaders emerged in many of the towns and villages throughout West Cork, and this led to people coming onto the roads and streets in groups to demonstrate public support for the prisoners. Local anti-H-Block committees came into existence in locations as far apart as Kinsale and

Castletownbere. Such public support for the plight of the hunger-striking prisoners was also in evidence in other parts of County Cork, including Cork city. Great numbers of people marched throughout the country. With no positive response forthcoming from the British government, the inevitable happened, and Bobby Sands MP died on 5 May 1981. This event brought huge sympathy and support for the hunger strikers' cause, not only in Ireland, but also in many countries throughout the world.

When Francis Hughes and Raymond McCreesh died shortly after Bobby Sands, the pressure was mounting on politicians to act. Hopes of some movement were raised when a meeting took place between relatives of the deceased hunger strikers and the then Taoiseach, Charles Haughey.

I remember distinctly the relieved demeanour of those relatives, shown on television, emerging from the meeting. It is my recollection that Charles Haughey told them that no more men would die on hunger strike. What a misleading promise! As everyone knows, seven more deaths were to follow the first three: Patsy O'Hara, Joe McDonnell, Martin Hurson, Kevin Lynch, Kieran Doherty TD, Tom McElwee and, on 20 August, Michael Devine.

Instead of honouring his promise, Charles Haughey called a general election for June 1981.

Prisoner-support groups in West Cork decided to put forward a candidate on an anti-H-Block ticket. At the convention in Dunmanway, that honour was bestowed upon myself. We had three weeks to get the vote out. People were generous in the giving of their time and financial support for the campaign. The coverage given to our efforts by the local print media and radio was also of considerable benefit.

I have an abiding memory of great numbers of dedicated people, men and women of all age groups, emerging from the towns, villages and rural areas of south-west Cork and putting their energy and commitment wholeheartedly into the election campaign. Former Mid-Ulster MP Bernadette Devlin McAliskey was guest speaker at a Bandon rally in May 1981. Experienced election observers said that the turnout of people for the visit was the largest that they had ever seen in the area.

In one humorous incident, one of our supporters was canvassing nuns in a convent in Dunmanway. One sister said of the candidate, "Sure that poor man being kept behind bars would not be able to do much for us even if elected." She didn't realise that I was a *non-prisoner* candidate!

I never witnessed before that time, or since, any event that captured the attention of people in such a way as the hunger strikes did. We received 1,097 first-preference votes, with a considerable number of other preferences cast in every polling booth throughout the constituency. Had further time been available to meet with and seek the support of more people, the prisoner issue would have generated even greater support I believe.

Haughey lost the election, his defeat inaugurating coalition government administrations ever since. A new government was formed with Garrett FitzGerald as Taoiseach. This new administration did not succeed either in getting the British to change their stance on the prisoner issue.

What is the legacy of ten young men sacrificing their lives for a cause they strongly believed in? It is my belief that in their doing what they did, the spirit of a nation was aroused. People who had been living quietly in their communities for many years suddenly came to life and, in many instances, demonstrated publicly their sense of horror and indignation at the way in which the prisoner issue was allowed to deteriorate.

The election successes of Bobby Sands in the North, Kieran Doherty and Paddy Agnew in the South, Owen Carron after Bobby's death, and other strong electoral performances, shocked the political establishments, North and South. There was a sense of alarm among politicians, and those in power now knew that they were not dealing with what they may have perceived as just a small group of prisoners but, with people who had strong support at the ballot box as well.

Almost twelve years after the IRA ceasefire of August 1994 and after the IRA's decommissioning of armaments in 2005, a stalemate situation exists. When the IRA campaign was in progress, politicians in both parts of Ireland and in Britain said repeatedly that if the campaign ended, talks to resolve the conflict could begin. Yet, the North remains under direct rule. I find this unacceptable and feel a sense of frustration at the lack of progress in resolving the problem.

How serious are politicians to be taken when they talk about bringing about a settlement? My main fear is that mainstream parties may accept the re-establishment of an assembly in the North as a solution to what is termed the Irish problem. The putting in place of such an assembly would not be a final solution and, in my view, cannot be allowed to be seen as such.

The prisoners' sacrifice no longer dominates the news headlines, but the memory of carrying such a sacrifice to its ultimate conclusion still lives on in the minds and hearts of those of us who want the Irish people to govern themselves.

A greater recognition of diversity within Ireland now exists, notwithstanding the divisions that remain between republicans and nationalists on one side and unionists and loyalists on the other. I hope that in time each tradition, with its own beliefs and ideology, can be accommodated in one administration within the island of Ireland. If we of the present generation are to remain true to the ideals of the hunger strikers, we must strive to persuade unionists that they have much more in common with the rest of us who live on this island than with the British people who reside across the Irish Sea.

THOSE CHERISHED PICTURES
Rita O'Hare, activist, former editor An Phoblacht

CHRISTMAS 1980. WE HAD JUST MOVED INTO OUR OWN HOUSE IN Dublin, having lived in rented accommodation for years. The 1980 hunger strike had ended shortly before, and the feeling of relief that a deal had been achieved that would end the obscenity of the H-Blocks and Armagh was palpable in our family and in *An Phoblacht/Republican News* where I then worked. It was as if we felt that we could enjoy the Christmas break with the family and friends without guilt at our self-indulgence when the prisoners were in such conditions. There was hope that the Brits would keep their word.

By early in the New Year of 1981, it was clear that this was not the case and that another hunger strike was looming.

In those days of censorship, *An Phoblacht* had a particular role and responsibility. It was the only vehicle that republicans could rely on for information on what was really happening in the prisons. With the onset of the 1981 hunger strike, *An Phoblacht* became even more central in the propaganda war.

The hunger strike, of course, dominated all else in *An Phoblacht* that year. It was our part in the battle. It had to be the best, the most comprehensive and informed. It had to be political and analytical, but it had also to be personal. These men were in the forefront of the fight, symbols of resistance for republicans. But they were ordinary human beings, sons and brothers, boyfriends, husbands and fathers. Not many were husbands or fathers. Most of them were too young, barely into their twenties or early thirties, on the threshold of adult life. They were so young, so heartbreakingly young.

Nowhere was that so poignantly portrayed as in the profiles

An Phoblacht carried of those prisoners going on the hunger strike, their families' accounts of them, where they were from, the photographs.

Those photographs. These were not old photos from musty albums, past history, men in old-fashioned clothes. They were recent. Boys in jeans and tracksuits. School photos from just a few years earlier. Photos of the football teams they played with. First Communion. First dance. Making the hay on the family farm. Harvest of just a few years previous. The families wanted firm promises that the photographs, these precious, irreplaceable memories, would be returned. They knew, these mothers, when they gave us those cherished pictures and told us the stories of these young lives, exactly what it meant. They knew what would follow, yet they endured it.

I heard of Bobby Sands' death on the early RTÉ news. No bin lids to herald the awful news in Dublin.

And it went on all that dreadful year.

But they endured it, those young men and their families.

In his book, *Ten Men Dead*, David Beresford ends with a quote from a Yeats play, *The King's Threshold*. He quotes the play several times to explain hunger striking in Irish terms. The King, of course, is Thatcher. A woman, a mother, but what a parody of both. The last quote reads:

> When I and these are dead
> We should be carried to some windy hill
> To lie there with uncovered face a while
> That mankind and that leper there may know
> Dead faces laugh. King! King! Dead faces laugh.

Beresford calls the poet's dying words, "as fitting an epitaph as any for the great Irish hunger strike of 1981".

I do not know if these or any words can ever be fitting to describe the suffering and the heroic sacrifices of the year of '81.

A FAMILY ALBUM
Trisha Ziff, photographer, filmmaker, curator

It is one of the peculiar characteristics of the photograph that it
isolates single moments in time

- Marshall McLuhan

I *GOOGLED* THE WORDS '*HUNGER STRIKE IRELAND*' AND HIT THE BUTTON
'images' on the search engine, curious to see what photographs might
appear. What would be the first image on my computer associated with
those three words? Unclear as to how the algorithm decides which image
represents those words, I wondered if someone else *googled* the same
words would the result be the same as mine?

On my screen appeared an image linked to *The Irish Times*. I had seen
various incarnations of it many times before. A grid of portraits of the
ten hunger strikers of 1981. Head and shoulders; ten young men's faces
staring out at me, most of them smiling. Portraits that immediately took
me back to a time impossible to forget. I was able to put a name to each
face despite the passage of time. Portraits invested with memories of
protest, of community, of anger and sadness, of a world I was welcomed
into despite my status as an outsider and my English accent. I associate
these photographs with a watershed moment that changed so many lives,
political directions and visions. Ten young men who, through their bodies
and with their political convictions, stood up to the might of British
imperialism. Humble snapshots perhaps, but the power of their gaze,
those eyes and the vision they represent, is still powerful.

I revisit each portrait remembering what we learned about each one
of these men as we counted their days of protest hoping for a political
breakthrough. Who were the men behind these portraits? Where were
they from? What were their stories, their families, passions, idiosyncrasies,

their activism? Each one unique, yet at the same time a neighbor, a brother, a friend, a comrade; ordinary young men in extraordinary times.

What do these portraits reveal? What are the small details we discover that makes them unique? Only one of them wore glasses - Micky Divine. Most were too young to even think about that and yet would all slowly lose their sight as the days without nourishment increased. Kieran Doherty and Kevin Lynch wear their manicured late '70s moustaches with flare! 'Burt Reynolds meets Frank Zappa'. Just one has a beard - Patsy O'Hara - before the no-wash protest, yet, later, they all would join him. Martin Hurson's portrait is probably taken from a wedding photo – he is the only one wearing a tie and just visible is a flower pinned to his lapel. Whose wedding, I wonder? Not his own: he died single at twenty-five. Francis Hughes looks directly into the camera, strong, confident – a rare moment perhaps when he was not on the run or on active service – a legendary warrior. Joe McDonnell smiles in an infectious happy-go-lucky way. He and Thomas McElwee's portraits are semi-profiles but they are caught gently smiling as they turn toward the camera. Thomas was Francis Hughes' cousin; families within families. Raymond McCreesh's fully blown grin. What happened or was said to make him laugh? Bobby Sands also smiling; his long hair and wild spirit, the poet. Photographs taken before they were imprisoned, or perhaps in the case of Bobby taken while he had political status in the Cages.

Ten young men whose images were captured at distinct moments when the idea of hunger strike must have been far from any of their thoughts. Together, these portraits form a unique family album. How many times have I looked carefully at these small postage stamp images or seen them reproduced in books, in newspapers, and on posters. Reproduced by artists, painted on gable ends, blown-up massive, and interpreted in color, or hammered out in copper on plaques, the image barely recognizable from the original photograph, like Chinese whispers. Portraits engraved in our memories; a sixtieth of a second becoming timeless and iconic.

A wedding photograph taken from its frame, another perhaps chosen from a strip of four from a photo booth, another cut out of another photograph - a group or family photograph where now one of the faces is missing. Photographs taken from an envelope filled with other snapshots, or carefully peeled from a family album. Precious photographs chosen by family members to represent a life. To those families, the photographs told other stories; a Christmas, a party, a birthday, a night with friends, stories unknown to most of us. I wonder who was behind each camera and what must it have felt like to have taken that photograph used now in this radically different context?

I think about a knock on the door; who was the person that was welcomed into a home, despite all the anxiety and stress and fear and, for sure, was offered a cup of tea graciously before collecting the photograph and taking it away. A family knowing their son had embarked on hunger strike, a parent or wife being asked to hand over a portrait of their loved one. How did they decide which one? Or was there only one? I think about the decision and the generosity of that act of parting with each precious photograph, only to see it reproduced a thousand times on posters and in print.

1981 – a time before cell phones, before Facebook and the onslaught of the selfie, when taking photographs was not an everyday occurrence but marked a special moment. A time when not everyone owned a camera. I think about the place these images lived before being shared with all of us. The family album, stiff sticky card pages covered with cellophane, where now there is a yellowed empty space – retrieved from under the cushion on the sofa or from a drawer or kept flat in between the pages of a book. Photographs taken from a place of familiarity and belonging, shared with a community, shared with the world both supportive and hostile.

The private image becoming public—the personal political.
I look at the photographs once more and wonder how different each of these men must have looked in those last days of their lives; gaunt, long-haired, bearded, pale, prematurely aged by hunger, so different from these portraits.

In the nineteenth century many believed the photographic portrait not only captured the image of a person but also on careful examination you could see the soul.

SHADOW

John Montague

Across these lands a shadow grows longer,
the mortuary visage of Margaret Thatcher,
flushed with righteous anger,
a games mistress, a grocer's daughter,
her thumb on the scales of justice

Satisfied that her name is linked forever
with lengthening dole queues, humiliated miners,
riot-rended football terraces, that absurd Armada,
and the dying hunger strikers
who wrought that Iron Lady

Into their chief recruiting officer.

SANDS

John Montague

This is a song of silence.
This is the sound of the bone
breaking through the skin
of a slowly wasting man.
This is the sound of his death;
but turn the hourglass,
also of his living on.

THE WRITING OF RODAÍ MAC CORLAÍ
Colm Scullion, former blanket man

Colm Scullion, H3, to his mother
May 10th, 1981

HELLO MA AND ALL AT HOME. HOW'S THINGS? WELL, I SUPPOSE YOU'RE all waiting to hear of Frank's death.

At the minute it seems unavoidable. We're expecting it and we're well prepared for it.

We were expecting Bob's death, but it still came as a shock. He died at twelve minutes past one and the doctors confirmed it at seventeen minutes past. His mother and sister had just left the room before he died. Then his father, brother and brother-in-law came in and were at his bedside when he died. He was in a coma and his breathing was laboured and it just stopped and that was it. Before he went into a coma he was in a lot of pain.

It's still very hard to accept that he's dead. You'd think that he was away on a visit or something and that he'd be back shortly. He came to our wing nearly two years ago and from then up until he left, he was the main man on the wing. The Irish teacher, lecturer, poet and O/C during the last hunger strike.

He knew even before he went on hunger strike that he'd never be back in the wing again and he was right. He said there was no chance of this ending before there would be several deaths. His would be the first and it wouldn't be in vain. When he went on hunger strike they kept him on the wing for three weeks and then the screws came one morning and told him he was being moved to the hospital. I'll never forget him at the top of the wing going out.

The last thing he shouted was "Goodbye, lads", and away he went. Well, at least he's happy now. Anyway we don't expect Frank to last long. Probably sometime next week or the week after. Mrs Hughes must be wrecked, God help the woman.

Well, we're pleased with the way the support is going but it's going to take something big to break the Brits. We think they're just going to dig in and sit it out. Anyway, the whole world knows now what we're up against. No matter what way this issue ends the Brits have created a lot of hatred which they'll feel for a long time.

Well, what do you think of the poem Bobby did? *Rodaí Mac Corlaí*. Look after it. I know it all anyway but just in case I forget. I'll get it done on a hanky sometime.

I discovered the above comm in an envelope that my mother Patsy had proudly kept in a drawer for years. It ends with a reference to the now famous poem that Bobby wrote about Rodaí Mac Corlaí, the United Irishman hanged on the bridge of Toome.

The story of Rodaí was conceived around the hearths in Ballyscullion after the 1798 Rebellion and passed on in the oral tradition. Almost two hundred years later the poem was born in a filthy, dark, H-Block cell. Ironically, Bobby, like Rodaí was to die at the hands of the British, fighting the same injustice.

The story was told to me by my father, Kevin, as he had heard it as a child, in the house he was born in and the very house Rodaí had taken shelter in.

Bobby was intrigued by the story and decided to compose his tribute. I repeated it over and over while he picked my brains on the names of hills, places and customs of the Ballyscullion /Lough Beg area.

He would pace the cell wrapped in a blanket, stroking his beard, then pause at a clear space on the wall and write a line or two. During the no-wash protest we would keep a piece of the wall clean at the door for writing. We would use the lead of a pencil about one inch long, which was easily concealed inside your body. I wasn't allowed to look anywhere near the wall until the poem was completed. I think it took Bobby a couple of days before he was satisfied, as he kept altering lines here and there. I remember he had mentioned the townland of Brecart between Moneyglass and Toome but later omitted it.

When his *Prison Poems* was first published in late1981 the first line includes a mistake. Bobby had written Duneane *not* Duneaney.

> I am Rodaí of Duneane – MacCorlaí - Antrim born!
> This day in Toome I meet my doom for an oath that I have sworn.
> On yonder oak on Roughery Hill a jackdaw I have heard,
> It waits to steal my very soul 'tis surely the devil's bird.

Roughery is a steep hill running towards Moneyglass.
Rodaí's father had also died at the gallows. Some say it was for making pikes, others say that he was caught stealing sheep.

> My greying mother tara the pity, cut my silent father free,
> Where he danced like a ship on an angry wave from yonder hanging tree.
> And he felt no touch nor heard no scream his deathly gaze a loss,
> As he slumped into her cradled arms, like the Christ did from the cross!

Bobby had a keen interest in the countryside. I told him stories from my childhood, working on Willie Thompson's farm with my cousin Leo in the evenings; stories about my grandfather Paddy ('Butterman') Scullion, well-known stiller, who was jailed twice for poteen; having our first taste of alcohol as teenagers in the Crosskeys Inn; the summers in the Moss, cutting and handling turf; then the poaching on the Bann and Lough Beg for salmon and eels with my father, not to mention the near escapes from the bailiffs.

Bobby loved it all. We made plans that when we'd get our freedom we would go poaching. We also planned to go to Gweedore, Donegal, to immerse ourselves in Irish. We had something to look forward to, away from the hell of H3.

> But yer they came the decent folk, from humble homes by moss and greenly glen,
> They came with trembling heart to die, those bold United Men.
> And 'twas at Crosskeys the pikes gleamed white 'neath a telling yellow moon,

As the common folk (and there, there the poacher's son) went out to
meet their doom.

The MacCorlaí's had left Ballyscullion with other locals, including members of the Brown family, and proceeded to Toome where they dismantled the bridge. They then marched on to Antrim where the battle was won and lost.

At Antrim town the cannon roared, the ancient Cú howled at the sight,
The primrose wept, the jackdaw danced, and black death ran through the night.

Another mistake in the original print is in the following verse where the word 'lough' (meaning Lough Neagh) was mistakenly published as 'laugh'.

In the morning mist that came in silent dread the great Lough whimpered sore,
For a thousand souls had trod her breast and the lark would sing no more.

When I was released, I continued my research, collecting more stories.

Brothers Paul, Pat and Simon Brown told me how their ancestor Paul Brown was stabbed during the battle of Antrim and died on his way back to Ballyscullion, along the roadside halfway between Toome and the Elk Bar, "at the big sheugh", known locally as "Paul's drain". They also showed me the location of the MacCorlaí home place on a hill known as "MacCorlaí's Brae", which is on the Ballyscullion Road, close to the present GAA grounds (where their nephew, Bellaghy GAA chairman Sean Brown, was later killed by loyalist paramilitaries, most of whom were state agents). They said that there was more than one MacCorlaí present at Antrim. Their story was supported in later years when I was researching in the Public Records Office, where I discovered a Francis McCorley (Rodaí's brother), the names Brown and Larkin (Larkin was my great grandmother, whose ancestors lived in our house), all working at the construction of the Earl Bishop's palace in 1796.

Rodaí was now on the run; he had teamed up with other United Irishmen and was hounded by the Redcoats.

> Oh! The spring was born by lough and land when I chanced by Springwell Brae,
> In the hope of a roof and a bite to eat and a ship to Americay.

Springwell Brae is a steep hill in Ballyscullion from where the locals fetched drinking water. As children, we spent many happy days playing on it with our sleighs in the winter.

Rodaí had left our house in Ballyscullion Mór and was taken across the Bann to Ballyscullion Beg on the Antrim side of Lough Beg. The story goes that he was staying with a family called McErlean.

Mrs McErlean was cooking brachan (or breach) on a crane over the fire. However, Rodaí noticed that every time the brachan heated up, the crane was pulled away from the glow of the fire allowing it to cool down while McErlean kept stirring it. She asked Roddy for his shoes; the plan was now in place.

> In Ballyscullion I spent some nights, in Bellaghy three or four,
> Then I crossed the Bann with a fisherman to my native Antrim shore,
> By the winding bog I came upon McErlain, and he with a grudge for me,
> But he bid me day and asked me stay and share his hospitality.

> The jackdaw fluttered and danced with joy and me the blinded fool,
> For I slipped into Hell and by the Devil's fire I rested on his stool
> 'You'll have some breach,' said a greying soul, 'and let me take your shoes,'
> And she stirred the pot and stirred the pot and I slept before her rouge.

The story goes that McErlean had sent a neighbour called Duffin to alert Sam Finneston or Fenton, a Yeoman, of Rodaí's whereabouts. Rodaí had had a fall out with the local priest. Apparently, he had entered the chapel and pulled the chalice from the priest's hands and thrown it into the congregation. This turned the locals against him.

> McErlean the Curse had sent a man on the road from Moneyglass to Toome,
> And Duffin the devil ran to The Rock for Cruel Sam to fix my doom
> And the woman McErlain she stirred the pot and stirred the pot and never would it warm
> 'Till came the Fencibles in their coats of red and n'er a one did warn.

When Bobby finished the poem, he called everyone to the door. I remember him shouting across the wing at Big Tom McElwee, "Suas ag an doras, Seo é." Men got up to their doors. The wing went silent as he recited Rodaí MacCorlaí. There was a mixed reaction. The wing cheered, while a couple of the jokers (Hector McNeill!) blew raspberries and farted out the side of the door.

I personally felt very proud of it. My simple story had turned into a beautiful poem.

It was as if Bobby knew every field and hill in Ballyscullion. He was able to take himself out of the cell and stand at the foot of our 'Stra Field' and look east across the Bann, towards the Largey Line, Crosskeys, Rougery, Moneyglass, Duneane and Toome, then west over Springwell Brae, Bellaghy, Slievegallion Braes and the majestic Sperrins guarding South Derry.

Some years later I was privileged to share stories with Bobby's mum Rosaleen, exchanging everything from his childhood to the final days on the blanket. My daughters, Aisling and Blaithin, were with me. The stories were both sad and funny and we all learned something. For example, Aisling was Bobby's favourite girl's name, therefore the name of my first born; or, that Bobby hiked to Galway to busk, with only a penny in his pocket and a guitar and getting a lift there with a group of Travellers.

I remember saying, "Ye know, we had planned to go and stay a few months in Gweedore to brush up on our Irish, but it wasn't to be." Rosaleen replied, "Bobby just got there before you, he's waiting on you."

And the sunset red on Slievegallion Braes, the jackdaw hid in shame,
The primrose wept for Rodaí boy, for McCorlaí óg was slain,
And all along the Largey Line a woman wails and tonight she'll roam the glen,
Oh, Rodai of Duneane! - McCorlaí - Antrim born -will e'er we meet again?

I'd like to dedicate this article to my mother Patsy and my late father Kevin Scullion in gratitude for the great hearth and home they provided their children

A PROFOUND AND HISTORIC EVENT
Robert Ballagh, artist, activist

THE ENORMOUS SACRIFICE OF SANDS AND HIS NINE COMRADES REVER-
berated around Ireland and the world in a way that no other
event has done in recent Irish history. No rationalisation and no
revisionist spin can erase the memory or blur the reality of that
act of self-sacrifice, and when historians, journalists, songwriters
and others reflect on the last thirty years, the names of Bobby
Sands and the other hunger strikers will loom larger than most
others.

Natural political instincts and even basic human sympathy
meant that ordinary Irish people manifested strong support for
the prisoners in 1981. Two prisoners – hunger striker Kieran
Doherty and blanket man Paddy Agnew – won Dáil seats in the
1981 general election, while Bobby Sands took a Westminster
seat. This caused apoplexy in Margaret Thatcher's government
and consternation in Charlie Haughey's Fianna Fáil, which
would otherwise have secured an overall majority in that election. Around the country, black flags festooned the less fashionable housing estates; there were marches, protests and even
strike actions in Ireland. Internationally the hunger strike
stirred the admiration and respect of most progressives and all
those movements which still found themselves in struggles for
their national rights.

However, the reaction to these momentous events from official quarters was one of shock (for example, nobody but the most
committed of the prisoners' supporters expected them to win
seats in parliaments, North and South). And while Thatcher's
government, red in tooth and claw, fought the prisoners with a

ferocity that shocked even some British civil servants, the Dublin body politic and media reacted with a mixture of paralysis and sullen hostility.

Twenty-five years on, it is possible to reflect more realistically on the hunger strike, its origins and effects. The prisoners' motivation arose as a direct response to the British government's disastrous criminalisation policy, which aimed to depict the entire Anglo–Irish conflict as a criminal conspiracy. Strip away all the recrimination and political pedantry, and one is left with one simple explanation for the hunger strike as expressed, with little sophistication but much meaning, in the words of "The H-Block Song":

> So I'll wear no convict uniform
> Nor meekly serve my time
> That Britain might brand Ireland's fight
> Eight hundred years of crime.

Emotional, admittedly, but by 1981, literally thousands of young people had been sucked into a violent conflict and ended up serving long jail sentences for their principles. Those politicians who stupidly imagined that the same young men and women were going to accept the status of criminals must have been suffering from emotional and political problems of their own.

The direct result of the hunger strike was that the prisoners had their rather elementary demands ceded to them, some immediately and others over a period of time. These were: no prison uniform, no prison work, free association, visits, letters, parcels and recreation facilities, and remission (though not in full). But the political effects were more fundamental.

On a superficial level, Sinn Féin and the IRA were immeasurably strengthened and replenished with mass support, recruits and a renewed motivation. But much deeper political waters were stirred by the hunger strike. Dr Garret FitzGerald has admitted that this period and the subsequent success of Sinn Féin at the ballot box caused him to instigate the Anglo–Irish Agreement. Sinn Féin, meanwhile, had discovered that the ballot box and wider political forms of struggle were, indeed, as effective as the Armalite.

It would be simplistic to argue that the hunger strikers consciously stimulated the peace process; they could hardly have anticipated such specific, long-term effects. But those who followed them learned many lessons from that period, in particular, that most Irish people support measures that will achieve political democracy as well as peace.

At the same time, the humility experienced by most people in the face of the hunger strikers' awesome sacrifice provoked another realisation which, over a period of time, contributed to a cross community awareness of how the Troubles have affected everyone. Today, both republicans and many loyalists – but, strangely, not the declining band of armchair unionists in South Dublin, nor those securocrats who still pine for "a bloody good war" – have learned to appreciate the pain and trauma of their political opponents.

A peculiar sociological and political fact of the peace process is that those who have fought and suffered the most are the most enthusiastic proponents of the peace process. At the same time, "constitutional" unionists in Belfast, along with their dwindling supporters club in corners of the Dublin media, are the most obdurate and bellicose opponents of political progress.

Twenty-five years after the hunger strike, another irony is that revisionism is in headlong retreat. Young Irish people feel none of the post-colonial shame that afflicted many in their parents' generation. They feel no need to apologise for Irish history, Irish political struggle or other aspects of their culture. On the contrary, they celebrate their identity.

Today, young people are intensely curious about the hunger

strike. But they also express bewilderment at the fact that they have been denied knowledge of the hunger strike by official sources.

Dublin people offered support to the hunger strikers in 1981, and today's generation want to know about those events even if others want to airbrush them out of history. None but the most bitterly prejudiced can deny that the fasting to death of ten young men in 1981 was a profound and historic event.

IN DEEP DESPAIR

William Brown, ecumenical Christian,
pro-Agreement unionist

THE HUNGER STRIKE OF 1981 WAS PIVOTAL FOR PROVISIONAL REPUBLI-
canism, stirring it internally and posing important questions.
Externally it refocused public interest in the Northern Irish situation, generating some renewed sympathy for the republican
cause. If anything, it hardened unionism, but its main significance was internal to Provisional republicanism. The hunger
strike gave it a modern icon, a heroic figure with whom it could
identify in an emotional sense, in a situation that could provide
opportunities and a new direction.

Bobby Sands, who was a determined young working-class
republican with obvious leadership qualities and a growing reputation as a poet and thinker, has primacy here. He was the first
of the ten hunger strikers to die, and, to an extent, his untimely
death recreated the sacrificial/redemptive ideology that Irish
republicanism had inherited from Patrick Pearse – but an ideology not without its moral problems.

Many were opposed to it even in principle; for a mass hunger
strike is a horrific instrument that is coercive in intent and violent
in its impact. And yet it is arguable that the personal sacrifice of
the ten prisoners was resonant with pathos in that it was a desperate attempt to persuade the world of their *bona fides* – that they
were not criminals; that there had to be reform appropriate to
their circumstances (in line with previous prison practice); and
that they should be accorded political status.

At a personal level, the real issue for me was whether such a
horrendous means, allied as it was to a republican physical-force

145

tradition, could ever be conducive to peace and reconciliation in a bitterly divided community – surely what "political status" ultimately had to be all about. As the poet, Yeats, put it in his "Easter 1916": "Too long a sacrifice / Can make a stone of the heart."

Whatever we think of hunger striking, the logic of this one was a clear political signpost, albeit on a long and tortuous road. Bobby Sands' by-election victory in Fermanagh and South Tyrone, when less than a month from death, was a sensational event. Though in a sense opportunistic, it became part of a process that paved the way for Sinn Féin to lay a new stress on politics. Unfortunately, for too long this would take the form of a halfway house – the "Armalite and the ballot box" – a policy that many regarded as contradictory.

Nevertheless, some believed that gradualism held the hope of light at the end of the tunnel, and that, once embarked upon, political involvement would inevitably lead Sinn Féin to the ballot box alone. Even so, negative and cynical political comment is in the ascendant in Northern Ireland and has often been a wet blanket on progress. Worse still is that when eventually proven wrong, the pundits of pessimism persist in proclaiming the old negative messages, while continuing to declaim against the liberals who sought to encourage progress by more positive analyses.

But then we must remember that the politics of sectarianism is intrinsically and inevitably negative, since its objective is to maintain the abject simplicity of a "them and us" status quo. Yet for all the grim foreboding that surrounded it, the hunger strike of 1981 strangely proved to be a pivotal event that, in the long haul, would contribute to the hopeful politics of a new beginning. It is significant here that Gerry Adams' book, *Hope and History – Making Peace in Ireland*, begins with the hunger strikes.

The hunger strike and its concomitant events were never remotely close to being seen in any such light by the vast majority of unionists. With the world looking on, they, of course, had to be interested and to respond to events as they unfolded, but their general attitude to it was quite similar to their reaction to the earlier dirty protest, ranging from studied indifference to scandalised disgust. It therefore made no positive impact on unionist thinking. In fact, unionists by and large continued to see the prisoners simply as criminals. They remained utterly opposed to the objectives of the hunger strike, and more especially its fundamental decriminalising principle.

Some went much further, being of the opinion that as IRA men the prisoners deserved all they got, even though from their perspective this was self-inflicted. Typical responses from extreme loyalists were cynical and self-fulfilling, and often in the form of sectarian jokes, ribald songs and macabre graffiti. Unionists' heroes were those who, like Prime Minister Margaret Thatcher, took the hardest and most uncompromising line by categorically rejecting the prisoners' five demands. Throughout the entire episode, she never once looked like conceding anything, nor was she ever likely to. Things were going backwards.

I was in deep despair over the hunger strike. I fervently believed that for humanitarian and political reasons, the prisoners shouldn't have died, nor been allowed to die in order to achieve what had been their lot under William Whitelaw. The whole business had been hopelessly misjudged and mismanaged. To me it showed just how far things could go wrong once we lost our sense of the importance of human dignity, our duty of care to our neighbour, or our respect for the sanctity of human life.

All of this was rooted in dire political failure – failure to engage in dialogue so that we might better understand and value each other, and prevent what the prisoners saw as the most terrible of last resorts. I, therefore, was in particular despair of unionism's self-righteous blindness to the *causal* violence and injustice of its own politico-military record, which had paved the way for republicanism in 1916 and again in 1969. And so I couldn't oppose political status for men whose people had suffered such grievances for so long and who were so sincere as to die for their political principles. Indeed, if ever in the world there was a bad, bitter and bungled crisis that called for an exercise of common sense and the thrice-blessed quality of mercy, this surely was it!

I was fearful that the serious trauma of a hunger strike, when added to our existing agony, might lead to some kind of new and terrible iconic ideology – that of a politically redemptive sacrifice as articulated by Patrick Pearse. I felt there were some signs that Bobby Sands might be accorded that status, but this never reached the extent I first feared. I recall a conference in 1998 where a dissident argued that "Bobby Sands didn't die for the Belfast Agreement", as though he had died for something far more noble and far-reaching. Anxious not to appear disrespectful, I pointed out that Bobby Sands had died for the five demands relating to political status. Political myths should be avoided.

Not that I ever doubted his sincerity, for I had always acknowledged his courage and genuine belief that he was a political prisoner, engaged in what to him was a noble cause. Obviously there were many reasons why I couldn't walk in his shoes, or see his war in the way he saw it, although I could well understand why and how it had happened – in which respect my sympathies were certainly not with ascendancy unionism. But I was certain that we should avoid new mythologies that would glorify suffering and death, leading to further violence and alienation, and impeding the making of peace and reconciliation.

So I couldn't see hunger strike as the right way to political status, and I recoiled from the idea of a national redemption based on Christological self-sacrifice. Christian redemption is not nationalistic, but universal: "For God so loved the *world* that he gave his only begotten Son". Yet like all democratic aspirations, nationalism has its legitimate place. I would contend, however, that this should be secondary, not only to Christian universalism (*catholicism* with a small *c*), but to the classical republicanism of the United Irishmen – that we are citizens of the world. This is increasingly obvious in the inter-related global village of the twenty-first century, so much so that universalism is now something of a truism.

A greater awareness of the important implications of this can make us better Irishmen and women, inasmuch as the great pluralist principle of the unity in diversity of Protestant, Catholic and Dissenter in liberty, equality and fraternity can be achieved only through the pursuit of broadly based and inclusive politics. Unity demands inclusivity. The message now, therefore, has to be one of dialogical engagement rather than sectarian violence, of pluralist politics rather than mere party interest, of community rather than self-serving or narrow tribal loyalty – a philosophy that requires us to live rather than die for Ireland.

Despite my misgivings, the hunger strike in quest of political status turned out to be a pivotal event. In time to come, it would lead to political participation and engagement, to the ceasefires, to the Agreement of 1998, eventually to long-anticipated demilitarisation – and thence to who knows what? In their own way, the ten hunger strikers made a most courageous contribution to a different, and in the end a much greater, purpose than they themselves could have imagined in their last dark and desperate days.

As with Patrick Pearse, it was not for them to know the outcome of their actions – the "terrible beauty" of how the future would unfold – which shows the futility of arguing that they didn't die for this or that cause or outcome. In the turn-out, what we try to live for, what we hope for, or even what we may choose to die for is never quite what we might have expected. There are things that are not for us to know, such are the mysteries of Providence. And although hope and history occasionally rhyme, hope in its future realisation can be very different and reach far beyond history as we have known it. It can transcend history, sometimes beyond our dreams.

We don't have all the answers, but we do have the shared moral truths of a common weal that includes our Christianity, to say nothing of our hard-earned experience, all of which can become the basis for renewed hope, if we so desire. We must learn the lessons of the past. Out of respect for the memory of Bobby Sands and his compatriots (as well as many, many others), we should re-evaluate our human consanguinity. This in turn could enable us to place a higher value on our own political status as fellow citizens and fit us to eschew narrow sectarianism by engaging in the pursuit of that which resonates with the best in our common Irishness, and with our common humanity as citizens of one world.

Such politics would demand that we resolve henceforward to work together as Protestant, Catholic and Dissenter for a continuing peace in which faith and hope can nurture the things that make for a better society, reconciled in liberty, equality and fraternity. And if we can continue to progress in that direction, then neither the hunger strikers nor any of the other victims of the Troubles will have died in vain. May they rest in peace.

(A poem by St Francis of Assisi written after receiving the stigmata. Irish version by Gabriel Rosenstock)

AG MOLADH DÉ
Froinsias d'Assisi

Taoi beannaithe, a Thiarna Dia, Cruthaitheoir na n-iontas.
Taoi láidir, Taoi mór is ró-ard,
Is Tú an Rí uilechumhachtach.
Is Tú, a Athair Naofa, Rí na bhflaitheas, Rí an domhain.
Trí Phearsa san Aon, a Thiarna Dia thar chách.
Is Tú an mhaith, an uilemhaith, an mhaith is airde,
A Thiarna Dia, is beo duit, is fíor.
Is Tú an grá is an charthain.
Is Tú an ghaois, an umhlaíocht is an fhoighne;
Áilleacht is ea Thú, is Tú an cheansacht, an tseasmhacht is ea
    Thú.
Suaimhneas is ea Thú, ríméad. Is Tú ár ndóchas is ár lúcháir go
    léir.
Is Tú an chóir cheart chothrom. Ionatsa atá ár saibhreas.
Taoi álainn, Taoi ceansa.
Is Tú an cosantóir,
    An coimirceoir
        An caomhnóir.
Is Tú an neart, is Tú an úire.
Is Tú ár ndóchas,
    Ár gcreideamh,
        Is ár ngrá,
Ár milseacht uile is ea Thú
Ár mbeatha shíoraí:
A Thiarna na n-iontas,
A Dhia uilechumhachtaigh, a Shlánaitheoir na trócaire.

MESSAGE FROM H-BLOCKS
Ulick O'Connor

Thinking of Apollo who went down among the swineherds
And of One who elected to be born in a stable,
I thought of those in Belfast who traced excrement on their cell
    walls
To send the world a message along the spirit's cable.

Then the final throw, the refusal of sap to the body,
The mind roaring along swerved avenues of agony,
Bishops shanghaied to tell them their soul was in danger
As the jailers discovered the value of Catholic theology.

That they should let you die rather than wear your own jacket
Defines the jackboot under that affable decorum.
Let it not be forgotten that this summer the Teagues in Belfast,
Out of the body's agony, made the world their forum.

(May–August 1981)

THEY DEFY COMPREHENSION
Jude Collins, writer, broadcaster

WHEN I THINK OF THE HUNGER STRIKERS, IT IS 1981 AGAIN, AND I'M
driving towards a fly-over. The fly-over is across the M2 leading
out of Belfast, and on the part of it that meets the grassy bank, in
huge letters, someone has painted the words 'Seven dead saves
are led'. It's almost certainly the work of young unionists from
the nearby Rathcoole estate, where Bobby Sands grew up, before
he and his family were intimidated from that part of Belfast.

The sight of that graffito stops me humming along to the car
radio and nudges two responses from me. First, the teacher part
clicks its tongue and wonders how people could go through life
believing that "our" is spelt "are" and "lead" is spelt "led". Then
the human part takes over, indignant. What sort of response is
that, to get upset about spelling matters when the message conveyed is so grim? The teacher part slinks back into my subcon-
scious, and I turn off for Glengormley, my good mood of a few
minutes ago replaced by unease and bafflement. The image of
seven young men, not ten miles from here, following one another into the grave, won't go away.

As with many people, the hunger strikes began a slow education for me. In 1981, I was recently returned from Canada. During the ten years away, I'd stayed interested in events at home,
but from a distance. Detached from the daily pain and rage, I
found myself adopting the commonsense view of the Troubles.
The conflict here was a clash between two tribes who, deaf to all
pleas, refused to stop fighting each other. Other countries had
given up religious wars centuries ago, but not us. Faced with this
backwardness, Britain was doing her best to hold the ring,

153

occasionally losing her temper as on Bloody Sunday, but for the most part playing a benign role and paying a price in soldiers' lives for her dedication to fair play.

Well, OK, maybe I knew it was a bit more complicated than that, but essentially the analysis seemed accurate. The problem came down to a small number of nutters with guns who were holding the rest of the Irish people hostage to their outdated thinking. And the solution? That lay with decent people, who must work even harder at getting along with each other, regardless of religion, and so isolate this unhinged minority. Had a member of the Alliance Party come knocking on my door in Winnipeg, I'd probably have signed up.

Then I came home. For the first twelve months or so, I was able to consign the Troubles to a space somewhere at the back of my head. However brutal, they didn't impinge on my daily life. But the hunger strikers were different. They would not stay on the periphery but kept crowding in to centre stage. As the weeks passed and the reports became more frightening, I ached for someone to talk to. Somebody must have a mental grip on this whole thing that would allow me to control it and put it to the back of my brain again. But who? My wife was busy trying to cope with four young children and doing a part-time degree. My colleagues were a mixed workforce whose unwritten rule was that politics must be avoided. The 95 per cent unionist neighbourhood I lived in was an equally unpromising option.

Which left my brothers and sisters. Like most Irish people of my generation, I came from a large family. And like most such families, when we came together, our talk was of children and parents and work and holidays. Politics? That wasn't so much forbidden as irrelevant – a backdrop to the real things of life. Except the hunger strike wasn't just politics and it wasn't a backdrop. This was life and death being played out centre stage. Every screen and every newspaper was full of it. Even letters from our

Canadian friends spoke of Bobby Sands – how could he do it? What kind of man was he? And so in the summer of 1981, I gathered with my siblings for a family occasion, and almost immediately the hunger strike came up.

There was almost instant agreement. These men were in prison because they'd killed or been involved in killing, and now they were intent on killing themselves and wanted sympathy. Well, sorry. John Hume had it right: a united Ireland was fine to dream about, but only a madman would say Irish freedom or even civil rights was worth a single drop of blood, let alone a precious life. These people were deranged, dangerous and intent on killing themselves. Maggie Thatcher was *not* to blame. They themselves were.

I looked at the heads around the table, eating and nodding, and suddenly realised I didn't agree with a single word that had been said. I wanted to, but I couldn't.

Because no matter how convenient it might be to cast these men as crazies and criminals, the unavoidable fact was that, unlike criminals, they hadn't broken the law for personal gain or satisfaction. Like it or lump it, they were political prisoners. Once you accepted that notion – that their actions were politically motivated – then their case for different prison treatment became unanswerable. True, Catholic bishops and nationalist newspaper editorials preached otherwise, and theologians competed with each other over what was the true definition of suicide, to see if death by hunger strike fell within that definition. But such debate at this point seemed quaint and even silly, in the face of the tolling bell that was the bulletins from prison.

As my brothers and sisters talked and reinforced each others' opinions, I thought briefly of Thatcher. Maybe it was personal distaste for her that was leading me to a position of dissent? Maybe her nasal intonation, her arrogant certainty were the things that had pushed me into opposition, not logic at all? But no. Even if her voice had been sweeter than a lark's in the morning, I would still have reached the unhappy conclusion that was hardening into certainty.

Then one of my sisters said, "They're not even dying for Ireland – they're dying for each other, which is just plain stupid." That's when I found myself shouting.

Not too smart, agreed: trying to point out the unreason at the heart of their comments, and doing so by shouting.

And when shouting didn't work, I tried nostalgia. Our mother used to sing when we were small, as she did the housework and work around the farm. And what were those songs? Yes, "If I Were a Blackbird" and "I'll Take You Home Again, Kathleen", but also "Kevin Barry" and "The Manchester Martyrs" and "All Round My Hat I Wear the Tricoloured Ribbon-o". If the men she sang about had died in a noble cause, wasn't it obvious that the hunger strikers were dying for the same cause, and dying more slowly and horribly than any Manchester Martyr or Kevin Barry?

An uproar of voices. Don't twist things, I was told. That was completely different – people like Kevin Barry had belonged to a totally different organisation from these people in the H-Blocks. They'd brought it on themselves and wanted to die, whereas Kevin Barry would have been glad of reprieve.

I recognised the argument. It had been on one of the leaflets left on my desk by one of my students a couple of weeks earlier. A beautiful, warm young Protestant, she'd been visiting me to talk about an essay and had left this pamphlet sitting there – presumably by accident – when she gathered her books. I looked at it. "They had a choice!" the headline shouted. "Their victims had none! Let them die!" I thought of the girl, compassionate in most things, her heart locked now against the men dying in Long Kesh. What had brought her to this place? What had brought the dying men to their terrible position?

And the face of another student came to my mind's eye.

Another young Protestant, a male this time, easily the most thoughtful of the students in his year. Since he'd decided from the start that the hunger strikers were right and Thatcher was wrong, when faced with sitting his final examinations or joining the anti-H-Block campaign, the decision was simple. He walked away from his studies and never came back.

And I saw – and see now – the face of a third student, from Poleglass. It's a week after Bobby Sands' funeral, and she closes my office door and sits down, her face shining. She wants to tell me about the night Bobby died. "It was the best night of my life – God forgive me!" she says. "It was that exciting, and sad, and – everybody was out and . . ." She throws her hands in the air, and then, still smiling, she starts to cry, and goes on crying until her face is red and swollen.

Like most middle-class, uncommitted people, I experienced the hunger strike at one remove, usually through the experiences of others. But even through the filter of television, it came across with shocking force.

The televised pictures from Bobby Sands' funeral. The mass of people walking behind his coffin, seeming to push against the edges of the screen, so tight it was surely impossible they could all find room to walk. But they did, only their heads visible, bobbing and rippling like grains of rice.

And I remember – why do I remember this? – Oliver Hughes being interviewed about his brother, Francie, whom he's just come from visiting. The TV reporters crowd around him, eager for news. What had he seen, how did he feel, what did Francie look like? Oliver Hughes stares at them for a minute, his eyes bulging, his face grey. "I'll tell youse what he looked like," he says. "He looked like a wee ould man, lying in there. A wee ould man."

And then, days later, when Francie Hughes' coffin is being brought from Forster Green hospital, I watch as unionist protestors crowd around the entrance. The coffin comes out and they clap, they cheer, they shout oaths and insults at the dead man, at the dead man's relatives, at all that the hunger strike represents.

Twenty-five years later, the images are still sharp, my thoughts jumbled. I still don't understand how these ten men could have done what they did. How they could have had such unrelenting purpose, to face down their natural instinct for self-preservation, which must have shrieked for them to give up, and kept on shrieking all those hours and days and weeks until they died.

Most events and people and places shrink with the passage of time. Broad childhood streets turn out to be narrow; people who were giants turn out to be of average height.

Oddly, I find, with the hunger strikers, the reverse happens. As time goes by, they seem to grow in stature . . . No, that's not quite right. They don't grow; they stand increasingly alone, sharper and more distinct. It's as if time had to burn off the trappings and counter-claims of the time, the let-them-die pamphlets and the banging bin lids and the jeering crowds. Those past distractions gone, I'm left with the actions of ten men that are so much above the everyday, so rare and rarefied, they defy comprehension. Yet, despite that, or maybe because of it, twenty-five years after their deaths, they shine a light that is purer than ever and that points a steady beam to our future.

THE NIGHT WE NAMED
BOBBY SANDS STREET

Pedram Moallemian, former Iranian student

SHORTLY AFTER THE REVOLUTION OF 1979, IRANIANS WERE BUSY changing names. Names of thousands of streets, buildings and even cities that had been named after the Shah, his family or others close to the former regime needed to be changed and replaced by names of new idols and symbols of the revolution. Perhaps the most prominent was Tehran's major thoroughfare going from Pahlavi Street to be named after the regime's renowned adversary, Dr Mohammad Mossadegh.

As teenagers, we didn't limit the move to names related to the former regime though. My family lived in a new development where streets were numbered, but that didn't stop us from changing 19th Street to Mehdi Rezaei Street. Mehdi was one of the youngest victims of the former regime, having been arrested, tried and executed, all before his twenty-first birthday. He was someone we could relate to.

The process was just too easy. We would make cardboard signs in the shape and size of actual street signs, replace the old ones or, better yet, glue new ones on top and wait until people started using the new name. In many cases, they were eager to do it, particularly when it was a name of a despised character they were replacing.

Other times, it never actually took. Shahreza Avenue, named after the patriarch of the Pahlavi dynasty, was quickly changed to "Enghelab (Revolution) Street," but our old street is still called 19th, to this day.

Imagine the chaos all of this had caused everyone, from cab drivers and mailmen to just ordinary people who were not sure what street their own houses were on any more. But chaos is just part of any revolution, and this was another ingredient of ours.

So, by that fateful day in May of 1981, when the news of Bobby Sands' death was received in Iran, we had plenty of experience, and there was no way the memory of someone we considered a great revolutionary who had stood up to the British for his people, and at the highest cost, could be forgotten.

It happened more on a fluke. I was part of a small circle of friends, all under fifteen years of age who were always attending speeches together, covering the local streets with political graffiti, distributing flyers and occasionally getting beaten up by those we pissed off. One of us lived on a street that backed onto the British Embassy in the heart of Tehran, and because of this central location and his parents' more liberal approach, we'd often gather at their flat.

Our original plan to honour Sands was far more risky. From their windows, you could see the Union Jack flying prominently in the embassy's yard. We wanted to sneak in at night and replace it with an Irish flag! That plan ran into a few problems. If there was a place to buy an Irish flag in Tehran, the thirteen- and four-teen-year-olds in our gang had no luck finding it. We made one, but it looked horrible, and because the colours we had used were closer to the Iranian flag, we were worried it would be taken as the wrong flag and maybe send the wrong message.

We finally decided on a big white sheet and wrote "IRA" across it. Even that was problematic: we tried it once on the roof, and it was so heavy that it would not wave and be seen fully. We were worried that if it just sat hanging from that pole, it would be only a white sheet and nothing more. There was also a concern about guard dogs we had never seen but could occasionally hear on the other side of the wall.

With all that, late one evening, with all of us frustrated and exhausted, the flag plans were abandoned.

Then somebody within the group brought up an old practice: let's rename the street. I honestly wish I remember who said it first to give him full credit, but I just don't after so many years.

The plan wasn't as exciting and adventurous, but we were desperate at this point. We all agreed and had soon bought large white construction paper and navy magic markers to make signs. I was the most graphically gifted of the bunch, so I'd draw the shape of the actual signs, copying the real ones made by the city, and the rest of the gang would colour and cut them. We made about twenty of them and went out when it got dark to cover the old signs.

Next evening, we returned to see if any of them were left, and to our surprise there were a few new ones made by others too, and thanks to the glue we had used, even the ones very close to the embassy compound had remained in place. However, the occasional missing corner was proof that someone had tried to remove them. Soon the entire street had new signs and the city officially changed the name also.

To me, the first big victory came a few months later when, at another Tehran street corner where passengers holler their destinations to passing cabs in hope of being picked up by someone feeling the route is profitable enough, I heard a woman yell, "Bobby Sands!" The name had stuck, and it was now certified in a way far more official than by the city putting up actual metal signs.

The larger victory, however, was when we discovered that the embassy had been forced to change its mailing address and all its printed material to reflect a side-door address, in order to avoid using Bobby's name anywhere.

What we had no idea about was how the news of our little "prank", which had turned much more significant now, had reached across the great distance to get to Ireland, its people, the activists and even some of the remaining prisoners.

Years later, I was told of how that little gesture had shown them they are not alone, and that even in far away places, people respect and honour their struggle.

Maybe one day I'll be walking down an Irish street and be pleasantly surprised when I get to Mossadegh Square. Maybe.

Footnote: In 1981, the Iranian government was officially represented at Bobby Sands' funeral and presented to Mrs Sands "a plaque from the people of Iran". In 2004, it was revealed that British Foreign Secretary Jack Straw had been lobbying Iran's foreign minister to change the name of Bobby Sands Street, which was formerly known as Winston Churchill Street. To date, the Iranian government has rejected the request.

AN INSPIRATIONAL ACT OF STRUGGLE
Paddy Prendiville, journalist, activist

PRIDE AND SHAME; RENEWED SELF-REGARD AND THE OLD SELF-loathing.

These conflicting emotions, as manifest in Irish people south of the border during the hunger strike, are the memories that endure for me. Most Irish people retained a respect (grudging at the very least, reverential and emotionally committed at best) for the hunger strikers. But that elite layer, the self-appointed guardians of public morality and "modern" values (academics, journalists, establishment politicians, captains of industry) could not hide, did not even try to hide, their antipathy to Bobby Sands and his comrades. Whereas among the silenced majority, censored republicans and the great mass of Irish people, the sense of solidarity was palpable.

This solidarity was sometimes hidden from view, sometimes fractured and atomised, sometimes helpless as our hand-wringing politicians shuffled around the stage with embarrassed expressions and were sometimes inarticulate as they were confronted with the voluble wordsmiths of what passed for an intelligentsia in 1981.

In the three decades of the Troubles, this was the elite's worst nightmare – a classic, Irish form of heroic and pacifist self-sacrifice that rang bells from Bantry to Belfast, Derry to Carnsore, across the nation and across the centuries. A protest that was running through the ordinary Irish population like an electric current, but threatening peace of mind in various boardrooms as well as in Mount Merrion and other sheltered oases of suburban bliss. If the victors get to write history, then that shallow, minor section of southern society which likes to see itself as metropolitan, not post-colonial, is still in the saddle, however precariously. They got away (barely and for the time being) with the imagined pretence that the "northern" hunger strike passed the southern population by.

But as each commemoration comes round and as young Irish people demand to know more about the epic events of 1981, the silence from the scribes of that time becomes louder and more damning of those same commentators who continue to lecture about transparency, ethical standards in public life, and so on.

I sat in a Dublin city-centre pub as the television newscaster announced that Bobby Sands had won the Fermanagh and South Tyrone by-election. My own elation was an insipid drop in the emotional tsunami that engulfed the rest of the room in a display of fervour that would have surprised the Falls Road. Every so often, "southern" Irish people express themselves in a manner and with a force that completely contradicts the desiccated media image of a people who are supposed to have matured beyond such backward, nationalist sentiments.

The industrial strikes that broke out spontaneously on building sites, in Dublin bus depots and in factories; the walk-outs and protest marches across the country; the seas of black flags that festooned working-class estates everywhere – these activities and many others went largely unreported. I well remember how, in Tralee, in the house of a wealthy and privileged relation of mine, a shudder passed through her as she stared at a sea of black flags in a housing estate several hundred yards away and articulated her distaste for this appalling spectacle.

If such energy had been undertaken by, say, local charitable groups or even tidy town committees, newspaper colour writers and camera crews would have descended on the well-intentioned folk who took up such forms of activity. There would have been interviews with Bernie and Aoife from the residents' committees and photographs of their efforts. But a dark, malevolent silence descended on the Dublin-based media in 1981 as editors looked away (and worse) and journalists kept quiet for fear of damaging their careers.

Whenever a risen people throws up inspirational acts of struggle or personalities, a constant, philistine response is that most people are more concerned with making ends meet than with the acts of dreamers and revolutionaries. As Yeats put it:

> Romantic Ireland's dead and gone,
> It's with O'Leary in the grave.

Certainly the dreary, would-be reformers of various anti-republican groups argued in 1981, and still do, that economic growth, not emancipation, is what matters to Irish people. Patrick Pearse called such people fools, and his argument is timeless. It's not even especially Irish; it's universal, as anybody remotely involved in campaigns for democracy and liberation the world over will tell you.

On a delegation of Irish journalists, academics and politicians to the Philippines, when the dictator President Marcos was still in power in early 1983, I was privileged to be granted an interview with the poet, academic and revolutionary, José Maria Sison. Not universally known in the West, Ma Sison has long been regarded as the Che Guevara or Fidel Castro of his people. When I met him, he was arraigned in front of a military tribunal, manacled alongside two of his comrades in the New People's Army on various charges, and he had undergone torture over a lengthy period.

I apologised for the intrusion as the non-jury, military tribunal proceeded, but the three NPA men were anxious that a western journalist should hear their arguments. In any case, Ma Sison dismissed the proceedings with a wave, claiming that they had, effectively, already been sentenced to "death by musketry" (an antiquated, Spanish, legal term for capital punishment).

Ma Sison then launched into an intense polemic about the domestic repression of Marcos and his subservience to US economic and military interests in the region. Suddenly, because of something I said, Ma Sison stopped, looked at me wide-eyed and exclaimed: "You're Irish?!" I replied "Yes", and asked him to tell me more about his own torture and possible death by firing squad. (This was a minor exclusive for me at the time, and I had been granted by the authorities just twenty minutes or so with him.)

Too late. Ma Sison refused to talk about himself, the Philippines, Marcos or world politics. He pleaded with me to explain to him what he described as the "magnificent commitment of these men" (the hunger strikers). How was it possible, asked the man facing death for his principles, for these men to show such determination, such resolve? His bafflement seemed to be entirely genuine, and his face radiated admiration. This reversal of roles became incongruous as the three Filipino revolutionaries fired questions at me about Sands and the others (Ma Sison was conversant with the different political currents within republicansim at that time) and I tried hard to resist exaggerating my modest role as a rank-and-file activist in the hunger-strike campaign. My embarrassment, alongside a feeling of pride, increased when the three manacled men raised their clenched fists to me as I left the military barracks for the airport, and as they shuffled back, surrounded by automatic-gun-toting soldiers, to their incarceration, or worse.

The faint feeling of fraudulence on my part was relieved only by the awareness that such respect was not for me. It was for my nationality, for the hunger strikers and for the inspiration that centuries of Irish history has bequeathed to the colonised of the world.

The previous summer, as the Israeli war machine surrounded the PLO in West Beirut, I had had a similar experience. The world's media were in the Lebanon, watching and waiting for the Israelis, egged on by the local Phalangist militia, to go in and finish off the PLO with their massive military superiority, provided by the West. My colleague, Gerry Lawless, and I learned fast that while the international press card was necessary in Christian East Beirut, the Irish passport was infinitely more useful in opening doors and gaining access to people in besieged West Beirut.

At the time, the only question appeared to be when, not whether, the Israelis would go in and raze West Beirut to the ground. Every Palestinian militant and young PLO member knew that, as front-line foot soldiers, they were unlikely to survive the massacre that lay ahead. And yet, as in Manila, the simple fact of our being Irish seemed somehow to be more important, more inspirational and more worthy of discussion than their own lives and deaths.

I recall leaving a very dangerous West Beirut one evening for the comparative safety and luxury of East Beirut when a dozen or so teenage PLO fighters hailed us. The usual, polite civility for western hacks was replaced with huge smiles and backslapping when, as usual, we quickly flashed our Irish passports.

"Bobby Sands! Bobby Sands! Bobby Sands!" they kept shouting.

One of them said some unmentionable things about Margaret Thatcher and drew his levelled hand across his throat with mock, yet deadly, intent as they vied with each other to strike the most pro-republican and anti-British note.

As in the Philippines, the incongruity of the situation struck me. We were leaving for the safety and comfort of western Europe while they were waiting to die for their cause in an area that was already war-torn and in semi-ruins. It is impossible to describe the sense of menace and doom that lay over West Beirut in those days. Even the Mediterranean air was suffused with the acrid smell of cordite from Israeli forays that would blitz whole areas.

Yet, as we left for the West, we were being feted like heroes by young Palestinians because we were Irish and because of the hunger strikers.

I have rarely felt ashamed to be Irish, even in the face of the profound, national, psychological illness that newspapers like the *Sunday Independent* exhibit. But returning to the rarefied environs of the Dublin media following the above two experiences in Beirut and Manila was a perverse experience. People thousands of miles away had more respect for the sacrifices of the hunger strikers than many of my colleagues and the people I had to interview and question in my working life. Such impressions can be superficial and serve only to remind that journalists are insulated, more than most, from the lives and outlook of the people they are supposed to be informing.

The year 1981 and the hunger strike was perhaps the last great hurrah for the great Irish pastime of censorship and denial. RTÉ, then riddled with "modernists" who knew full well that Bobby Sands would not, could not, win the Fermanagh–South Tyrone by-election, got found out as they tailed the world's press to the election count. What utter humiliation they should have felt, even if they did not. Sands' election victory was not on the news schedule in the RTÉ newsroom because the broadcasters' political experts said it wasn't going to happen.

But as the cheers of people in pubs and elsewhere around the country rang out, that evening showed that most Irish people knew what Sands and his comrades were doing; they knew the hunger strike was another chapter in the great drama that is our history. And just like the disgraceful censors masquerading as journalists in RTÉ and elsewhere, they knew which side they were on. The other side.

Listening to Michael McDowell describe Bobby Sands as a criminal on RTÉ more recently, I wanted to throw the television out the window – a violent, typically republican, response, I suppose. Hughes, McCreesh, and the others – each of them, had more principle and idealism in his little finger than McDowell has in his entirety. God knows, Irish working people, republicans and supporters of the peace process have much reason to remember the PD politician with distaste.

But for that remark about Bobby Sands alone, McDowell deserves to be branded with infamy as long as his name means anything in Irish history – which will be nothing like as long as the names of the hunger strikers.

AN tAMHRÁN ÉIREANNACH

(I gcuimhne ar Bhobby Sands)

Giuseppe Conte

(Leagan Gaeilge le Pádraig Ó Snodaigh)

An cuimhin le héinne Bobby Sands,
a ghruanna rua-indiacha,
a gháire dhordánach,

a ghártha áthais is réabhlóide?
An cuimhin le héinne é,
buachaill charcair na Má?

D'iompraíodh séiléirí don chill
Chuile lá oráistí agus arán donn,
iad ag plabadh doirse, is ag gáire

os ard eatarthu féin, ag rá "An fíor é?
an é nach mblaisfidh sé den ghlóthach féin feasta?
an leanfaidh sé air go deireadh a shlí?"

Is bhainidís de, iad gach maidin
go scáthshúileach á iniúchadh
ó scornach síos go heasnacha.

Is san idirlinn bhí an Mhárta ar fáil
is lasmuuigh an geimhreadh ag cnagadh
ar chaoráin, ar theangacha gainimh

mar a raibh an mhuir ag creimeadh go mall
faoi na failltreacha ar bhruach
na hinnilte, mar a raibh

caiple fiáine glasa
ina seasamh go huaigneach ar fiar
in aghaidh shíor-rith na néalta.

Lasmuigh bhí na tonnta fós
ag síothlú san fheamainn dhonn,
is na locháin ar lorg a chéile, le gean, mar

a bheidís titithe ar bhior a gcinn idir na cnoic.
Buachaill charcair na Má,
ba mhian leis scríobh, dánta a scríobh.

Is chonaic lá amháin tríd an ngríl
na grabhóga aráin a chaith cara leis
amach, is chuala na cantairí beaga

ag tuirlingt á bpiocadh: "Ar a laghad
tá neach éigin ag ithe!" Smaoinigh sé.
Seanfhís de chuid a óige bheith eolach

ar dhóigh na n-éan, mar a dtéann siad
sa spéir shamhrata, mar a bhfilleann said
istoíche. Éin! Éin dhubha, na

fiacha a chuala sé ag tuirlingt anuas
ar chópáin fhairsinge na ndíonta
ó Ard Mhacha go dtí an Clochán, bhí ársaíocht

iontu ó thaobh eitilte is fuirigh.
Tá na céadta bliain ag na fiacha le himeacht.
Éitlíd os cionn failltreacha is gaineamh is bailte móra

a bhfaca said a n-éabhlóid mar a fheicfidh
a dtitim. Go minic b'ionadh leat
a neamhchorraí a bhíonn. Minic a n-uaill

níos piachánaí ná uaill an anaithe.
Is d'airigh sé na crotaigh is na ríthe rua,
a nglaonna iargheimhridh ag comhcheiliúradh

plúiríní sneachta is sabhaircíní.
Is d'fhan leis na fuiseoga a chlos,
anamacha sona arbh fhéidir go bhfuil

eolas éigin acu ar an mbás
de bhreis orainne; d'fhan leo: "Má thagaid
go luath agus eitilt go hard, samhradh

tirim te an tuar, samhradh
nach gcaithfeadsa." Is chuimhnigh
ina leanbh dó nuair a d'amharcadh orthu

mar théadh scread na saoirse osdaonna
is fís ba ghile ná an spéir féin
i seilbh air. Céad tá laistiar de na ceolta

de na guairneáin solais atá thar rochtain na gcróc
is na gcocán dearg thíos anseo?
Ó, is é a thug gean dóibh uilig, do na

héin is na heitiltí go léir. Anois bhí na séiléirí
ag tabhairt prátaí bruite is arán donn leo,
iad ag gáire ag doras na cille,

ag bualadh a mbos go tréan.
"An fíor nach mblaisfidh sé faic feasta?
Caillfear seo, caillfear amárach é."

Is ar feadh meandair thothlaigh sé
cáis ollannach is mil, ach
le haoibh ansin: "Ní fada go rithe ina slaoda

trí mo scornach oscailte
drúcht na maidine agus réaltbuíonta.
Beidh srutháin nach n-aithníonn éinne

go luath do mo thionlacan, ceolta
bodhrán is triantán ar ghrinneall na mara.
A Eoraip, nach n-éisteann a thuilleadh

le guth na n-imeallbhord is na bhforaoisí

le guth na dtonnta is na leapacha ancairí,
a Eoraip gan dánta, a Eoraip bhalbh

na dteampall seasc, cam,
a deineadh de ghloine is d'fhéar lofa,
a Eoraip loitithe, thitithe.

Cá bhfuil na healtaí faoileán
a d'éiríodh gach lá thar na Rosa
mar ar scaip tú seileastram is ór Mhuire?

Is na coillte naofa, na ciorcail cloch
ar bharr do chnoc, iad ailínithe
le grian is réaltaí, cá bhfuilid?"

Bhí sé ag fáil bháis: is fairis ansin bhí
an oiread sin daoine, na sluaite daoine.
Thug na séiléirí leo don chill

an tráidire lán is an ghloine,
ag plabadh an dorais go láidir
ag gáire os ard eatarthu féin.

"Imeoidh duine éigin an turas seo!"
Chríochnaigh míúd an Mhárta '81
Is tháinig míonna na glaise is na glé-

spéire, ach thit buachaillí charchair na Má
mar sheileastraim is mar ór Mhuire
a stoithfeadh spéirling den

ghas: Bobby Sands, Francis Hughes,
Raymond McCreesh, Patsy O'Hara
is Thomas McIlwee, a gcónraí

folmha á n-iompar ar ghuaillí tráthnóna ar bhóithre
na Gaillimhe mar a bheannaíos ceannchromtha dóibh

Tusa, a Dhia spéire is talún is

uiscí, a Dhia na mearú súl, na taoide
líonta is na ngálaí, a Dhia-Linbh
arb áil leat cathanna is stoic

is atá lonnaithe san uile chamhaoir is san uile
luí gréine, tusa arb eol duit dólás
an té is deartháir duit sa bhás, fáiltigh romhaibh.

Buachaill charcair na Má,
ba mhian leis scríobh, dánta a scríobh,
ach shíothlaigh a neart is a thaibhreamh.

Sa chill bhí na séiléirí ag ithe
oráistí is arán donn, iad ag gáire go hard
eatarthu féin. Do b'fhíor, bhí sé imithe

ar aghaidh ar a shlí féin, thar chuile
dhoras idir iata is oscailte
thar an uile lúcháir is bhrón

bhí a imirce i gcrích anois. Ar maidin
bhaineadar de, iad scáthshúileach
á iniúchadh ó scornach síos go heasnacha.

Is tá an Mhárta imithe is tagaithe arís
lasmuigh tá an tEarrach ann mar aon le
bruacha de bhláthanna corcra is craoraga

néalta ag eitilt sa spéir
mar éin imirce i dtreo
brúchtadh bogthe abhann. Buachaill

charcair na Má, cuimhnigh air!
Ansin in airde fara fuiseoga solasmhara.

DEAD MEN LIVE

Tom Hayden, Irish-American social and political activist

"The blame for this sorry story, if blame there be, must lie with those who, many years ago, decided that in emergency conditions in colonial-type situations we should abandon our legal, well-tried and highly-successful wartime interrogation methods and replace them by procedures which were secret, illegal, not morally justifiable, and alien . . ."

— Lord Gardiner's minority report on British prisons, filed on Bloody Sunday, 1972

THOSE TEN DEAD MEN ARE ALIVE IN IRISH CONSCIOUSNESS, IN THE global human rights movement, in cages from Abu Ghraib to Kabul and Guantánamo, in a welcome corner of my mind. They endured the most, and their ghosts still thwart the morticians of oblivion.

As others have said, the election and death of Bobby Sands MP was the turning point that launched Sinn Féin's electoral strategy and fostered the possibility of the peace process. Across the world, the hunger strikers today are honoured more than Margaret Thatcher.

In America, the hunger strikers broke the muzzle which the Irish-American establishment had placed on the voices of Irish republicans. US House Speaker Tip O'Neill could no longer prevent the ninety-three-member House Ad Hoc Committee from holding hearings on human rights violations in the North. Sympathetic media coverage increased. Contributions to NORAID soared. Huge picket lines filled Fifth Avenue. The Massachusetts legislature "wholeheartedly" endorsed "the ultimate objectives of the IRA".

Patricia Harty, now editor of the respected *Irish America* magazine, was a young immigrant in San Francisco, living with two English roommates and working for an American company that supplied airline food. While she herself participated in demonstrations outside the British Consulate, her co-workers couldn't get their heads around the hunger strike at all. They were "sympathetic, but horrified. Like, 'How could they do that?'" However, she remembers, there was "awe, that these young men in the prime of their lives could do this".

Looking back, she believes, most of those people she worked with forgot the hunger strikes shortly after, "but maybe, maybe they did learn something, that being Irish wasn't just all jigs and reels on St Patrick's Day". The wheels of assimilation were set in reverse.

Some Irish-Americans could be counted upon to blame the hunger strikers themselves. In the centre of Irish Boston, for example, the Irish-born historian Padraig O'Malley, whose name seemed to bloom with authenticity, attacked the hunger strikers for a primitive, degenerate nationalism. Stating openly what a majority may have privately believed, O'Malley wrote that the Irish were their own oppressors: "We need England. We need it to disguise the sordid and sad reality of our murderous designs on each other." (*Boston Globe*, 6 May 1981, suggesting that O'Malley wrote these words on the very day Bobby Sands died.)

I was in West Belfast in 1976 about the time Bobby Sands was re-arrested and taken to Castlereagh. I did not have the chance to meet him, but like millions of others, he and the other hunger strikers have continued to live in my consciousness. When I returned to Los Angeles, I joined many others in writing letters of solidarity to the Irish prisoners and picketing the British Embassy.

I began feeling like a stranger in my own land as I encountered the blank stares of my non-Irish friends (not to mention some of Irish ancestry who seemed to feel "outed" by the hunger strikers). I remember not being able to get their suffering out of my mind, not being able to purge a sense of guilt, not being able to avoid the tears in public when the devastating finish came.

Were these feelings born of romantic republicanism, morbid Catholicism, or a vicarious fascination with death? Of course, there was a long, historic – and officially discouraged – tradition of hunger strikes in Ireland, and, of course, the Republic itself was inspired by the martyrs of 1916. And yes, there was something Christ-like in the persona of Bobby Sands, just as there was in Che Guevera. I was influenced by all these things, but most of all by admiration at the hunger strikers' collective revolutionary will. Years later when I interviewed a survivor, Laurence McKeown, he showed no sign of desire for martyrdom. "We were captured soldiers, and so we used our bodies as the last weapons we had," he simply said.

At least they did not die in vain, or invisibly, like many of the demonised across the planet. They bested the British, defeated oblivion, awakened a whole generation, but also contributed to a global movement for the human rights of political prisoners and families of the disappeared. That movement sometimes achieves surprising successes, as in Chile, Argentina and Uruguay in recent years, where the memory of ghosts is stronger than amnesia.

Another reason the example of the Irish hunger strikers still resonates is that the empire, however weakened, continues its cruelties. By "empire" I mean the arrogant Anglosphere of the British and their grown and twisted children, the Americans. The dysfunctional family has joined together as the hated Multinational Coalition in Iraq and Afghanistan.

In his prison poem, "Modern Times", Bobby Sands foretold

the present, "where the oil flows blackest, the street runs red".
And again he was prophetic in "The Torture Mill", written about
the H-Blocks:

> They chop your neck, then walk your back,
> Spread-eagle you like pelt.
> For private parts their special arts
> Are sickeningly felt.
> They squeeze them tight with no respite
> Till a man cries for the womb
> That gave him birth to this cruel earth
> And torture of that room.

There is a straight line from tiger cages in Vietnam to broken
bones in Palestine to death squads in Chile to the concertina
wire and renditions in Afghanistan and Iraq; from the Brits who
disguised themselves as Arabs in places like Aden to carry out
the theories of Frank Kitson and the neo-conservatives of the
Reagan–Thatcher era to the imperial fantasists of today.

Just as in the 1970s the British carefully designed techniques
to circumvent the technical definition of torture, pleased
instead to be condemned only for "inhuman and degrading
treatment", so they and the Americans mask themselves in the
same disguise today. Gentlemanly authors of torture-by-another-
name, they use their Oxford and Ivy League educations, and in
some cases their medical-school training, to inflict torments that
neatly evade the legal prohibitions of torture. Pain, for example,
if it is to be prohibited, must be of "an intensity akin to that
which accompanies serious physical injury such as death or
organ failure". Mental pain, to be considered torture, must leave
"lasting psychological harm", not simply suffering at the
moment of infliction.

Such methods, originating in the British empire, tested on
Irish prisoners, now are unleashed in the covert war on terrorism

as "counter-resistance techniques". Hoods. Standing on toes for hours. Blinding light. Forced nakedness. Threats of castration. Beatings. Waterboarding. All the disciplining gifts of Anglo civilisation to the lesser breeds. And always accompanied by innuendo and slur. The prisoners are savage, filthy, blanket men, ragheads, beyond redemption.

The occasional lapses into (impermissible) torture, as opposed to (permissible) interrogation techniques always are due to the store of bad apples kept on hand for blaming. After seven official investigations by the Pentagon, none fix blame on civilian decision-makers (*New York Times,* 24 April 2004). In the British case, both Tony Blair and the Tories are "united in ascribing the abuses in Basra to a tiny minority of British troops" (*New York Times,* 20 January 2005).

This has been a colonialism enacted with scarcely concealed religious fervour. It was Bob Jones University in South Carolina that bestowed a divinity degree on the Reverend Ian Paisley. Murderous loyalists like Kenny McClinton belonged to the evangelical Prison Fellowship, a global network including American Watergate felon Charles Colson (according to *God and the Gun* by Martin Dillon, Orion, 1998).

In the Iraq crusade, Protestant evangelicals like Franklin Graham, son of Billy Graham, condemn Islam as a "wicked" religion and speak at the President's prayer breakfasts. A chaplain critical of the rise of evangelical Christianity among the US military's chaplains is forced to resign, while the Muslim-hating General William Boykin becomes the Pentagon's point man for intelligence. The soldier convicted of sexual humiliation at Abu Ghraib sought clemency on the grounds that he distributed Bibles to Iraqi children. When the number of Christian missionaries in Muslim countries has quadrupled in the wake of the first Gulf War, have the Crusades not returned, at least covertly?

At the time of writing, there are 17,000 prisoners being held in Iraq, mostly on "suspicion", charged in the Baghdad version of Diplock courts. Seventeen thousand Bobby Sandses.

The folly of empire is evident only in retrospect. Do Brits today really believe that denying the hunger strikers political status was important enough to justify their death by starvation? Do the Americans really believe that the tiger cages of South Vietnam were effective in preventing communist-led revolution? Are they ever asked to reflect on their behaviour, or apologise? The answer, of course, is no. But before we lose heart, it always must be remembered that the authorities go to their extremes of obfuscation because they fear public opinion and the growing reach of human rights laws that have been erected largely through the sacrifices of political prisoners.

Somehow, Bobby Sands knew this, had a universal heart, knew that the human spirit could not be tortured into silence. He wrote of "flowers in the dark", or "bluebells" lifting their heads, just as the hounded African-American artist, Tupac Shakur, wrote of "roses that grow from concrete". A remarkable quality of Bobby Sands was his ability to write poetry on toilet paper, to smuggle intimate thoughts from the bowels of the self to the published page, without computer or yellow pad. He was a guerrilla poet. He properly condemned a world where journalists write "not a single jot of beauty tortured sore" and "poets are no more". But he resurrected a profound counter-tradition, where the needs of the soul are asserted against hopelessness, by any means necessary. That is the only hope of prisoners around the world today and the threat that the captors cannot suppress.

HOW THE SACRIFICE OF THE HUNGER STRIKERS AFFECTED AMERICA
Frank Durkan, human rights lawyer

He dared prepare for, dared aspire to take,
The sacrament of hunger; he conformed with
All our famine-tried; erect he entered
The tower of hunger alien hands had raised.

THE ABOVE STANZA WRITTEN BY THE IRISH POET, PÁDRAIC COLUM, commemorates the sacrifice of Terence MacSwiney who died on 25 October 1920.

MacSwiney – then the elected mayor of Cork city – had been tried in a Dublin court and convicted of sedition. He was sentenced to a prison term to be served in Lincoln Gaol in England.

Long an activist on the Irish revolutionary scene, MacSwiney decided to protest his treatment by entering into a hunger strike.

"I have taken no food since Thursday, therefore I will be free in a month," he declared. He was true to his word. His long, agonising ordeal lasted seventy-four days.

Not since the 1916 executions had an individual act of self-sacrifice such as this galvanised the resentment of the Irish people towards British misrule in Ireland. It excited the interest of people all over the world and, most significantly of all, among Irish-Americans who had now come to realise what it was that their forebears had been forced to endure. The growing interest in the "Irish problem" in America ultimately had its effect on the British government and helped bring about the Treaty which resulted in the creation of the Irish Free State – later to become the twenty-six-county Republic of Ireland.

It is said that those who ignore the lessons of history are condemned to repeat its mistakes. So it was with the British government in its attitude toward the revolutionaries in Northern Ireland in the 1970s and 1980s. The heavy-handed approach by the British military towards the nationalist community in Northern Ireland ignited a flame of resentment which translated into what amounted to a full-blown rebellion. The nationalist hunger for civil rights was ruthlessly met with extraordinarily repressive and brutal measures that not even Britain's vaunted propaganda apparatus could conceal.

The appellation of "terrorists" to the northern rebels soon lost its significance in the face of wholesale indiscriminate arrests, internment without trial, torture in various detention centres like Castlereagh, the Diplock courts, the "shoot-to-kill" policy, and the harsh conditions in the men's detention centre in Long Kesh and the Armagh Women's Prison.

Irish-America stirred uneasily as evidence of Britain's maladministration seeped out. Except for isolated pockets of protest in urban centres like New York, Detroit, Boston, Hartford, Chicago, San Francisco and others, there was not any appreciable protest from the Irish-American community as a whole. A few civil libertarian members of Congress came to the fore, among them Senators Edward M. Kennedy and Abraham Ribicoff, Congressmen Mario Biaggi, Thomas Manton and Jonathan Bingham. But by and large, the political weight that could and should have been brought to bear on indifferent administrations in Washington (President Carter excepted) was not at all commensurate with the Irish-American muscle available in Congress.

The hunger strikes changed all that. The prisoners being held in Long Kesh had insisted that they were political prisoners – not criminals. They refused to do prison work and wear prison clothes. Their only attire was a blanket. The authorities countered with brutal beatings and deprivation of privileges: no radios, no TV, no visitors, no letters. The seven men commenced a hunger strike led by Brendan Hughes in October 1980. The resultant publicity conjured up memories in the minds of the authorities of Terence MacSwiney and others like Sean McNella, Michael Gaughan, Frank Stagg and Hugh Coney (shot in Long Kesh), whose deaths did so much to further their causes and embarrass the governments of the day.

At the end of the first hunger strike in December 1980, Bobby Sands' misgivings about the British and their unwillingness to honour their own statement about radical changes to the prison regime were proven to be right. The government reneged on the deal, and the punishments increased in their severity and intensity.

Stung by the betrayal, Bobby Sands, followed by nine of his comrades – Francis Hughes, Patsy O'Hara, Raymond McCreesh, Joe McDonnell, Martin Hurson, Kevin Lynch, Kieran Doherty, Tom McElwee and Michael Devine – commenced a hunger strike which culminated in the deaths of all ten of them.

The ordeal of the hunger strikers – as each one died in his turn – became international news the world over. The will of the prisoners to have their political status restored ran up against the obstinacy of British Prime Minister Margaret Thatcher. No entreaty, no request from whatever source, could move this woman. She let them die as surely as if each one were standing on the scaffold and she releasing the trapdoor.

The publicity for this progressive march to death made tremendous headlines all over the world and particularly in the United States. The fact that Bobby Sands was elected a member of the British Parliament while on his hunger strike had an enormous impact. Thousands who would otherwise not have bothered to interest themselves in Irish affairs now began to ask questions. How could this be? Why would a government let one of its parliament's elected representatives die rather than grant him the right to wear his own clothes?

Editorials ranging from outright support of the prisoners to bewilderment that such a situation had come to pass dominated the American media in May through July 1981. Television brought lurid pictures of the men's funerals, the military's attempt to disrupt them, and the disrespect shown to their families. The bitterness of the nationalist community in the North became solidified and inflamed. Many would begin to question whether "criminals" would choose to die such a cruel and agonising death. Streets in Iran and elsewhere were renamed after Bobby Sands. Churchmen waffled in their attempts to come to grips with the "morality" of the issues raised, and official Washington finally began to take a closer look at the Irish scene.

This came about because Irish-America finally woke up to the reality of Britain's maladministration of the North. Elected representatives and would-be representatives began to hear more and more from their Irish-American constituencies. Hearings were scheduled in Washington on the "Irish question". Speakers were invited from across the Atlantic to enlighten us.

The day Bobby Sands died, Irish pubs and restaurants closed their doors and black flags flew in protest. A boycott of British goods was highlighted by reports on TV showing students pouring English gin into the East River in New York. A Leitrim saloon keeper named Tommy Madden threw all British products out of his Triangle Bar in Eastport, New York.

The most significant result achieved by the sacrifice of the ten men was its impact on the United States Congress.

Representatives without any Irish connection, such as Nita Lowey (Jewish), Robert Menendez (Hispanic) and Donald Payne (Afro-American), were prominent, with Irish-American congressmen and women such as Peter King, Joe Crowley and Carolyn

McCarthy, in confronting the issue of the Irish question and gaining the attention of the government of the day.

The election of William Jefferson Clinton to the presidency of the United States marked a watershed in the relationship of the American administration towards the "Irish question". Prior to his election and as part of his platform, he attended a conference organised and arranged by New York Assemblyman John Dearie and former New York City Council President Paul O'Dwyer.

On that occasion, he promised, among other things, that he would issue a visa to Gerry Adams to visit the United States, and he promised to appoint a special envoy to go to Northern Ireland and report back on what the US government could do to help the situation there.

Following his election, when he attempted to fulfil these promises, he met with a storm of protests from all quarters. The British press was livid, the American press accused him of harbouring "terrorists", and every agency that had the remotest connection with the issuance of the visa loudly denounced his decision. To his eternal credit, he prevailed, and following Adams' first visit to New York, Clinton appointed Senator George Mitchell to go to Northern Ireland as his special envoy. The rest is history.

The Good Friday Agreement which came about and which is the template for peace and justice is a direct result of the publicity engendered by the deaths of the ten hunger strikers. Without their sacrifice, there is little doubt that Northern Ireland would not have achieved its present status on its road to becoming part of a thirty-two county, united Ireland.

WORKING CLASS WARRIORS
Terry O'Sullivan, Laborers International Union

BOBBY SANDS. FRANCIS HUGHES. PATSY O'HARA. RAYMOND MCCREESH. JOE MCDONNELL. KIERAN DOHERTY. KEVIN LYNCH. MARTIN HURSON. TOM MCELWEE. MICKY DEVINE. For me, as a proud citizen of both Ireland and the United States, and as a trade unionist, these names are as significant as the names of some of the greatest warriors of the past; those who faced strife and struggle, who fought, who bled, and who died, in the pursuit of justice. Giants like Wolfe Tone and George Washington; Daniel O'Connell and Frederick Douglass; James Connolly and Terence Powderly; Constance Markievicz and Mike Quill; Big Jim Larkin and Mother Jones; Martin McGuinness and Martin Luther King, Jr.

These courageous souls remind me that in both the Labor and the Republican Movements, we must never forget that we would not be where we are today without the hard work, dedication, and sacrifice of all those who came before us. The peace and prosperity that all of Ireland has experienced over the past two decades were paid for with the sweat, blood, and lives of those who faced down Black-and-Tans, paramilitaries, and British troops.

The ten H-Block hunger-strike martyrs were combatants, not criminals. They were brave warriors on a battlefield of concrete walls and iron bars who made the ultimate sacrifice for the cause of a free and united Ireland. Although their primary target was the United Kingdom's hypocritical 'Criminalization' policy, their ultimate goal was to secure for all the people of Ireland the rights bestowed upon us by our creator: life, liberty, and the pursuit of happiness.

All of the hunger strikers were from working- and middle-class backgrounds, and had witnessed, and suffered from, exploitation, abuse, and discrimination. Confronted with hatred, prejudice, and violence, they, and thousands like them, decided to rise up and break the shackles of oppression. In another place, in another time, their lives would have taken different, more peaceful paths. But that was not the time and place into which they were born, and so, like the Minutemen at Lexington and Concord, like the United Irishmen of 1798, like the Fenians of 1867, and like the volunteers of 1916, they fought against a foe much larger and stronger than themselves. When that foe tried to criminalize not only them, but the entire cause for which they fought, they resisted this lie, and stood for the truth; first by refusing to wear prison uniforms and finally, by refusing sustenance.

The H-Block hunger strikers took to heart the prophetic words of an earlier Irish hunger striker, Terence MacSwiney: "It is not those who can inflict the most, but those that can suffer the most who will conquer." Following in the footsteps of Mahatma Gandhi and the Reverend Dr. Martin Luther King, Jr., the hunger strikers turned their oppressor's ruthlessness, rage, and resolution against him. Just as American civil rights marchers conquered hearts and minds with their willingness to endure humiliation, beatings, attack dogs, fire hoses, and murder, so the hunger strikers aroused the conscience of the world by refusing to eat. When Margaret Thatcher and her allies in Westminster and Stormont turned a callous, contemptuous, blind eye, they revealed themselves as monsters and the hunger strikers as heroes.

The willingness of the ten men – and others behind them - to lay down their lives was one of the most powerful weapons ever deployed in the struggle for a free and united Ireland. It not only proved fatal to the policy of 'Criminalization', and restored Special Status; it set us on the path towards the Peace Process.

The actions of the H-Block hunger strikers inspired and moved many of Ireland's exiled children in America. We followed the progress of their individual strikes. We marveled at their strength and determination. We mourned as each one died. We have never forgotten their sacrifice, or their names. They became for many of us, myself included, powerful symbols of resistance to British occupation and rule.

As a father, I am awed and inspired by the courage and fortitude, not only of the hunger strikers themselves, but of their parents; mothers and fathers who supported their sons' decisions, resisting every natural impulse to force them to change their minds. As a proud son of Ireland who has never had to risk life or limb for the cause, I am humbled by, and grateful to, all those who risked, and too often lost, their homes, their liberty, their loved ones, and their lives. For these brave Irish patriots, the Peace Process holds out the hope that no one will ever have to suffer such losses again.

At this uncertain moment in history, the greatest homage we can pay to Bobby, Francis, Patsy, Raymond, Joe, Kieran, Kevin, Martin, Tom, and Micky is to do whatever we must to see their dream of a just, united Ireland fulfilled.

A CAUSE THAT WILL SUCCEED
Tony Benn, veteran political activist

BOBBY SANDS GAVE HIS LIFE FOR THE PEOPLE OF IRELAND AND THEIR right to be free from British domination, which for centuries has cast such a dark shadow over its history.

He joined the struggle that had gone on for so long and which will continue until his dream of Irish unity and freedom is realised, and in making the final sacrifice he kept faith with those who had gone before and inspired those who followed.

In Britain, we are often told that there is an Irish problem, but the truth is that there is a British problem in Ireland, and every attempt to deal with it has failed. Occupation failed, partition failed, Stormont failed, direct rule failed, strip-searching, plastic bullets and the H-Blocks failed because they were all designed to retain British rule.

Bobby Sands' election to the House of Commons proved that even when the campaign was waged through the ballot box, it was still not accepted by those in power in London.

I am sure that the opportunity that seemed to be opening up with the Belfast Agreement is one that he would have welcomed, but, like many republicans, he would not have been surprised to see it frustrated and undermined by the hostility of the unionists and the weakness of the governments in London and Dublin.

Every excuse for delaying the implementation of what was promised on Good Friday has been trotted out from the original demand, years before, first for a ceasefire, then that it be permanent, then that the arms be decommissioned, that decommissioning be photographed (in order to humiliate), then because of a bank robbery and the brutal murder of Robert

McCartney by individuals, and it has been delayed even after the IRA put all of its weapons beyond use and declared an end to its armed struggle.

But Bobby Sands' cause has prospered and will succeed because peace and justice are what the people need and want.

Bobby Sands said, before he died, "Our revenge will be the laughter of our children" – a phrase that says all we need to know about him and looks beyond the bloodshed to true peace.

COMMON CAUSE
Ken Loach, film-maker

THE HUNGER STRIKERS STAND IN A LONG LINE OF THOSE WHO HAVE given their lives in the attempt to rid Ireland of the British. Living on this side of the Irish Sea, we are very aware of the distorted way that the struggle in the North is reported. It is seen as sectarian, an intractable religious divide, but rarely as the ragged end of a long and dishonourable rule by an imperialist power.

As always, it was the ruling class, not the people themselves, who caused the trouble. The same class that oppressed the Irish also exploited the farm labourers and mineworkers who were my father's forebears. Of course, if this story were told from that perspective, there would be the terrible danger that the people of our two countries would make common cause.

There was an early example of such solidarity in Cromwell's time. In 1649, some of his soldiers, weary of his tyranny, refused orders to fight the Irish. A group of them, Levellers, were trapped in the church at Burford, a town in England's west country. They were shot in the churchyard for their pains.

It is fashionable to say we should not live in the past, that we should put it behind us, and so on. On the contrary, I think that as we pause to remember the hunger strikers, we should also remember the long struggle of which they were a part.

ANNIVERSARY MARCH
Ann Zell

A millipede. Or actors in a budget film
stepping in place while the backdrop is scrolled past.
The last open field on the road comes by.
Two piebald horses and a boy on a motorbike race
up-and-down, up-and-around, patterning the long grass.
The unmuffled noise of the bike mixes
with the whump-growl-whine of helicopters
and the off-key fluting of the nearest band.

The boy waves to his friends, pretending he is
herding the horses. Dogging the heels of the march
mechanised cowboys with plastic bullet guns
gun their engines as we stop for stragglers,
pretending they are herding us down the road.
We move only when we are ready, along a route
our feet have memorised; family groups
keeping no order, keeping the children close.

Often photographed but seldom seen
we appear no better and no worse than
other people, on the rare occasions
when our film is screened. It is not apparent
that we are also with the horses
whose manes and tails float on the slipstream
of their running. Who gallop out of the field
and up towards the mountain as the footage ends.

(*May 1991. First published in* Weathering, *Salmon Press, 1998*)

READ ALL ABOUT IT

Roy Greenslade, author and media commentator

THE STORY ON THE FRONT PAGE OF *THE TIMES* ON 2 MARCH 1981 began in that newspaper's deliberately understated, formal journalese: "Mr Robert Sands, described as leader of the Provisional IRA men at the Maze prison, began his threatened hunger strike yesterday." It went on to explain that his protest followed the aborted fifty-three-day hunger strike by seven republican prisoners the previous year and concluded: "Provisional Sinn Féin said he is prepared to carry out his threat to fast to death." That low-key start to what was to become a cataclysmic event was echoed throughout the rest of Britain's London-based national newspapers. In keeping with their journalists' ignorance of the dynamics of the Irish situation, they were slow to catch on to the significance of the hunger strike. But ignorance has never prevented papers from having strong opinions, especially about the IRA.

When the British papers woke up to the seriousness of the protest by Mr Sands and his comrades in the Maze, and to its effect, there was a collective scream of anger. The so-called diverse and pluralist press was united in its opposition to the republican prisoners achieving their ambitions. Most of them stood four-square behind Prime Minister Margaret Thatcher, in her determination to face down the hunger strikers. She wouldn't give an inch, and they reinforced her trenchant attitude, echoing her view that "crime is crime is crime". There would be no granting of political status, no compromise, no sell-out, no surrender. The prime minister and the press were unmoved when three more men – Francis Hughes, Patsy O'Hara and Raymond McCreesh – joined the fast. There were other events to divert editors: the gang of four broke away from Labour on their way to setting up a rival party; President Reagan survived an assassination attempt; riots broke out in Brixton; Lady Diana fever had gripped the tabloids; and, most importantly, Mrs Thatcher was growing unpopular in a period of economic gloom. She needed to reassure an increasingly sceptical public that she was a tough leader, and the hunger strike offered her, and her press cheerleaders, the opportunity to do so.

But the IRA wrested the political initiative away from Thatcher when Sands stood in the Fermanagh and South Tyrone by-election. His victory both perplexed and outraged the press, but editors realised at last the wider implications of the hunger strike. Several remarked on its becoming a major propaganda coup, especially in the United States, the Republic and among the nationalist community in the North. The *Daily Express* could not fathom the breadth of interest and tacit support. It whimpered: "In a world where the agony of Afghanistan continues unabated, where Catholic Poland fends off Communist Russia and where tyranny exists in most countries, it is fantastic that one man, deliberately taking his own life in a democratic nation, gets such attention." While several papers demanded that the H-Block MP be disqualified, and called for a change in the law to prevent prisoners from standing for Parliament, Sands' condition was deteriorating. With death nearing, the papers sought to bolster Thatcher's position: she could not give in, said the *Daily Mail*, because of the consequent "sense of betrayal" among "the Protestant majority". The *Mail* even told the pope to keep his nose out of affairs.

Editors could not understand how an act they regarded as an unacceptable form of "blackmail" could be viewed within Ireland so sympathetically. Nor were they prepared for the support offered to the fasting men from around the world. When the *New*

York Times – America's most respected paper – remarked in a leading article that "by appearing unfeeling and unresponsive", Thatcher and her government "are providing Bobby Sands with a death-bed gift: the crown of martyrdom", the British *Times* responded with incredulity. It argued that the *NYT*'s "well-meaning" but "dangerous" advice "exemplifies the muddled refusal to face reality" by underrating "the seriousness of the Republican position and its capability for propaganda", adding: "There is no evidence that the British Government can save Mr Sands' life except by an act of appeasement that would be even more damaging than his death to the future stability of Northern Ireland."

We will return in a moment to these "damaging" acts of appeasement, but let us first note how the papers greeted (and I use that word advisedly) the death of Bobby Sands.

Two days before he succumbed, the Thatcherite editor of the *Sunday Express,* John Junor, wrote: "I will shed no tears when Sands dies. My only hope is that if and when he does every other IRA terrorist will go on the same sort of hunger strike in sympathy. And stay on it until they are all in wooden suits." From the opposite end of the (British) political spectrum came the *Guardian*'s lament that "a blood sacrifice" was about to happen which, though "an act of personal heroism", was fuelled by "a misconceived belief". Again, we'll return to that misconception.

Once Sands died, the papers derided his heroism. "Courage, he certainly had," admitted the *Daily Telegraph*, "but it was the courage of the ruthless and corrupted sort which holds human life in contempt." According to the *Daily Mail*, it was "a regrettable act of suicide" and "terrorism as theatre", in which "Sands' performance . . . was a moral fraud." As far as the *Daily Express* was concerned, he was "a fanatic who would have been unnoticed in life but imagined – God help us! – that he would serve Ireland in death". The *Sun* thought it "foolish to hand to him the martyr's crown", and said confidently: "Blackmail has failed, and the society which has stood firm against violence in long blood-stained years will remain unshaken."

This "failure" was a familiar theme. The *Daily Mirror* told its readers that Sands' death "advances no cause". The *Express* agreed: "Sands will find no victory in the grave. The British government stands Everest-like in its resolve never to concede political status . . . the shadow of Bobby Sands will pass." *The Times* sought to explain away Sands' election triumph. It "was not a vote for violence, nor for a united Ireland, nor even necessarily for political status . . . It was, to some extent, a vote expressing sympathy for Sands and concern over conditions at the Maze, but it was above all a rejection of Mr Harry West . . . The myth of Fermanagh must not be allowed to gain credibility." However, there are myths and myths: their myths and our myths.

Sands' funeral was marked by an outpouring of grief in Belfast's Milltown Cemetery and an outburst of vitriol from London's Fleet Street graveyard of truth. A *Daily Mirror* writer saw it as "a pathetic end for a man who never played more than an average part in the deadly moves called by his IRA masters". The funeral was "a macabre propaganda circus", claimed the *Daily Mail*. "The ritual of so-called full military honours at the graveside . . . is a gangster parody of the moving tributes which fighting men traditionally pay to comrades who fall in defence of honourable causes."

Then came press parody in the *Daily Express* with a picture of the Sands cortège, in which his eight-year-old son, Gerard, appeared next to the pall-bearers. Headlined "Sad Pawn of War", the article began: "They told him his daddy was a hero. Then they sent him out into a scene he could never understand and made him the centrepiece of an IRA martyr's funeral." He was "cruelly manipulated" in a way that supposedly "sickened all impartial observers" (i.e., British reporters). It was, said the piece, a "ruthless exploitation of a young life". This assertion rested on slim evidence: the boy looked sad and bewildered; the boy carried out his family's bidding by tossing earth onto his father's coffin; the boy witnessed gunmen firing a volley of shots over the grave.

At this point, let's stop and think. There had been many funerals for British soldiers in the previous years, often attended by sons and daughters, nephews and nieces. These children also looked sad and bewildered; they took part in rituals they hardly understood; they stood by as riflemen shot into the sky. Yet no paper dared to call their presence at the graveyard a form of exploitation. They were never presented to the British public as pawns of war.

"Impartial observers", far from being sickened, spoke of these children as innocent victims, bravely facing up to an awful destiny. But they were used as propaganda tools, too. And that, of course, is the central point of this retrospective study of the British press coverage of the hunger strike. There are their soldiers and ours; their victims and ours; their morals and ours; their deaths and ours. Their deaths are noble, heroic acts in defence of freedom. Our deaths are ignoble, cowardly acts, attacking (so-called) democracy. Most notably, there is their propaganda and ours. And theirs, sanctified by the state and promulgated by the national press, is inevitably seen as legitimate (good) propaganda while ours is viewed as illegitimate (bad) propaganda. Their views are apolitical common sense, based on fact; ours are politically inspired mischievous bias, based on lies. Indeed, their lies – whether about shoot-to-kill, collusion or, as we shall see, the aftermath of the hunger strike – are merely means justifying ends; our lies, our means, are despicable. How else to explain the view of the *Sunday Telegraph*'s columnist, Peregrine Worsthorne, who mid-hunger strike delivered himself of this gem: "The English have every reason to feel proud of their country's recent record in Northern Ireland, since it sets the whole world a uniquely impressive example of altruistic service in the cause of peace."

His article was deliberately provocative, but papers imbued with anti-republican bias were guilty of breathtakingly casual insults. The *Daily Express,* exasperated by worldwide sympathy for Sands and his comrades, cried out: "We are letting the IRA win too many easy propaganda victories." Easy? For men to fast unto death as their jailers tempted them with food? Easy? For relatives to watch their kin starve themselves to death? Easy? For fellow prisoners, who knew their likely fate, to volunteer to replace dead friends? But the newspapers, normally so critical of their governments, wrapped themselves in the Union flag and spoke with a single voice against the hunger strike. Even the lone liberal voice of the period, The *Guardian,* thought Thatcher's "policy has been correct," though "her posture has been disdainful". But that was hair-splitting: policy and posture were entwined.

As nine more men died in the following months, the papers reiterated their support for Thatcher's inflexible stance. The *Daily Mirror,* the paper then advocating British withdrawal from Ireland, predicted that "the IRA cannot and will not win the hunger strike". *The Times* admitted that the deaths were rousing the North's nationalists "to a measure of active sympathy with the Provisionals that has not been seen since the Army shot thirteen men dead in Londonderry in January 1972". It added: "Nevertheless, this is an issue where the government must stand its ground." One of Thatcher's journalistic fans, Paul Johnson, conceded in the *Sun* that the strike "has been turned into a calamitous propaganda defeat for Britain . . . All over the world Britain has been vilified." The *Sunday Times* agreed: "Ulster is widely seen outside Britain as the West's last unliberated colony; and the hunger-strikers, irrational to the point of absurdity though they look from Britain, have contrived to dramatise that suggestion of oppressive colonial rule." The following week, the *Sunday Times* proved it by conducting a survey among foreign paper editors: thirty-six said Britain should withdraw from

Northern Ireland; five said it should remain; and only one, at a Turkish conservative daily, unequivocally backed Thatcher's stand against the hunger strike.

There was further predictable press upset at the success of hunger-strike candidates standing for the Dáil, but the message remained the same: the government would not, could not, offer concessions to the prisoners. But now we must move on to look closely at the "damaging" appeasement and the "misconception" mentioned earlier. When the strike came to its end in October, the papers hammered home the "fact" that the republicans had "lost". The deaths were "senseless" (*Daily Telegraph*); they were "ten wasted lives" (*The Times*); the "final impression is not so much one of IRA heroism as of IRA cynicism" (*Sunday Telegraph*). *The Times* reported that the newly appointed secretary of state, James Prior, would be offering reforms to the Maze regime, but these would fall short of the prisoners' five demands: free association; the right to wear their own clothing; restoration of full remission; no compulsory prison work; and increase in personal letters, parcels and visits. The government had always maintained that, taken collectively, these amounted to political status.

According to a *Times* leading article, the collapse of the strike "usefully deflates the myth of the invincibility of the IRA. It also opens the way for minor, and only minor, changes in the prison regime." Every paper sought to stress that the inevitable reforms would not mean the granting of political status. There would be only "limited concessions", said the *Daily Telegraph,* because the government "has no intention of allowing the Maze to become a 'prisoner of war' camp run by the prisoners". The *Sun* said: "The demands of the hunger strikers to be treated as political offenders were absurd . . . They should be treated as violent criminals with no special privileges." The following day, the *Daily Telegraph* reported that Prior's reforms meant prisoners would wear their own clothes, would get back half their lost remission, would receive extra visits and letters and would be allowed to communicate and, on occasion, "share association in recreation rooms and exercise areas". They would be expected to work, but not as in other jails. Both the government and newspapers indulged in spin to present this fudge as anything but a climbdown. Anyway, the prisoners had to agree to the reforms, and they were not prepared to work. But the London-based newspapers affected not to notice what happened in the weeks afterwards.

The hunger-strike story suddenly vanished from the pages of the national papers. When *The Times* reported on 13 October that Prior had given the IRA until 1 November to decide whether to accept his new prison rules, it was the last reference to the reforms. As far as its readers were concerned, Thatcher had prevailed because the paper told them that the strike had been called off "on terms in which the IRA can take no satisfaction". Similarly, *The Sunday Times* observed that "the changes now in prospect infringe no principle, since they will still make no distinction between Provisional IRA prisoners and ordinary convicts".

Every newspaper reported Thatcher's defiant statement, "I shall never give them political status – never," as if it were an incontestable truth.

To continue the story just a little, we must turn to the *Belfast Telegraph*, which reported on 26 October that almost all the prisoners were now wearing their own clothes, but prison work was "still a sticking point" to a settlement. After the Prior deadline, the paper went on reporting that work remained an obstacle. None of this appeared in the British papers, so their audiences were left to believe the myth of Thatcher's victory. As we now know, the prisoners eventually avoided work and were allowed to associate freely. The hunger strike achieved much more, of course. Most notably, it was the precursor to the peace process.

Finally, let us recall another example of British newspaper prescience. A *Daily Telegraph* leader pronounced with typical condescension: "Hunger striking is a fairly familiar device which normally fails even to procure lasting fame for those who employ it." And whose iconic picture stares down from walls, and remains on the lips of republicans and non-republicans alike twenty-five years after his death? Bobby Sands'.

IT'S TOO SOON TO SAY

Anne Cadwallader, journalist

IT SEEMS INDECENTLY EXTRAVAGANT TO LINK MY EXPERIENCE, EVEN tenuously, with the 1981 hunger strikers. The only possible justification is to show how wide its ripples spread. Wide enough to change the life of an English woman with no previous interest in Ireland.

For people of my generation in Britain, even for the politically aware, Irish history was a gaping hole in our education. We were vaguely aware of the potato famine and knew subliminally that Cromwell wasn't exactly a local hero in Drogheda – and that was about it. Blissful in our ignorance, we allowed successive British governments to muck things up. Ireland barely registered on our political Richter scale. The battle against apartheid in distant South Africa was of far greater appeal. But the hunger strike began to force some of us to consider Irish politics. Most of us in Britain then regarded the ten men as extraordinarily perverse. I had no strong views either way, but as an idealistic young reporter who believed good journalism could change history, I felt obliged to take an interest.

My career was just starting on the *Bradford Telegraph & Argus,* an evening newspaper in west Yorkshire. I was also a member of Bradford South Labour Party and my union, the NUJ. As the news increasingly focused on events in the Maze, I became more intrigued. The newspapers didn't sate my appetite, so I pounced on the first hapless Irish person I came across. As the venue for this encounter was an extremely noisy nightclub, late one Friday night in late 1980, the conversation was somewhat restricted. We met the next day for lunch to continue the interrogation. He was originally from Portglenone in County Antrim and had lived in Yorkshire for about five years, earning a meagre living by writing and performing plays on Irish political themes in the local pubs, where he also sold *An Phoblacht.*

His explanation threw up even more questions than it answered.

In common with my peers, I viewed the IRA with unmitigated disgust on two fronts. Firstly, the IRA indiscriminately murdered people, including civilians. My personal experience of this was limited to sitting in union meetings in central London during the 1970s, listening to bombs going off near by (causing the book-shop I then worked in to tremble from roof to basement). Secondly, I had read, repeatedly, that the IRA, in a horribly exploitative and unsavoury way, oppressed its own working-class community through operating shady drinking dens, one-armed bandit scams and dodgy taxi firms.

The Official IRA, we were led to believe, was different. They were the good guys, who had been undermined by the Provision-als. The Officials had laid down their arms and were campaign-ing for working-class unity against sectarianism. Right on, comrade. Until early 1981, it had never occurred to me to ask why any ordinary people supported the IRA. I wasn't even aware that they did. My Irish friend in Bradford drew a messy map on a serviette, explaining the schisms in republicanism. He told me about the Easter Rising, the Civil War, the battle for civil rights, Castlereagh and the H-Blocks. He even claimed that the Provi-sional IRA had popular support in Belfast and Derry. How could this be?

I was training to be a sub-editor and studying newspaper design. When he produced a copy of *An Phoblacht* for me, it was not what I had expected. It packed a powerful punch, it spoke a political language I understood, and it was even humorous in a blackly sardonic way. All this intrigued me.

A couple of months later, at the 1980 NUJ annual conference, I coincidentally met a middle-class, Irish-speaking RTÉ producer who had a somewhat different interpretation of events in the North. Was he right about the IRA? Or was my friend in Bradford right? It seemed there was only one way to find out. Reader, I became a political tourist!

My Conservative Party card-carrying parents were not impressed at this news. Margaret Thatcher, they felt, was not nearly tough enough on the wretched Irish. They had no doubts about the hunger strikers. Bobby Sands was a murderer who deserved to die. He was doing the world a favour by killing himself.

By now, I had read up a little and knew that he had been intimidated out of his home as a child, that the long sentence he was serving was for possession of a quarter of a gun and that a non-jury court had convicted him under special laws and sent him to a special jail. The only thing that wasn't special, it seemed, was the terms under which Sands and the others were serving their sentences. They wanted the return of political status, and they seemed to me to have an arguable case.

On a family trip out to Leeds Castle in Kent (of all places), my parents and I had one of our furious rows. We had had plenty of these before over the miners' strike, trade unions, public ownership, taxes and so on. This one, however, was particularly bitter. It made no difference. I was determined to go and find out for myself.

I took the Liverpool boat to Dublin and the train to Belfast. Nothing could have prepared me for Belfast in April 1981.

The atmosphere was brooding, sinister, frightening. The grey, rainy streets of central Belfast were grimy and pockmarked with dereliction. To get the full-on experience, I eschewed hotels for a squat off the Lower Ormeau Road. Neighbours were stockpiling flour and medicines. Life revolved around the half-hourly radio bulletins as people waited for Sands to die.

The newsreader announced one evening that the UDA was staging a "show of strength" on the Shankill Road. I blithely set off to witness this event. Fools rush in. If I had been frightened before, I was terrified by what I saw there: masked men carrying cudgels, openly drilling up and down a street, watched by police officers who made no attempt to intervene. In the UK!

That Sunday afternoon was unseasonably warm, but I noticed people on the Ormeau Road pulling their children in off the street and closing their doors and windows. Inquiring, I was told an Orange parade was about to march past.

This sounded like more instructional fun, so I set off to watch. I had covered several National Front marches in Bradford and had watched as the Union Jack was used to intimidate black and Asian people. But that was nothing compared to the deeply disturbed feelings of confusion and dismay I felt as the same flag was waved during this Orange parade. Inexplicably, tears stung my eyes. Questions began to bubble up. I was British and proud of it. My great-grandfather's statue stands in the Central Lobby of the House of Commons. My uncles, going back generations, were farmers, clergymen, accomplished horsemen in the comfortable English shires. My mum and dad had both served in the British army. Even when I stopped going to church regularly, I never missed Remembrance Sunday.

Psychologically, I was deeply disturbed by Orange marchers waving the Union flag. It had no connection to any Britishness I knew. The next day, I walked up the Falls Road and interviewed Richard McAuley in the Sinn Féin press centre. He was intense, driven, had an answer for everything (some things never change).

I was flabbergasted at the murals. I was astonished at the pages of the *Irish News*, listing all the streets that supported the hunger strikers. I was intrigued that the protest marchers included young mums with prams, and grandparents wearing hats, not just young people in jeans. I loved the Irish music in Kelly's Bar on the Short Strand and the slogan written on a wall outside: "Rise with your class, not out of it."

I also visited Derry and got a quick lesson in history gazing down from its walls on the geography of the Bogside. I met Mary Nelis in the kitchen of her house where her washing machine had just broken down. As she mopped the floor, she spoke about her sons – the ones in jail and the ones she feared would inevitably end up there. She was taking a couple of days off from the protest marches, where she was habitually clad only in a blanket. Mary seemed like so many other people I had met, a thoroughly decent person. How could she and others support the hateful IRA?

My empathy with the hunger strikers and their families was growing against the backdrop of that unanswerable question. Every bone in my body rejected the idea of bombing or shooting people, so why were so many supporting the ten men? Even when it became clear that Sands would die, there were the increasingly familiar names of those who would die next: Francis Hughes, Raymond McCreesh and Patsy O'Hara. Their faces were everywhere. It seemed to me a case of the irresistible force (the hunger strikers) meeting the immovable object (Margaret Thatcher). Which side would give way first? The question consumed my every waking moment and most of my sleeping ones.

I phoned the Ulster Unionist Party, determined to try to investigate their side of the story, but was told there was no one available to speak to me. The response to my queries was cold, distant and uninterested in the questions of a naïve British journalist, but time was running out and I had to leave.

I arrived in Dublin, full of what I believed were original insights and with the fervour of the political convert. My RTÉ producer friend was amused but gently dismissive of the somewhat radical views I transported into the calm of his south Dublin home. He woke me the next morning with the news that Bobby Sands had just died. I sat at his mother's impeccably dressed breakfast table and miserably ate toast and marmalade in silence. We then drove to O'Connell Street to see the protests and watch people signing the book of condolences at the GPO.

The next day, we drove out into County Wicklow, and I fell in love with the Irish landscape, but already wanted to return to Belfast. The time came to go home. I didn't want to leave Ireland and wept like a baby on the boat. Although I had been in the country barely a week, I felt like a plant being ripped from its roots.

Back in Bradford, I discovered that all the many photographs I had taken in Belfast and Derry were out of focus because I had been shaking either from fear or from the high excitement of witnessing history in the making. I spoke about my experiences at several local Labour Party branches in the Yorkshire moors and dales, bringing along the plastic bullet I'd been given in Derry (most of us still believed they were the size and consistency of jelly babies) and the pages of street names from the *Irish News*. I expected a hostile reception, but people were genuinely interested. I sold dozens of copies of Michael Farrell's *Northern Ireland: The Orange State*. The experience convinced me that it was possible to interest British people in Irish politics. Life in Bradford, though, was never the same again. There was no going back. I was sitting on my back doorstep in the sun when the news came in that Owen Carron had been elected. It seemed to confirm my view that there was a lot more going on in Ireland than met the eye.

Centuries ago, Aristotle wrote about the compelling push/pull effect of simultaneous attraction and repulsion. I was hooked. I vowed to return to Ireland in virtually any capacity and spent the next six months applying everywhere. Rejection letters came back by the armful, but eventually I managed to find work in Belfast. I intended to give it six months before taking the next step up the career ladder. My father, who must have known me better than I gave him credit for, somehow knew instinctively that he was "losing" his daughter. He tried to disssuade me from going. It's only for six months, I reassured him.

Twenty-five years later, I'm still here. My views have become far, far more complex than they were in the wake of the hunger strikes of 1981, but of one thing I am as certain now as I was then. If the British public knew more about what had been done in their name in Ireland, the violence here would have ended far quicker than it did.

Since then, I have met Kieran Doherty's father, Alfie, Francis Hughes' brother, Oliver, and Bobby Sands' sister, Bernadette. I have talked for long hours with some of those who shared a prison cell with some of the ten men who died.

I interviewed Pat McGeown on the hunger strike's tenth anniversary. He told me of how, pulled off the strike by his family, he had come round from his coma to find a nurse standing over him with a puzzled look on her face. The syringe she had been using to give him a vitamin injection had bent after striking his bone. Recollecting the story, he smiled. I winced.

If asked to assess the significance of the hunger strike, I always quote Chinese premier Chou En-Lai's response in 1949 to a question about the impact of the French Revolution in 1789. "It's too soon to say," he replied.

The hunger strike remains for me a personal milestone. I still can't comprehend, of course, what the men went through. I wish I had known them. I wish, above all, that they could see the results of their actions for themselves. I wish they hadn't died. I wish no one had died.

DO BHOBBY SANDS AN LÁ SULAR ÉAG

Michael Davitt

Fanaimid,
mar dhaoine a bheadh
ag stánadh suas
ceithre urlár ar fhear
ina sheasamh ar leac na fuinneoige
ag stánadh anuas orainn
go tinneallach.

Ach an féinmharú d'íobairtse?
ní géilleadh, ní faoiseamh;
inniu ní fiú rogha duit
léimt nó gan léimt.

Nílimid cinnte
dár bpáirtne sa bhuile;
pléimid ceart agus mícheart
faoi thionchar ghleo an tí óil;
fanaimid ar thuairiscí nua,
ar thuairimí *video*.

Fanaimid, ag stánadh,
inár lachain i glcúmh sóch,
ar na cearca sa lathach
is an coileach ag máirseáil thart
go bagarthach ar a ál féin,
ar ál a chomharsan
is i nguth na poimpe glaonn:
'coir is ea coir is ea coir.'

Thit suan roimh bhás inniu ort.
Cloisimid ar an raidió
glór do mhuintire faoi chiach,
an cumha ag sárú ar an bhfuath:
is é ár nguí duit
go mbuafaidh.

"THIS MORNING REFUSED BREAKFAST . . ."
Kevin Rafter, broadcaster, journalist

MEMORY CAN PLAY TRICKS. MY RECOLLECTIONS OF THE EVENTS OF 1981 now mix with material gleaned from books as a student and seen first hand as a reporter of the more recent narrative in Northern Ireland. I have images in my head of black flags hanging from lamp-poles, but I don't think they are personal copyright, rather transfers from television footage watched in later years. I am certain I remember election posters for Charlie Haughey and Fianna Fáil, but I know my recognition of H-Block posters is not directly linked to 1981, but again something stolen from elsewhere and tucked away in my own memory.

I was eleven years old when Bobby Sands started his hunger strike. I don't remember the news bulletin which carried the announcement. But, in my mind now, I can hear the newsreader on BBC radio stating that a prisoner in the Maze Prison "this morning refused breakfast". I listened to an archive recording of the broadcast a short time ago. Now it fights for a place with my real recollections.

Something about the prison campaign connected with me. Was I politicised? Was I radicalised? The answer to both questions is, most definitely, no. Did I find a hero in Sands? Did I understand what was happening north of the border? Again, the answer is no. But as a young boy, taking in snatches of the events in the wider world, something about the hunger strikes made a connection with me.

We lived in Waterford. Home and school were side by side. I had a Raleigh bike which I cycled to and from school most days. But I know that for a time in 1981 I took an early morning diversion before the nine o'clock school bell sounded. The Cove Stores was the nearest newsagent. The shop was almost straight opposite the entrance to school. The building was a funny shape, almost fifty-pence-piece style. It was dark and poky inside.

The shop must have sold other newspapers; it most certainly did, but I recall only copies of *The Irish Times* and the *Irish Independent* piled up on the counter. I wonder now what the shop owner must have thought about his new regular customer – a primary school boy neatly decked out in a grey school jumper, grey shirt and black and red tie. I seem to remember I bought the *Independent* more often than the *Times,* but I suspect that had much to do with the bolder front-page cover on the *Independent.*

Did I read every line of the analysis articles and news reports on the hunger strikes? Was I ever late into class, having been distracted by the latest developments from Northern Ireland? What did I think of Bobby Sands? I have no real answer to those questions. I simply don't remember what I felt, let alone understood, as an eleven-year-old back in 1981. What I do know is that after school had ended and I had cycled home – most days – I took a scissors to those papers. I kept a scrapbook of newspaper cuttings chronicling the day-to-day movements in the hunger strikes.

My family was not political. There was no talk of politics, that I can remember, or even of the conflict in Northern Ireland. I think my grandmother was different. She read the *Irish Press.* She nodded approvingly at Charlie Haughey when he was on the television news, although, if I'm honest, I'd have to admit that she never actually said anything political that lodged permanently in my memory. Maybe I take my interest in politics from her, maybe not. I never asked enough questions when she was alive, but then, why would a young boy seek out such information? Sadly, when the time comes to appreciate knowing such matters, age tends to rob us of the memory points.

My grandmother had been a young girl during the War of

Independence. She carried messages across the checkpoints in the slip of her skirt. The Black and Tans never thought to stop a girl. My grandmother was a Reilly. Her mother was a Breen. Their cousin became a republican hero Dan Breen. He hid in my grandmother's thatched farmhouse. They hid his guns in the thatch. That's what I have been told.

The chair he slept in now stands in my living room. A few years ago, it was rescued from a farm outhouse. A dog had gnawed at one of the wooden armrests. It's restored now, but the damage marks are still visible. My children love hearing the story of how Dan Breen was sleeping in the chair when a gunman snuck up, but the bullet missed their distant relation, instead leaving its mark on the armrest. They touch the place deferentially, like a pilgrim would a holy object. I'll tell them the truth one day.

Breen was a wanted man. The police posted notices seeking information about his whereabouts and tempting those with information to tout. There was a reward of £1,000 on his head. The notice read: "Daniel Breen (calls himself Commandant of the Third Tipperary Brigade). Age 27, 5 feet 7 inches in height, bronzed complexion, dark hair (long in front), grey eyes, short cocked nose, stout build, weight about 12 stone, clean shaven; sulky bulldog appearance; looks rather like a blacksmith coming home from work; wears cap pulled down over face."

In the mid-1970s, they built a modern bungalow opposite the old thatched house in which Dan Breen slept. I have my own memories of the old house. There was an open hearth. A turf fire. A photograph of JFK was propped up on the living-room dresser. A pope was his neighbour. My guess now is that the pope was John XXIII.

We were still visiting the family farm on the outskirts of Tipperary town in 1981 when I was compiling my scrapbook of newspaper cuttings on the hunger strikes. I remember the farmyard with the green gates and the crab-apple tree in the corner which led to the cattle fields. There was a fairy tree in one of those fields. Hop around it three times and make a wish, the visiting children were told. I don't know if I ever succeed. I have a medal – one of the veteran medals issued by the Fianna Fáil government in the 1930s. It belonged to my grandmother. It's a link to the past that I don't recall.

I now have my own memories of the H-Blocks. It was a misting November morning in 2004. A reporter's visit. The camera captured hours of footage in case I ever want to check a detail. We climbed to the top of a sentry tower and gazed across the vast complex. What my eyes could see – the overgrown vegetation, the rabbit warrens and the rusted iron work.

I stood in individual cells in H4. Looking past the window bars, I tried to find some detail from the outside world in the prison yard. The frustration at my failure made me angry. The claustrophobia in the cell made my head spin. The locks on every cell door had been stripped out after the prisoners left. But the keys for the medical room were still hanging on the key rack.

I was an intruder in someone else's story.

THE FULL SANCTION OF HIS OWN LIFE
Brian Keenan

(Reproduced from *An Evil Cradling* with the kind permission of the author, former Beirut hostage, Brian Keenan)

HUNGER STRIKE IS A POWERFUL WEAPON IN THE IRISH PSYCHE. IT overcomes fear in its deepest sense. It removes and makes negligible the threat of punishment. It powerfully commits back into the hunger striker's own hands the full sanction of his own life and of his own will. I was desperate for information. I needed to know something, anything, even a lie, something on which the mind could fix and, like a life belt, cling to for survival. I simply stopped eating. I recall now that in those first few weeks I had eaten very little and felt little need to. Hunger never seemed to affect me. Perhaps the mind, constantly shifting and readjusting and falling back, grew so preoccupied that it never turned its attention to the needs of the body. But because of this I felt supremely confident about what I would do. So each morning as breakfast arrived, I would simply consign it to a corner and forget about it. It was not an effort. The food accumulated in my plastic bag. I considered it to be a wise move not to inform the guards of my intention but to go it alone until I could use the threat of my own death to obtain the information for which my mind was ravenous. I thought I would leave it for some days until I was fully launched on this course and fully committed to it, until I was so fixed on it that they could take no action to break me from it.

Day after day, the food piled in the corner, forgotten, untested and unconsidered. I thought that this rotten food might infest the cell with the horrors of the toilet. In the mornings I concealed what I could of the food in my shirt, carried it with me to the toilet and got rid of it there. I thought also to keep enough sitting in the room so that when I revealed my intentions to them, they would see I was serious. After seven or eight days, I thought it was time to make a move. I had felt myself growing dizzy as I stood up in the mornings to walk to the toilet: that short walk of some thirty feet exhausted me. To let this thing run too long and not to pressurise them when I was sufficiently alert and strong would put them under little enough compulsion to respond. I took from my briefcase a stub of pencil which the guards had not found and scribbled on the cover of one of the textbooks a note to the chief, declaring what I was doing and why I was doing it.

When I had been given my food and before the guard had left, I called him back. The Grim Reaper arrived, and squatted in front of me; I simply handed him the note and told him to take it to his boss. He was puzzled. His English was very poor, so with some pidgin English, mixed with pidgin French, I was able to communicate the purpose of my note. He understood the word "Boss" and looked at the note. He did not understand what I had said, but pointed to my name at the bottom and then with his finger pointed at me. I nodded "Yes". He explained falteringly that he would take this note to his "deck boss". I understood that term to mean some junior lieutenant. He left and locked the door.

One way or the other I was committed to confrontation. But the days of hunger, or rather of indifference to hunger, had steeled my purpose. I remember as I refused to eat each meal feeling myself grow stronger. A fierce kind of pride met a fierce determination of will as the food heaped in the corner. My resolve was banked equally high and my purpose became more strongly fixed. Within the hour, the door of my cell was opened and in came the kidnapper who had been in the car when I was taken. He read the note quietly to himself, pointed to some words he was unsure of and I explained them at length. He looked around the cell. I lifted the plastic and pointed to the food. He appeared very anxious and upset by this. There was no anger. His voice was pleading when he asked, "Why don't you eat?" Again I told him that I would not eat until someone came here and told me why I had been taken; how long I was going to be held; what was being done and whether they had had any communication with representatives of the Irish Government. I was amazingly calm. I had not lost that defiant self-confidence but for some reason, whether it was the effect of a long period without food or the mind fixing itself so definitively on its purpose, I felt no need for anger or aggression. My stubbornness had interiorised itself. The guard left, telling me he would return with his chief.

The next morning, after I had been brought back from washing, my kidnapper and a man I presumed to be his boss came to my cell. The chief stood just inside the door while the kidnapper squatted beside me and talked to me. His chief would say something to him in Arabic. He would translate it for me. I would answer but he never translated the answer. I was sure that his chief spoke English and knew exactly what I was saying, but for some reason, and this was to happen again and again, the chiefs when they came would not let their voices be heard speaking English. I repeated again what I had earlier told him, so that this boss might hear my reasons and my purposes. I spoke slowly and calmly. I recall that this seemed to cause them some concern. They were probably worried that I was already becoming ill. They explained that they had no doctor. I answered that I did not want a doctor. If they brought one I would refuse to see or speak with him. I was made to stand, then to sit, then to walk in the passage. I assumed my light-headedness and my weakness were obvious to them, for they quickly brought me back to my cell and told me to eat. I refused. They said that I would die. I simply shrugged. I was then told that they did not care if I died, there were many hungry people in Lebanon. I said, "Feed them with this food, for I shall not eat it." Words were exchanged between the chief and the young kidnapper and they left, saying simply, "OK, you die." I smiled.

The next day, they were back, the young kidnapper and the prison chief and The Grim Reaper. They checked that my day's ration of food was untouched. Again the question, "Why you don't eat?" I answered, "I will not eat until you tell me *why?*" They talked outside my cell. For a moment I thought that they would try to punish me, but I was beyond caring. The young guard came back and told me that he did not know, it was simply his job to do such things. I told him that I still wanted to know and would not eat until I was told. He left, and as the door closed I heard him speak outside the cell. I knew that his chief was standing there, listening and saying nothing.

For the next few days nothing happened and I ate nothing. I was confident, I was strong-willed and almost ecstatic as I pushed each meal from me. Occasionally one of the guards would come and tempt me with an apple. But I was beyond desire. Things would come flying through the grille. A piece of cheese, and different pieces of food. I remember carrots were occasionally flung at me. I laughed and laughed. Here was a game I was winning; I was in control and control could not be taken from me.

My hunger strike ended the day the cell door opened and in came my young kidnapper. He had with him copies of *Time* and *Newsweek*. There were dramatic headlines on the front cover of each magazine about the attack on Libya by the US Airforce, the death of some of the family of Colonel Gadaffi, and the bombing of Tripoli. My kidnapper told me, "My boss he say this why you here." I was amazed, half-laughing and half-angry but holding both in check I said, "What the hell has this got to do with me? . . . I am not American. I am not British. I am Irish." The young guard talked excitedly about the events in Libya. I could follow only part of what he was saying, but he concluded: "Now we give you what you ask . . . now you eat?" I simply answered, my mind reeling with what had happened and my sudden involvement in it, "I cannot eat." The shock waves of what I had become associated with made it doubly impossible for me, at that moment, to consider food. Exasperated, he walked out and left these magazines with me. I had become a tiny, insignificant pawn in a global game over which I had no control.

MEMO TO BOBBY
Edna O'Brien, writer

At the dying moment
Did you whisper a word?
We shall not know.
We can only guess at hunger
The hunger of hunger
Gargantuan, garrulous.

In your pig-sty with thousands
Of hours to fill –
Guard dogs,
The Prophet Sirah,
Blackberries in Rathcoole
A mouthful of cement.

Until the blessed morning –
Dementia and the letting go.
Your radiant smile
From a weather-beaten mural
How beautiful it is;
Such abundance.
Manna, it says, fell from Heaven, Once.

COIRPIGH NÓ FÍRÉIN?

Tony MacMahon

Is MINIC A BHÍONN AN CUMAS AG DÁN, AG AMHRÁN, NÓ FIÚ AG BLÚIRE de scríbhinn ar pháipéar salach, scéal as an ngnáth a insint – i slí níos treise agus níos iomláine ná a dhéanfadh. . . . TV . . . raidió . . . nuachtán. Do sheas mé i dteach carad, Tom Hartley, i mBéal Feirste in 1983 ag féachaint ar thaispeántas beag a bhí ar bhalla na cistine aige – ceithre phíosa páipéir thoitín, trí orlach gach taobh ar a mhéid, agus lámhscríbhinní orthu chomh hálainn, chomh slachtmhar agus chomh deorach is a chonaic mé riamh. Nuacht ó phríosúnaigh a bhí ar stailc ocrais a bhí iontu, ag cur síos ar phianta an bháis, ar aislingí na saoirse ag trá.

Tamall gearr roimhe sin, do chuala mé Séamus Mac Mathúna ag canadh amhrán nua-chumtha ar ócáid bhás an tríú stailceora, Raymond McCreesh. Is iad seo na véarsaí a chuaigh go smior ionam:

> And in the hell of the H-Block cells
> Where tyrants strive to break men's wills
> Where boots and bars leave life-long scars
> Those brave men's spirit ne'er did yield.
> And words of Christ rang in men's minds
> "Who shall lay down his life for his fellow man?"
> The Volunteers, without dread or fear
> Were O'Hara, Hughes, McCreesh and Sands.
>
> For three score days these brave men lay
> In their duel with Thatcher's tyranny
> And Britain's churchmen came to say
> That no clergyman their souls could free.

But far and wide, through tears and pride,
Their story's told through foreign lands,
So your voices raise and we'll sing the praise
Of O'Hara, Hughes, McCreesh and Sands.

Cuireadh an cheist seo ar Mho Mowlam tráth a ruaigeadh as a post í mar Rúnaí Stáit ar na Sé Chontae ó thuaidh:

"Cad é an difríocht idir príosúnaigh dhílseacha agus príosúnaigh den chlann phoblachtánach?"

D'fhreagair sí: "The loyalist prisoner is pumping iron while the republican prisoner is studying for his university degree!"

Lucht físe, fealsúnachta agus intleachta ab ea na príosúnaigh phoblachtánacha.

"Ní coirpigh sinn," a dúradar, "ach lucht prionsabail agus polaitíochta. Ní cuspóirí salacha beagintinneacha atá ár dtuomáint ach idéll arda na saoirse."

Sa tseanaimsir in Éirinn nuair a bheadh easaontas idir taoiseach agus duine dá chlann agus gach doras leighis nó réitigh dúnta ar chách, d'fhanadh an gearánaí os comhair dhoras an taoisigh ar stailc ocrais nó go bhfaigheadh sé nó sí sásamh. Mura bhfaigheadh, stailc go bás a bhí ann.

Bhí sé amhlaidh i 1981 nuair a chuaigh gasra poblachtánach ar stailc ocrais sa phríosún ar a dtugtaí na H-Blocanna. Bhí an tír, thuaidh agus theas, corraithe go mór. Ní raibh a leithéid tarlaithe ó 1920 nuair a thug Ardmhéara Chorcaí Traolach Mac Suibhne a chorp agus a anam do chúis na fírinne agus na saoirse ar stailc ocrais i bPríosún Brixton i Sasana. Bhí an domhan mór corraithe ag íobairt an tSuibhnigh.

Is iomaí stáitse amharclainne gur sheas mé air i dteannta an fhile Michael Davitt le blianta beaga anuas agus sinn i mbun ceoil agus reacaireacht na filíochta. Dán amháin de chuid Mhichael a théann i bhfeidhm go mór ar an lucht féachana ná an dán a scríobh sé in ómós do Bhobby Sands. Sa dán seo deineann sé cur síos ar an dráma mór a dhein na meáin chumarsáide de bhás Bhobby. Seo iad an dá véarsa tosaigh i nGaeilge agus ansan i mBéarla:

Fanaimid,
mar dhaoine a bheadh
ag stánadh suas
ceithre urlár ar fhear
ina sheasamh ar leac fuinneoige
ag stánadh anuas orainn
go tinneallach.

Ach an féinmharú d'íobairtse?
Ní géilleadh, ní faoiseamh;
inniu ní fiú rogha duit
léimt nó gan léimt.

We wait,
like people
staring up at a man
tensed on a fourth-floor
ledge
staring down at us.

But is your stand suicide?
No surrender, no escape;
today not even the choice
to jump or not to jump.

Scríobhadh an dán san an oíche sara bhfuair Bobby bás: "Thit suan roimh bhás inniu ort." Gan amhras bhí muintir na 26 Contae faoi phúicín stáit Section 31, a chuir bac ar agallaimh raidió agus theilifíse le Poblachtánaigh. Ní raibh á chur inár láthair ach an leagan "oifigiúil" den scéal. Ní raibh cead ó dheas scéal an phobail náisiúnaigh ó thuaidh a insint ina iomláine. Bhí mearbhall ar na daoine. Ach bhí a fhios againn inár gcroí nach aon choirpeach an té a thabharfadh a bheatha ar son an ruda gur chreid sé ann. Agus níl aon chinsireacht stáit in ann an méid sin a cheilt, ná na "coms" beaga ealaíonta sin a chur faoi chosc.

THE DESIRE FOR FREEDOM
Medbh McGuckian, poet

I WAS THINKING TODAY ABOUT THE HUNGER STRIKE. PEOPLE say a lot about the body, but don't trust it. I consider that there is a kind of fight indeed. Firstly, the body doesn't accept the lack of food, and it suffers from the temptation of food, and from other aspects which gnaw at it perpetu- ally. The body fights back sure enough, but at the end of the day everything returns to the primary consideration, that is, the mind. The mind is the most important.

So wrote Bobby Sands to himself at the outset of his fatal campaign in March 1981. Why, we may ask, is there no poem of the stature and resonance of "Easter 1916" for these ten men? Because Yeats was a bourgeois, aspiring to aristocratic norms, and that was a mid-dle-class struggle? Because these were merely "the scum of the earth" and deserved no epitaph? It was as if it was impossible to write a thing of even terrible beauty about such depths of desper-ation, though its shock and shame pierced the verbal atmosphere. Everyone wrote – but what could have been adequate?

A student once said to me that I used the word "sand" as a ref-erence, and, yes, I was haunted by its associations and alluded to them in a 1988 collection, *On Ballycastle Beach*, which was to be prefaced by a quotation from Roger Casement. A sense of numbed confusion and not knowing where to go pervaded, influ-encing even such a slight response as the following:

> Not like a camera I plucked you;
> Your eyes closed in obedience to my dream,
> And opened on a clearing to another dream
> Which was the gold of your own body disentangled.

A beach more than a house is a place
Of oppression. It feels at once excluded
And enfolded, can be both an answer
And an obstacle, a path through all the tangle

Of an unknown woman's dream. That second
My hand shook like a sound or step
On some most celibate shore. Was it the poet
Or the yellow path that dreamt me to a stop?

Since I was actually unknown to them, although they were known to me, this is a weak romantic pondering of the choices facing them. But when I learned of the Irish-speaking prison block called after the lapwing, I was able to dedicate a poem, "Gaeltacht na Fuiseoige" in their memory.

I heard the name Thomas Ashe for the first time from Gregory Peck*, and even the current inhabitants of the cells had never been told his story. The three poems for him had clear connections to the present, and one of the inmates designed a Sam Browne belt with Ashe's and Gregory's names on it, which he was proud to wear.

I had, like most people, no stomach for the details of those starvings, but was once consoled by an anecdote from one of the women, possibly Dolours Price, who relates that when Cardinal Ó Fiaich visited her, presumably to reason with her, she was so incapable of talk that in a moment of human compassion he just held her like a child.

Around forty years earlier, the Russian-American Expressionist painter, Mark Rothko, who was to commit suicide in 1970, had written:

---

* Gregory Peck's paternal grandmother, Catherine Ashe, was an immigrant from County Kerry and a relative of Thomas Ashe, who fought in the Easter Rising in 1916 and died on hunger strike in 1917, demanding prisoner-of-war status.

Most societies of the past have insisted that their own particular evaluations of truth and morality be depicted by the artist . . . Today the compulsion is Hunger, and the experience of the last 400 years has shown us that hunger is not nearly as compelling as the imminence of Hell and Death. Since the passing on of the spiritual and temporal patron, the history of art is the history of men who, for the most part, have preferred hunger to compliance, and who have considered the choice worthwhile. And choice it is, for all the tragic disparity between the two alternatives.

The freedom to starve! Ironical indeed. Yet hold your laughter. Do not underestimate the privilege. It is seldom possessed and dearly won. The denial of this right is no less ironical: think of the condemned criminal who will not eat and who is fed by force, if need be, until the day of his execution. Concerning hunger, as concerning art, society has traditionally been dogmatic. One had to starve legitimately – through famine or blight, through unemployment or exploitation – or not at all. One could no more contrive to his own starvation than he could take his own life; and for the artist to have said to society that he would sooner starve than traffic with her wares or tastes would have been heresy and dealt with summarily as such. Within the dogmas of the totalitarian states of today, you may be sure, the artist must starve correctly, just as he must paint by the dictates of the state.

As Rothko was writing this to himself (in the late 1930s), he could not have known that on the beautiful Riviera beaches of southern France we sunbathe on obliviously today, thousands of Spanish Republican refugees were being incarcerated without shelter, proper food or water, and daily suffering complete mental and physical breakdown.

The sand was the actual and only camp, so I thought there was little improvement between that kind of fascism and this, and that my book commemorating Emmet's self-sacrifice in 1803 might have meant something to that other Robert, that other artist who wrote:

> But then where does this proper mentality stem from? Perhaps from one's desire for freedom. It isn't certain that that's where it comes from.
>
> If they aren't able to destroy the desire for freedom, they won't break you. They won't break me because the desire for freedom, and the freedom of the Irish people, is in my heart. The day will dawn when all the people of Ireland will have the desire for freedom to show.
>
> It is then we'll see the rising of the moon.
>
> (*Diary of Bobby Sands*)

THE SANDS OF ST CYPRIEN
Medbh McGuckian

Frozen sand: it looked so innocent
It erased footsteps and soaked up blood
Like water.

Behind the barbed-wire perimeter
Of that motley group of huts,
His very being was fistfuls of hardened sand:

Sand running through his veins.
Neurosis of sand. Sand induced fits.
The pull of molecules of sand.

In the sand-jail where consonants burned away,
The air was filled with particicles
Of excrement, little L-shaped pieces . . .

Discoloured liquid
From standing pools of urine
Blew their imagined wholeness in their faces.

I don't know if I read it in a newspaper,
Or if someone told me,
Or I heard it after twenty-four hours had gone by:

But nothing reported could have been
Further from the truth,
How slowly, slowly, crushed by sadness

From a skeleton in a blanket
To a carcass in manure,
He backed into the calyx of the brown flower.

Whose tin of champagne sticks in our throats
So we barely make it go down
Because God is forbidden to perform miracles in this
place.

DERRY AGAIN, IN SLOW MOTION
Eugene McCabe, writer

As THIS PIECE OFFERS NO CHANCE FOR LEVITY, I'LL START BY RECALLING one of the kindest of creatures who ever drew breath. Annie Kennedy, "May she rest aisy," lived beside us here at Drumard on the Monaghan/Fermanagh border. She came up to the byre every morning for milk. At the start of the hunger strike she was impatient: "What about their fambleys? God help their poor mothers, sisters. And the lassies they're great with. All that filth in their cells; you wouldn't find weemen at the like; tell you what I'd do; I'd put a pan of rashers under their noses and they'd soon quit their carry-on."

When Bobby Sands died, there were tears in her eyes as she said, "And all the poor lad wanted was to wear his own trousers."

More seriously, what comes next to mind is Auberon Waugh's reference to Tomás Ó Fiaich as "that wretched Irish Cardinal", because of Ó Fiaich's compassionate pleading with the strikers to call off the strike and his outspokenness on their behalf. The gratuitous use of the word "wretched" seems the abiding Tory establishment's response to all things Irish, a gross, ex-Empire arrogance still dormant in the closet. At the moment, it is wide awake and walking backwards in Iraq with Mr Bush: a doomed, disappointing involvement because no English prime minister since Gladstone has been so committed or determined as Tony Blair to achieve a fair and final settlement in Ireland. Unfortunately, he'll not be around as PM to complete the task.

What I was aware of during that time (1981) was a sense of guilt about the extent of my anger (hatred's twin) for the Tories and for Thatcher in particular. We all know how we felt after Bloody Sunday, that mix of rage and utter helplessness that made Bernadette Devlin cross the floor of the Commons to claw at Reggie Maudling. I read the *De Profundis* on the Diamond in Clones and was asked by RTÉ what I felt about British soldiers killing unarmed civilians in Derry.

"No response to *that*," I said, "would bother me in the slightest."

Later, on reflection, I was startled, indeed ashamed, by what I'd said. I did not use the word retaliation, but that gut reaction was wrong for someone espousing non-violence. But then the temptation to hit back is one of the worst aspects of human nature. The hunger strike was Derry again in slow motion, creating an almost deeper anger that was hard to reconcile with the ideals of peaceful protest.

In the debris of the Brighton bombing, Mark's mammy, old bosom friend of the mass murderer Pinochet, uttered something heroic and defiant. I've forgotten what. That bomb was calculated, callous and indefensible. The vast majority of us here didn't want her or anyone maimed or killed, but I'd still like to see her tried and shamed for her crass indifference to young men prepared to starve for a principle they believed in, literally "unto death". Such a trial won't happen. The statue is already up celebrating her glorious reconquest of a sheep island off Argentina. Certainly she'll have the honour of immortality in the Irish psyche, alongside Oliver Cromwell.

I realise now it's not possible to know what you think or feel till you've written it down.

A couple of years back, I met Bobby Ballagh at a function. We related well. When the hall was empty, we stayed on talking amicably. Finally, Bobby said, "I was down checking out that blown-up bridge near your farm. On the way back, I paused at your gates, not knowing whether to call up or not."

"You should have," I said.

"I wasn't certain of your thinking," he replied.

"That," I said, "makes two of us."

Reading the contradictory, ambivalent emotions and reactions of the above, I can understand his uncertainty. To explain mine, I have to call on the support of Catullus who wrote 2,000 years ago:

> I hate and love: you ask how can that be?
> I have no answer, but it torments me.

That torment was the conflict between mind and heart.

Better say clearly now that I am, and always have been, openly opposed to violence as a path towards change and peace. Ghandi, Martin Luther King and Daniel O'Connell accomplished more by non-violence, and John Hume had a sporting chance of negotiating a fair solution had the gun (inevitably) never arrived to defend and then dominate, divide and deepen the existing injustice and hatred.

One very great man did emerge from the heartbreak of those thirty years. Gordon Wilson is an exemplar for all time. A modest, Protestant, Fermanagh draper, he will be especially identified with that almost unattainable directive from Christ: "Love your enemy."

That, for us, includes Thatcher, Paisley and even Cromwell, God rest his tortured soul. He was troubled enough once to write down the questioning of a friend who asked him: "Think you in the bowels of Christ, Sir, you could be wrong?"

As for the future? Who knows? Ulster's had a long gestation as the Mississippi of Europe with its 400-year mix of Scot's borderers and English colonisers escheating the native Irish. God knows, and the whole world knows, things haven't changed all that much up there. The deep-rooted differences are as passionate today as the grievances dividing Greek from Turk, Arab from Jew, Serb from Croat, Basque from Spaniard, and now, on a world scale, extreme Muslims from the entire Christian West.

These hatreds, stemming from religious and cultural dislike of the unlike, show little sign of change. The "terrible beauty" of the civil rights marchers and those who armed to defend them has long since been replaced by the awful ugliness of a mendacious, cunning, two-headed beast – extreme loyalism and extreme republicanism. Common sense, that most uncommon of qualities, may hopefully persuade both sides towards the difficult path of reconciliation. That implies the courage to forgive, to eschew ancient resentments and the pitfalls of blind nationalism and loyalism.

It was a soldier with the Irish name of O'Flaherty (VC) who said in 1915, "You'll never have a quiet world till you knock patriotism out of the human race."

How? Knock is a violent word.

One image that's stayed with me for years is an observation of Biblical resonance from Kathy Sheridan in Marie Heaney's collection, *Sources:* "The late Bedouin King, Hussien, began his political life by witnessing the assassination of his grandfather and ended it by weeping over the bodies of the children of his enemies."

SWIMMING IN EDEN
Shane Connaughton, writer and playwright

DACHINE RAINER LIVED IN KENT IN A BEAUTIFUL TUDOR HOUSE surrounded by fields through which the River Eden ran. She'd come to England from America in the 1960s when property was cheap and the dollar strong. Though Jewish, she'd been instrumental in founding the Committee for the Liberation of Ezra Pound, with the help of others such as Dwight and Nancy Macdonald, W.H. Auden, e.e. cummings and his wife, Marion Morehouse.

Whenever I argued with her, she'd say, "Just because a man is a great poet doesn't mean he is incapable of nincompoop political opinions. Pound and Yeats and all other great poets – go back to their words. You will find them there. They give a good account of themselves."

Brought up in the Bronx, New York, as a child she'd been gripped by the events surrounding the execution of Sacco and Vanzetti, the poor fish peddler and cobbler. They had committed no crime. What was dangerous about them was their radical opinions. Nurtured on the teachings of Prince Peter Kropotkin and Tolstoy, she came to believe the state should be abolished and that cooperation not conflict was the chief factor in evolution. During World War II, she and her companion, Holley Cantine, edited *Prison Etiquette,* a collection of the writings of conscientious objectors imprisoned in America. Christopher Isherwood wrote the introduction.

Though Dachine's novel, *An Uncomfortable Inn,* had been highly praised by Norman Mailer and Rebecca West, she was essentially a lyric poet.

I spent a lot of time with her in 1981. The weather was good, and we swam in the river every day. In the evenings, we sat out-side and barbecued steak and drank wine. And carried on talk-ing. I remember her saying, "More people fail for lack of character than lack of talent."

The subject exercising her most in those dreamy days was Bobby Sands. The idea that there were young men slowly dying on principle, just an hour or two from our idyllic existence, obsessed her. I said to her one evening, "Oh, maybe Thatcher will give in."

She replied, "The power maddened can't give in."

Journalists of a certain type she called, "Whores of the state generously rewarded."

She began to write a poem.

One morning, in her quiet, insistent American voice she read it aloud.

In Memoriam
Robert Sands MP 1954–1981

One need only have seen the beauty in his joyous face to
know its goodness,
to feel the radiating passion of his will. There is, as Keats
was quick
to learn, no distinction between truth and beauty.
Newspapers
Inadvertently permitted us to interpret this calm Bobby
Sands:
a face defied the cold deranged violence of English
propaganda. Determined in his gentleness. We
watched all week,
the final week, read reports from his prison hospital bed.

He could not have wanted to die in this green Irish spring,
trade the young, friable earth for the clay dun of death.
He whispered

with his last exemplary breath, "Liberty for Ireland!"

I wait in a London house, wondering how many there are
     like me, ashamed
for England. Despairing. Although I withdrew from every
     belief in government
half a century ago (no person is good enough to rule
     another: assumption brutish)
and know that war is the hard currency of each state,
I feel guilty by having discovered no way to halt the
     English army. Guilt,
Americans have taken three hundred aggressive years to
     learn, is a terrible companion.

Bobby Sands will die in this lush Irish spring,
will trade the young, friable earth for the clay dun of
     death, whisper
with his last exemplary breath, "For united Ireland!"

As he ebbed towards death, I surprised myself hearing my
     prayer and cries in empathy
– as a mother with his agonising mother, with his father
     and his grieving sister
and as a radical, in a furore of sympathy with his enraged
     guerrilla cohorts: more than thirty thousand voters
     elected his heroic stance.
In what contempt Brit parliamentary democracy shows
     itself!
Weave slowly, thousands, black flags of Durutti,
waving and weeping across Belfast to the open earth.

He could not have wanted to die in this sweet Irish spring,
trade the young, friable earth for the clay dun of death.
     He whispered
with his final breath, "Liberty for Ireland!"

"It's very romantic, Dachine. It's . . . good."

She fixed me with a baleful and deadpan stare.

"I haven't finished yet, dumbo!"

"Oh, sorry. How does he compare to cummings, Pound – Bobby Sands?"

"Pound, cummings, Buster Keaton, were nineteenth-century Americans. Estlin was politically astute. Ezra wasn't. His was the error of any cheerfully dispositioned Jeffersonian democrat whose platonic self-deceptions were utopian and relatively conventional."

She had lived lives beyond me. I poured coffee, sat silent as she continued.

> It is curious how composed the English state in its perfidy.
> Composed
> and cunning. How it bends our honest language towards
>   deceit, abuses the words
> of Shakespeare and of Joyce: each report from Ireland
>   must be translated. Belfast's
> "teenaged criminals", "terrorists", please read, "young
>   men of a guerrilla army" fighting the English invasion;
>   for the hypocrisy of "security forces" truth reads
>   "English army assaults Celtic populace",
> Uproots its cities into battlefields.

> Bobby Sands will die in this burgeoning Irish spring,
> will trade his vivid earth for the drab and stench of
> death, whisper
> with his last exemplary breath, "Peace for beloved
>   Ireland."

As she paused to sip her coffee, I reflected, only an opera could do Bobby Sands justice. Such were the huge emotions aroused, it would take a Verdi to cope.

For English "security" translate "force" that divides a
    population
and rules
with tank and gun a land for ever foreign. On this
    battlefield,
Robert Sands,
the Statesman, taught his fellow prisoners the Gaelic
    language.
Who is this force
that crosses the frothing Irish Sea? Innocent soldiers,
    teenaged, deluded,
culled ("it's a job") from England's unemployed North;
    trained
delinquents to coerce
the Irish into submission, murder dissidents; for Ireland is
    England's Poland.

Whist! He has died in an Irish spring,
his brief life abandoned to the clay dun of earth
his young whispering breath, "For a reunited Ireland!"

"Please, Dachine. If you don't mind – 'Whist!'? It's a bit Lady
Gregoryish. Likewise the 'Celtic'!"

"You are going to condemn the poem, which I haven't finished reading yet by the way, because of one word? Have you ever
thought of being a critic? It's a lucrative career."

The radical fanatic is an artist. Dedication to justice, which
    like beauty
is another way of being honest, now as when Michaelangelo
    did battle
with the harassing Pope, is as heroic. He grasped
    endurance, a tenuous nettle,

Sands' Irish language, his brave eyes bright until he was
   blinded by
English terror.
England's Poland: nuclear installations sited on Irish
   earth.
The implacable cause of England's violence by her
   maddened
politicians.
Against such perfidy, Bobby Sands gave himself to die in
   an Irish
Spring
trading the wondrous soft air for the heavy clay of earth,
muting his whispering hope, "Liberty for Ireland!"

"Dachine, sorry to interrupt, if that's what I'm doing, but I'm not
aware of any nuclear stuff in Ireland."
   "Yet."
   "Hmm. I hate to say this, but I can't see anyone publishing it."
   "Not to inconvenience you, I haven't finished yet."
   "Go on, then. Sorry."

Before England's villainy is routed, young men all sides,
   will be
Murdered.
Before our century is out, the lingering death of our
   demented species,
unless the gentle cause of human liberty spurns lessons of
   a treacherous history.
Sighs and curses stampede the living air of his cell. There
   was no way to starve his spirit
determined to win Ireland from English slavery. Bobby
   Sands has acquired that same glory
that belonged to young Byron, that won for the "terrorist"
   Courbet!

> Bobby Sands could not have wished for death in this fresh
>   Irish spring,
> to trade the young friable earth for the dun clay. He
>   whispered with his dying breath, "Liberty for Ireland!"

"Now you may comment."

"I like it because of the emotion. It's operatic."

"Emotion is an organiser of form. Audible forms."

After she died, I went to Venice, the wet dream, her beloved city, and took a *vaporetto* across the *lacuna morte* to the cemetery. It was bucketing rain. When I got to the place, there wasn't another soul there save a man in his thirties, with carefully coiffured black hair, pale face, brown eyes, a smart suit, beautiful dark-blue wool overcoat and carrying a red rose.

We ignored each other. In the sprawl of tombs he seemed as lost as myself. I was searching around for the grave of Pound and Olga Rudge. I was going to read one of Dachine's poems. Aloud.

The rain was so hard it mashed strewn graveyard flowers into the soil.

Lost in the maze of death, myself and the smartly dressed man stumbled towards each other. He couldn't speak English, but I gathered he was a Russian now living in Israel. He had come to Venice to lay a rose on the grave of Joseph Brodsky. In the torturing rain we bumbled about, smiling helpfully at each other.

We found Stravinsky's tomb, Diagelev's. Dachine loved both. She loved ballet. Her daughter was a dancer.

At last we found Brodsky. The stranger laid his red rose down. The tomb was scattered with letters left there by Russians. The letters were love letters of a kind. Political love letters.

I eventually found the simple flat stone beneath which lay Pound and Olga Rudge.

I tried to explain to my fellow pilgrim about Dachine. Exasperated at not being able to communicate properly, tapping my chest with my fingers I said, "IRE. LAND. I'M. FROM. IRE-LAND."

His face lit up the gloom.

"Eerlan? Ah. BOBBY SAN."

Despite intervening governments, the selfless deeds of heroic people leap languages and time.

DIARY OF A HUNGER STRIKE
Peter Sheridan, author, playwright

IT STARTED WITH A CIGARETTE PAPER. I OPENED AN ENVELOPE WHICH seemed empty, but there it was, nestling down at the bottom, a single Rizla cigarette paper. On it was a script in blue biro, block capital letters, meticulous, the smallest handwriting I'd ever seen. It was from a republican prisoner in the H-Blocks, and it was a plea for help. It asked me, as a writer, if there was anything I could do to bring attention to what was going on inside the prison. It was a simple request, direct, the best kind and the hardest to refuse.

I put the cigarette paper in a tray on my writing desk. In those days, I worked from the bedroom of my home in Ballybough. It stared up at me from its perch by day, and it was the last thing I saw before I retired at night. I had to do something about it, I knew that, but I didn't have the time. I was working on a stage adaptation of Christy Brown's book, *Down All the Days,* and throughout 1980 it was my main preoccupation. Meanwhile, the situation in the Maze Prison went from bad to worse. Secret footage shot inside the Blocks appeared on our television screens, depicting shit-smeared walls and men in blankets with long beards. It was like a scene of degradation from the Bible, and it was worse than anyone could have imagined. It was so distressing to contemplate fellow humans living under those conditions that many people chose to shut it out and deny that it had anything to do with them. I didn't have that option. I had my cigarette paper.

Down All the Days opened at the Oscar Theatre on 30 April 1981. By that time, Bobby Sands was two months into his hunger strike and he was also the member of Parliament for Fermanagh and South Tyrone. It seemed inconceivable that a man who had the votes of over 30,000 people would not be afforded the political status he claimed was his right. Indeed, there was an argument put forward that Sands should be taken off the fast, that he was a more potent symbol of resistance and a greater embarrassment to Thatcher as a living MP than a dead republican. That proposition, of course, raised serious questions about where the impetus for the strike was coming from and whether Sands was open to such persuasion or not. The IRA and their Sinn Féin comrades of that era were not yet converts to the efficacy of political action and still believed predominantly in the militarist solution. The surge in popular support that followed on from the hunger strike did not provide a platform for British disengagement. Ironically, however, it did lead to the politicisation of Sinn Féin and a re-evaluation of tactics that ultimately put them on a purely political path. All of that had its origins in the crucible of the H-Blocks.

The Oscar Theatre was situated in Ballsbridge, less than a mile from the British Embassy. We struggled, against emotive nightly street marches and protests, to keep the show open. People were afraid to come out, particularly to that part of town. Bobby Sands slipped into a coma on Sunday, 3 May, and he died two days later on Tuesday, 5 May. The situation in Dublin was desperate, and the show closed three weeks early. I'd broken the golden rule and borrowed from the bank to invest in the play. It was an awful summer in every way. I worked at whatever I could to try to repay the bank, and I watched in horror as nine more coffins came out the gates of the Maze Prison.

I went back to my desk that winter and contemplated what to do next. There was the cigarette paper, as before, niggling at my conscience. I'd failed to respond to its plea for help, and I felt bad. I wasn't even sure what I could have done. I certainly wasn't going to find out sitting on my arse in Dublin, so I headed for Belfast. I wanted to gauge what feelings on the ground were like now that the strike was over.

I met people from all walks of life – my interviews were organised by the Association for Legal Justice – and my complacency was shattered by those who engaged with me. People were seething with anger at how the hunger strikes and the struggles of the prisoners had been portrayed, particularly by the southern media. It was arranged for me to visit the gaol, and the atmosphere inside the Maze was unlike anything I had ever encountered before. Sitting in the back of a truck, we were being taken from the arrivals compound to the Blocks proper, when the back door of the vehicle was opened by a prison officer who stood there and eyeballed each one of us in turn. The hatred in his eyes was palpable; his whole demeanour was one of pure aggression. Everyone averted their eyes from him, but I held his stare. It lasted a full sixty seconds, and I wasn't going to back down, having suffered at the hands of a bully when I was at school. He wilted, finally, and then slammed the door with such ferocity that the children jumped out of their skins and started to cry. I understood, too late, why nobody engaged in the battle of the stares.

I will never forget meeting the girlfriend of one of the hunger strikers, who abhorred all violence. With every fibre of her being, she wanted to intervene when her boyfriend lost consciousness, yet she knew that to save him also meant she would kill their relationship. They had made a promise to one another because he could not live with the degradation any longer. Imagine how angry she felt at the accusation that the men were pawns and were being used by the IRA for their own ends. She admitted to me that she was torn apart, on a personal level, and angry at the misinformation by the government and the media.

I left Belfast, ashamed at how shallow my understanding had been. There was widespread nationalist support for the hunger strikers and their five demands, and nobody subscribed to the notion that these men were criminals. You would never have known that, living in the Republic of Ireland. That was because, after partition, we had abandoned them to their fate. We had failed our fellow citizens. We did not want to be reminded of our constitutional dereliction. It ameliorated our guilt to portray the hunger strikers as criminal conspirators rather than as the victims of political abuse.

In my interviews with ex-blanket men, I asked them what the defining event was that led them to join the IRA. Not surprisingly, Bloody Sunday featured strongly in the responses to that question. For many, that day in Derry was the watershed, the point of no return, the day when peaceful politics failed and violence seemed like the only adequate response. Was any other form of resistance possible after that? many of them wondered.

Diary of a Hunger Strike opens with a Gaelic lesson being conducted by the OC, Pat O'Connor. When it's over, he and his younger cell mate, Sean Crawford, talk about how they got involved.

O'CONNOR
I was born into the republican movement.
CRAWFORD
How?
O'CONNOR
My father was active in the forties and fifties. And his father before him.
CRAWFORD
Interned?
O'CONNOR
Of course.
CRAWFORD
But there must have been a day you decided. Some day when you…

O'CONNOR

Not really. The RA was always there, around me, the family…well, I suppose Bloody Sunday in Derry was the turning point. There was no room for sitting on the fence after that.

CRAWFORD

Bloody Sunday. Jesus, I was only ten years old when that happened. Imagine, I was a snotty nosed kid in short trousers when you held your first Armalite rifle. And here we are today sharing a cell. Incredible, isn't it?

The play opened at the Edinburgh Festival in August 1982, produced by Hull Truck and directed by Pam Brighton. It generated huge controversy. It subsequently toured England and was seen for a week at the Belltable Arts Centre in Limerick, but could not find a venue in my native city. The Dublin Theatre Festival, despite my best efforts, refused to have it as part of its programme that year. The abandonment of the North was not just political; it was cultural, too. I directed the American premiere at the Los Angeles Theater Center in 1986. A bilingual version of the play, *Dialann Ocrais*, was staged at the Peacock Theatre in 1987. (You can say anything once it's in Gaelic!) It was produced in the North by Gearoid Ó Cearralain for Aisteoirí Aon Dráma in 1989 and again in 2001, the twentieth anniversary. It was an intensely emotional play to write and, had it not been for a cigarette paper, it never would have seen the light of day.

1973, 1981, 1991, 2005
Timothy O'Grady, writer

1973

I flew out of America for Dublin on a June day in 1973, seated between a North Antrim Protestant and a Galway Catholic, like the white stripe on the Irish flag. I'd been offered the use of an abandoned house on a deserted island called Gola off the coast of Donegal. I was, unbeknownst to myself, emigrating, leaving an America living through the death throes of the 1960s in the evacuation of Vietnam and the Watergate hearing and entering a world of silence and mystery and timelessness on the west coast of Ireland. Even the faces seemed to reach back into antiquity.

On the island, I wrote letters, cooked, read, walked. I watched a spider weaving his web on a window. In the evenings, I'd walk over to a rock and listen to ferocious lectures in Irish history delivered by a former schoolteacher who'd been born on the island and returned to pass the summers there with his wife. He had a little dog named Oscar who ran around nipping at the legs of the cows. The IRA, he told me, had trained on the island. He'd had to retire early due to a shredded throat having taught extra hours and shouted at his students for thirty-five years. In doing so, he raised the educational level of this impoverished part of Gweedore and gathered to his school an improbable number of scholarships. He told me about the island, the life there and its vanquishment. I'd walk around then and look through the windows of homes, at this life suspended at the point of departure – a jacket on the back of a chair, a tin of soup with a spoon in it, a discarded shoe. Like García Márquez's Macondo, Gola had lived in solitude for one hundred years, and then died.

I moved to Dublin when the cold autumn winds made life on the island no longer possible. The bus climbed the coast road, and I looked back, the island a bright disc in the grey sea. I passed Errigal, bogland and heather, Letterkenny, low-running dogs, men on bicycles, ladies in housecoats leaning on their gates. Birds turned high over the land. Just short of Strabane, we hit the border, a new experience for me. The door opened and two British soldiers got on, their faces taut with fear and venom, their fingers on the triggers of their rifles. They walked along the aisle of the bus with a roll of photographs, looking into our faces. Something seemed to come in with them: an extreme tension, a barely contained explosiveness and a desolate loneliness. Nothing in bog or pasture or roll of hill or the faces of the passengers looking on with implacable distaste and lack of welcome accorded with the curt truculence and anxiety of the soldiers. They seemed stripped of everything bar the wish to hurt and the will to survive. They were in a different register from all that was around them. No force or act of the imagination could bring them into the same rhythm. Nothing could give them the feeling of familiarity, ease.

They didn't see anyone on the bus that matched their photographs, and they got off. The door closed with a hiss, and we crept on through Strabane. Fire was everywhere there, coming out of shop fronts, windows, breaking through roof tiles. I didn't know what any of it meant, but it all passed through me with the force of a storm. It left me altered in some way, or at least deeply curious. I thought that if I looked at this country and its life-and-death conflict of identity, talked about it and read about it enough, I could somehow get to the bottom of it.

1981

When the hunger strikes began, I was writing my first book, *Curious Journey: An Oral History of Ireland's Unfinished Revolution*. It covered the period from the lead-up to the Easter Rising through to the end of the Civil War through the voices of nine then very old people who had participated in these events as republican activists. Writing it, it was impossible not to be struck by a powerful sense of familiarity with respect to the historical period I was writing about and the epoch we were then moving through – a mandate for independence being met alternately with equivocation and repression, unionists manipulating weak British governments, censorship, vilification, covert murders, the terrible cost to everyone involved of living in such close proximity to violence. That was, of course, the point of writing the book at all.

There were hunger strikes then, too, an Irish response to injustice from antiquity, as nearly everyone now knows. The British, however, were taken by surprise by it. One of the nine subjects of the book, a Donegal man named Joseph Sweeney, was arrested in March 1920, just before sixty republican prisoners in Mountjoy Prison in Dublin began a hunger strike to demand prisoner-of-war status or immediate release. He joined the hunger strike in Crumlin Road and continued it in Wormwood Scrubs in London. He terrified a medical officer there by lying down on the stone floor of his cell just before a medical visit. His pulse dropped precipitously, and when it was checked, he was sent directly to Marylebone Infirmary. The Irish Labour Party and Trades Union Congress called a general strike in support of the prisoners, and within ten days of starting their fast, all hunger strikers were released, including Joseph Sweeney in London.

It was never again to be so easy. Terence MacSwiney, then Lord Mayor of Cork, began a hunger strike a few months later against British harassment of Irish elected officials. No one had foreseen that his fast would last seventy-three days before he too would become one of the Fenian dead, the nation agonising over him day by day and the world watching in appalled fascination, as they would watch sixty-one years later when other Irish elected officials died of hunger in Long Kesh.

> You that Mitchel's prayer have heard,
> "Send war in our time, O Lord!"
> Know that when all words are said
> And a man is fighting mad,
> Something drops from eyes long blind . . .
>> "Under Ben Bulben"
>> – William Butler Yeats

A hunger striker fights, but not to kill or cause physical damage to others. Instead, he uses the slow ruin of his own body. The intention, though, is that "something drops from eyes long blind". A hunger striker exposes and clarifies. It is the ultimate act in a long process that takes in the politics of parliamentary democracy, street demonstrations, civil disobedience, boycotts, cultural nationalism and war itself. It declares that the combatant's own tortuous death is worth it in the making of a point. It is carried out in public – on the doorstep of the transgressor in the ancient world; in the media of the modern world. Everyone is invited to watch and to feel the hunger striker's painful disintegration. It can be worth it only if the point being made is about the violation of a principle. The principle of a hunger strike is always a principle of justice. It can have the power of revelation if the principle is perceived to be sufficiently fundamental. It can transform.

The 1981 hunger strikes were about five demands to do with clothing and remission and slopping out, but they were really about Britain's long colonial defilement of Ireland and the criminalising of those who resisted it. Only if the hunger strikes were perceived to be about these things could they seem to be worth the suffering and death of any of the ten. And on they went, month after month, death after death. They were seen to be about these things. They expressed and clarified. They revealed and transformed.

Around this event, many were defined. Southern politicians looked for words elastic enough to make them appear both against it and for it. The Church wondered if it was a sin and failed to find unanimity in the matter. The unionists perhaps caught their first sense of the power of suffering, which they were to use so improbably years later. Margaret Thatcher summoned Cardinal Ó Fiaich and John Hume to Downing Street in the midst of it. They went, believing they were to be made an offer which they could take to the prison. They sat in the hallway for nearly an hour, and when the cardinal felt sufficiently insulted to get up to leave, Hume persuaded him to stay on the basis that she was the prime minister and might have a crisis to deal with. Thatcher appeared at the top of the stairs after a while and invited them into a drawing room.

"I've got Irish whiskey just for you, gentlemen," she said. When she had her own in hand, she turned to them and said, "Tell me, these hunger strikers, are they trying to prove their virility?"

Meanwhile, thousands marched on the British Embassy in Dublin with the intention of burning it down. And thousands had voted for Bobby Sands and Kieran Doherty. Many before had been equivocal, but about this they were not. It was a defining moment, a time when the conflict was stripped down in a way that it hadn't been before, naked will facing naked will, bone to bone: cruelty, dissembling and power on the one hand and on the other a mute testimonial, an ultimate act at the end of an exhausted discourse. It might have failed, dissolved, been ignored, but instead the meaning of it ran like a runaway flame all over Ireland and out into the world.

1991
One warm Saturday in 1991, Gerry Adams came to the Conway Hall in Red Lion Square in London to speak on the subject of the respective anniversaries of the deaths of James Connolly and

Bobby Sands. The hall was full. He had spoken often enough by then, but seemed curiously shy. He mumbled something I didn't wholly catch which included the line, "I wish I was back home in Derry," from a song written by Bobby Sands and sung by Christy Moore. He raised the decibels a little when he began the speech, but kept the tone soft, more conversational than oratorical. He said that all present knew of the manner of death of these men: Connolly strapped to a chair, his leg gangrenous, killed by firing squad in a jail yard; Bobby Sands' system shutting down section by section, feeble, vanishing. But maybe we didn't know that Connolly organised pensioners' outings to the seaside or that Bobby Sands could be a short-tempered footballer or that he edited a community newspaper.

We knew instead the images of sacrifice and death. Too often, he said, he had stood by graves and heard said, "We owe it to our dead to continue." Death succeeded death. But, he went on, is it in death that we should find justification? If the movement is to have any value, if it is to mean anything at all, it must be about the affirmation and the enriching of life. That is its meaning and that is its power. James Connolly and Bobby Sands had been living men, flawed, contentious, funny, brilliant, brave and committed to the liberation of their people, far longer than they had been dying ones.

2005

Bobby Sands was put forward as a candidate for the Fermanagh and South Tyrone seat in a British parliamentary by-election taking place on 9 April 1981. Kieran Doherty stood for a seat in the Dáil on 12 June 1981. It was an audacious step for them to run, for it risked a loss of credibility for the prison protests and a vindication of Britain's policies in Ireland from which it would take the republican movement years to recover. In the event, both won, and "the political wing of the IRA", sensing the power inherent in elections, began its long, slow, uncertain climb to ascendancy over the military.

In August 2005, I was in West Belfast for its annual Féile. Two weeks earlier, the IRA had announced its effective removal from the Irish political landscape. I didn't see a Saracen, a foot patrol or even a cop in the time I was there. The barracks across from Milltown Cemetery was a disorientingly vacant space. On that day, the district's MP, Gerry Adams, was in Downing Street with the British prime minister. His party had delegates in town and county councils all over Ireland, as well as in the Dáil and the European Parliament, and was continuing to grow.

Ex-prisoners were exhibiting their paintings, giving lectures, reading poems and completing their degrees. People were ordering their lunch in Irish on the Falls Road. It would put you in mind of the story about Ian Paisley falling off the back of a flat-bed truck and being unconscious for twenty years. When the ancient figure's eyes began to flicker, Peter Robinson was brought hobbling to his bedside, at which ensued the usual exchange with rejoicings and gravity and the describing of the great changes that had taken place, followed by the question from Robinson, "Do you want the bad news or the good news?"

"I'll take the bad news first," said Paisley.

"I regret to tell you, Ian, that we now live in a thirty-two county republic," said Robinson.

"That's dreadful!" said Paisley. "If only I had been there to prevent it! Quick, give me the good news."

"Well, just last Sunday, Linfield beat Shamrock Rovers."

"Good to hear it," said Paisley. "What was the score?"

"3–12 to 1–16," reported Robinson.

What was happening? Stormont was back, the Union Jack flew, the border was still on the map. Unionists were answering "No!" as ever, to every question. But the towers were coming down, the prisoners were out, and everyone knew that the croppies would never lie down again. And something was moving, or at least had the capacity to do so.

In the year of the hunger strike, the two forces in the North were philosophically, morally and emotionally mutually exclusive in each of their tenets. Orangeism was sectarian, retrogressive and oligarchical. It was fanatically loyal to the British monarchy, but suspicious of the British Parliament. It drew its sustenance from the historical moment when the consolidation of the English conquest of Ireland coincided with the Reformation. It thus endlessly celebrated the Protestant victory over the Catholics and had no other purpose except to preserve this dominance. Republicanism was secular, progressive and democratic. It grew from an ancient and popular resistance in Ireland to British rule, adapted to the ideas of the French Revolution, then later to Pearse's Celtic nationalism and Connolly's revolutionary social-ism, and still later to other ideas of liberation and community politics, both imported and invented. There could be no recon-ciliation, it seemed. One or other of these two forces had to tri-umph. They mean the same now, too. But the circumstances around them have changed.

The Good Friday Agreement possessed the genius of allowing each of these sides to gain a victory of a kind, while not losing too early anything essential to its identity. Far more importantly, everything remained still to play for in terms of the final consti-tutional configuration of the island. It would depend on the nimbleness, the skill and the will of the players. And while they were playing for their particular party goals, all politicians involved would have to get to know each other and to work together. You could not gain the outcome you desired without doing so. This would be played out in a context from which the hardening impact of violence had been removed, and in which borders in Europe were losing their significance and national-isms were being marginalised. The Agreement contained a dynamic through the establishment of cross-border bodies with the possibility of an ever-widening remit that could create an evolving *de facto* all-Ireland government under which the border could slowly evaporate. There was a scenario – I would think the most viable scenario of all – in which Ireland became a thirty-two county republic not only without a further shot being fired, but in an atmosphere of geniality.

The philosopher and statesman, Benedeto Croce, wrote of the years which followed Italy's achievement of unification in 1870, "Prose had succeeded to poetry." "Poetry" here refers to the romance of Garibaldi's struggle and "prose" to the anti-climactic and unglamorous business of concession and compromise and budget-making to which Italians had then to apply themselves. The same, more or less, was said of Ireland in the aftermath of the Treaty, but the Treaty's "unfinished business" kept alive the poetry at the expense of the prose.

The poetry, in this particular sense, was timeless, outraged and single-minded. It referred to a pre-conquest past as a pretext for a Utopian future. It celebrated in exalted phrases heroic endeavour and suffering for the sake of the cause.

Prose is inclined to be less rarefied and pure, and to be more complex and mundane. It finds its meaning *in* time rather than, like poetry, trying to transcend time. Its form is more elastic, less bound by convention and, above all, more accessible to the process of synthesis than poetry. The prose in which history is written, to pursue the crude political analogy, could, as it grows more confident and sophisticated, come to draw on an amalgam of traditions: the tenacity of the Ulster planters along with the elegance of the Georgian gentry; the spontaneous intricacy of the medieval scribes along with the earthy sensuality of the bards; the vibrant metaphors of the West and the caustic wit of the streets of Belfast. A varied, clamorous prose that does not take itself too seriously nor is overly eager to please.

Are the first crude and tentative sentences now being written? It is too early to tell. Unionists are still blocking the mechanisms of the Good Friday Agreement which would allow the event-making and record-keeping to begin. Ian Paisley continues to sound his single, shrill note. But there are men in his party who want power and who know they cannot get it without working with Sinn Féin. And when in an interview I asked his daughter, Rhonda, what "Britishness" meant to her – her father's giant shoes sitting on the floor, so much statuary and portraiture and other iconography of him around the walls that his Cypress Avenue home seemed a Pharaoh's tomb – she replied, "Britishness? Britain is to me a place where old people are treated badly. I'm not British; I'm Irish. That's important to me both as a painter and as a person. Fortunately, we have an all-Ireland rugby team here to which I can give my support. Unfortunately, we have two football teams. But the Republic's team is strong and I can cheer for them. I particularly do so when they are playing against England."

She spoke slowly so that I would have time to write down every word. A Shankill Road loyalist ex-prisoner who had killed three Catholics in the 1980s told me, "There's going to be a united Ireland. That's clear. And you know, I really don't mind, so long as I'm allowed to support Glasgow Rangers."

A Protestant woman I met in Portrush told me her husband had just come back from a ceremony instigated by Mary McAleese for families of First World War veterans.

"He was rather impressed with Mrs McAleese. It seems we're going to have to get to know Mrs McAleese, and perhaps even to like her. And it seems we're going to have to stop speaking about 'Ulster' and start speaking about 'this island of Ireland'. I'm actually looking forward to it."

There is, I would say, a light now present that was not there in 1973, 1981 or 1991. Such a light, I think, can only grow brighter.

The great Irish historian, Nicholas Mansergh, wrote: "Historians are apt to reduce to terms of cause and consequence matters about which contemporaries felt in terms of challenging, desolating or terrifying personal experience. [They] are disposed to exaggerate the consequences and to discount the price."

The hunger strike of 1981 is now a part of Irish history, but at the time, the participating prisoners, as they weakened, gagged, went slowly blind and paid the price of their lives, could not have known what the consequences of their actions would be. Twenty-five years later, though, I believe it can be seen that theirs was the action which transformed the nature of the conflict, and that Sinn Féin's un-ignorable presence, the openness of the British to productive negotiation, the engagement of the United States, the taking down of observation posts and barracks, the releasing of the prisoners and above all a new and growing sense of power by those who had so long been quarantined and kicked around, are the direct consequences of the dying hunger strikers placing themselves before the electorate and winning.

They acted, as Gerry Adams said, in the service not of death, but of life.

THE MYTH OF MYTH

David Lloyd, writer on Irish history, culture and colonialism

EVEN TWENTY-FIVE YEARS AFTER HIS DEATH ON HUNGER STRIKE, THE memory of Bobby Sands will doubtless continue to be enshrouded in the haze of myth. I do not mean by this the myths that he and other Irish republicans are so often assumed to have perpetrated, but the myths that have been projected upon him and the other hunger strikers by journalists and historians alike.

As so often, where understanding meets its own conceptual limits, recourse to mythology takes its place. The social critics, historians or journalists, limited by rigid categories and ideological assumptions from grasping new forms of struggle and resistance, fall back on the ascription to those whose acts they do not understand of a consciousness outside the pale of modernity and civility. "Modernity" and "civility" being the terms that legitimate the state, whoever opposes the state must be consigned to the pathology of pre-modern modes of thinking. Myth represents the primal violence and disorder which the state, with its therapeutic modernity, comes to cure. Violence is not a product of the coercive dynamics of the state but the atavistic response of those who have yet fully to enter the condition of modernity.

To understand social conflict in these terms is not an innocent act, not a merely descriptive effort of the understanding. The mythologisation of struggle, its rendering in terms of "blood sacrifice" or primal rite, is the mystifying counterpart of criminalisation. Both practices partake of a counter-insurgency discourse that seeks to locate the roots of violence in the pathological state of individuals and communities rather than in the economic and political inequities that the state itself maintains and reproduces.

Against the "normalised" good conduct of the citizen, resistance takes on the symptoms of an aberrant pathology: if, on the one hand, popular culture provides the image of the "godfathers of violence", the terrain of myth furnishes the terms by which the mentality of republicanism becomes "atavistic", primitive and reactionary. Mythological analysis furnishes the deep structure of motivation that underlies and belies any claim on the part of the republican movement to represent a radical and socially progressive tendency. In this respect, the ascription of mythological thinking to republicanism is more insidious than the effort to criminalise it: its function is to insinuate that, beneath whatever rhetoric the republican articulates, there lurks a deeper tendency towards fascism. That tendency is, by the nature of mythic motivation, scarcely conscious: it is a drive unsusceptible to argument or discussion, and thus beyond the pale of civil society. It can be confronted and contained only by coercion.

Like the drumbeat phrase, "the men of violence", whose repetition served to insist, against all historical record, that there can be no convergence between feminism and republicanism, the mythological analysis of republicanism seeks to suggest that there can be no accommodation between it and a liberal civil society.

Although it was probably an essay on Yeats and fascism by Conor Cruise O'Brien, written on the eve of the fiftieth anniversary of the Easter Rising, that inaugurated revisionist efforts to recast the history of republicanism, the clearest statement of the connection to be made between republican violence and mythological thinking was Richard Kearney's "Myth and Terror", published in *The Crane Bag* (a journal not itself shy of indulging in mythic thinking and formulations like "the Irish mind" or "the Irish psyche").

Appearing in 1975, the essay anticipated the advent of the prison struggles and the British campaign of "criminalisation" that impelled them. Though it cannot be criticised for not taking into account in its analysis the dynamics of the subsequent prison protests or the transformation of the republican movement that they shaped, there is no doubt that the essay supplied a kind of template for subsequent analyses, journalistic and academic, of the prisoners' mentality and motivations. It does so precisely because it offers to provide a "deep structural" account of "terrorism" that would supplement the political ("constitutional"), economic and historical analyses then available.

In fact, as a modest supplement to more socially grounded analyses of the Northern Irish conflict, Kearney's "mythological perspective" rapidly comes to supplant them, claiming to provide "a sort of depth-hermeneutic which would be capable of detecting the more occult motivations operative in Ulster terrorism". Inevitably, this uncovering of the determining "cultural deep-structure" tends to displace prior "orthodox interpretations", making them more or less epiphenomenal, determined by rather than determining the nationalist movement's "mythical-nucleus". It is as if this mythological deep-structure is a kind of symbolic grammar that determines and constrains the acts and statements of republicanism.

Several further assumptions flow from this assertion of a cultural deep-structure. The first and foremost is that republicanism is a phenomenon without effective history, that its forms and practices remain the same across generations, manifesting always and everywhere the same "mythological essence": the Fenians, the IRB, Pearse and MacDonagh, presumably the republicans from 1922–1969, all recur to and draw from the same mythological figures and formations as Kearney assumes drive the Provisional IRA in the 1970s. The immediate source of their imagery, their "symbols", comes, incidentally, from poets as problematic for nationalism as "Thomas" [sic] Mangan, Samuel Ferguson and Aubrey De Vere (the latter both Protestants and Unionists), but those symbols none the less channel ancient Celtic motifs. The symbolic core of those motifs is the blood sacrifice – the idea that the land can be restored to fertility only by being watered by the blood of young men. Terror is thus in the first place intimately bound for Kearney to the symbols of republicanism, within which the baroque imagery of Catholicism fuses with a primordial Celtic mythic nucleus, on account of its commitment to bloodletting.

But terror is more deeply entwined with the mythological essence of republicanism by virtue not only of this sacrificial content but by its forms. The appeal to myth collapses historical process into mere immediacy. Myth preempts history: "the 'mythic' recourse to miraculous powers of transformation is primarily motivated by the apparent occlusion of all normal channels for effecting political change in history . . . A certain fatalism is inherent in all mythic invocations of the Past." Immediacy manifests itself in a double form.

In the first place, it is the immediacy of a revolutionary terror that seeks to anticipate, to pre-empt, the historical process of change and, moreover, the transformation of popular consciousness, by symbolic rather than strategic or tactical acts of violence. It is a critique of terrorist violence that goes back to Hegel's analysis of the Terror of the French Revolution and maintains its force in Marxist critiques of terrorism even now. But immediacy also manifests itself in the evacuation of historical process and its reduction to recurrent manifestations of the same mythic content: history becomes the eternal repetition of the same cycle of sacrifice and rebirth. As Kearney puts it:

> By means of such periodic blood-letting, the cult enables man to violently pre-empt history. It empowers him to give the lie to the intractable world of fact, sanctioning his accession to a mythic world where different laws apply and where he may be relieved of all the onerous inconveniences which bear him down.

Myth accordingly appears as a means to escape, but one which insistently commits the subject to repetition. Those who seek to escape their history, one might say, are doomed to repeat it.

Mythological thinking is, then, the recourse of those incapable of taking effective measures to change their conditions and is deeply related to a sense of historical impotence: "The experience of terror central to myth – and particularly the myth of sacrifice and renewal – is perhaps most plausibly explained in terms of a community's original experience of total impotence before a cruel and ineluctable destiny." Myth is thus the expression of a collective sense of victimhood, the articulation of what reactionary obfuscation of social movement politics has dubbed the "victim mentality". It is the recourse of those who are not fully the agents of their own existence.

Myth, to close the circle, is the expression of those who are subject to, rather than subjects of, their history: what is at first understood as a motif (and Kearney makes the inevitable association with the Wagnerian *Leitmotif* that embodies the essential characteristics of a personage in his operas) becomes a motivating force. History's victims, unable to take control of their own destinies, are unconsciously driven by mythic forces that they are impotent to control.

Of course, a deep irony underlies Kearney's approach. In unfolding his analysis of the mythic drives that motivate contemporary republicanism and make of terrorism a pathological and reactive response to victimhood, he neglects to observe that he is captured by the very irrationality whose mythic structures he pretends to critique. For his argument to have validity, Kearney must assume that the deep-structure of the "mythic nucleus" is in fact an effective underlying motive force in contemporary Ireland. In thus taking myth at its own word, so to speak, he in his own turn short-circuits historical process, reducing the long and highly differentiated history of republicanism to the eternal manifestation of the same mythic motifs and the history of the present to a manifestation of deep mythological powers. The further contradictions that ensue from this are manifold. Not the least of them, which has not lost its currency, is the invocation of W.B. Yeats, cultural nationalist and anti-republican Free State senator, as the privileged mouthpiece of this atavistic mythological mentality. But the failure to acknowledge so glaring a contradiction at the heart of the method of analysis itself indicates the degree to which the critic has balked at the attempt seriously to understand the dynamics of conflict in the North: mythic explanation, projected onto what he fails to grasp in its historical dimensions, itself pre-empts and mythologises history.

This fact has not prevented Kearney's essay from providing, together with Yeats' work, a kind of explanatory template for writings about the hunger strikes.

Given the short space remaining to me, I will focus on a single but typical work among the great number on the prison protests, Padraig O'Malley's *Biting at the Grave*, which indeed takes its title from Yeats's play on hunger striking, *The Threshold of the King*, and its section epigraphs from his poetry. More significantly, the very terms of his analysis of the hunger strikes are deeply informed and guided by Kearney's analysis, only amplified into a yet more strident register. The book stands as an index of the extraordinary extent to which discussion of the prison protests, both in Ireland and across the Atlantic, was saturated by the kind of psycho-mythological analysis that Kearney articulated. O'Malley's initial rhetorical question so sets the terms of his reportage that it more or less predetermines the answers his journalistic investigation will come up with:

> Who were we, I wondered, who could incubate and breed such merciless young who would prefer to do right by denying life instead of affirming it, whose

sense of victimhood had become such an integral part of their personality that they needed to affirm it by destroying identity itself? And who were they, I wondered, who could harden themselves to abandon life with a casual disregard for the terminal consequences of their actions, eyes fixed on a star in a galaxy of patriot-ghosts imploding in their imaginations, their bodies sacrificial offerings to the glutinous [*sic*] gods of a degenerative nationalism, minds impervious to the importunings of those who did not inhabit their closed universe.

The terms are precise and damning in advance: victimhood, sacrifice, "patriot-ghosts". What the hunger strikes bring out, for O'Malley, are "the psychic undercurrents of religion and tribe" and "the ancient mythologies carefully nurtured for decades, an idea of Ireland imbued with memory traces of blood sacrifice".

Correspondingly, O'Malley's bio-portrait of Bobby Sands is imbued with pathologisation, the mythological explanation extended by pathologisation. Sands' actions as a republican are derived from the "trauma" of ethnic violence, leading him to seek "a structure that provided security, comradeship, and support" rather than to any analysis of the Northern situation or of colonial dynamics in general. (Absurdly, Frantz Fanon's careful if debatable diagnosis of the violence of decolonisation that Sands read in the Cages of Long Kesh is reduced to a "cult of violence", in keeping with the mythical projection O'Malley requires.)

Almost climactically, the journalist's character sketch concludes by citing Kearney:

In death he would become intertwined with the mystical body of the Republican movement, his imminent martyrdom what philosopher Richard Kearney calls "a sort of leitmotif recapitulating the eternal song of sacrifice and rebirth which subtended and harmonized all [the] dead generations of Irish heroes."

This heady mix of private trauma and mythic fantasy, the peculiar stew of victimhood and megalomania, is not only the staple of counter-insurgency reportage on the prison protests (even so stolid and prosaic a historian as J. Bowyer Bell speaks of Sands as an "intense burning symbol"); it also points towards the solution to Ireland's problems in a sphere far removed from anti-colonial struggle. The hunger strikes become a symptom of an Irish malaise: they expose

> ... the extent to which Northern Ireland is a paradigm for what political scientist Robert Elias calls a "political economy of helplessness", a victim-bonded society in which memories of past injustice and humiliation are so firmly entrenched in both communities and the sense of entrapment so complete that the hunger strikes are a metaphor for the entrapment of the larger society. Moreover, this sense of victimhood extends to the South, the pervasive passivity there a product of an inherited sense of powerlessness.

Analysis of the hunger strikes – in keeping with this mythological mode of analysis, of course – permit us "to understand how those who remember the past are especially condemned to repeat its mistakes".

O'Malley's implicit prescription, to forget the past, composed on the very threshold of the "Celtic Tiger" decade, is at one with the ethos of that moment as it is with the ethos of counter-insurgency. A therapeutic modernity calls on the nation to put the past behind, to move on, as a healthy mourner moves on from what she has lost, forgetting the injustices and forms of exploitation that have been the history of the present.

But to cure memory in this fashion is to forget more than the past. It is to forget that the path to the present, in Ireland as in other colonial sites, has been one of modernisation under duress, to turn a phrase from Theodor Adorno: the forms of our modernity are not ones we have chosen, nor are they necessarily ones we should freely choose. It is no less to forget, and to ask us to forget, the present, the continuing "low-intensity" violence and injustice that subtends the state and society now, where the distribution of the benefits of prosperity grows increasingly lopsided and the intensification of coercive force is more and more evident domestically and globally.

The struggle over the meaning and the ends of modernisation, the struggle over the content rather than the form of peace with justice, are not over, their outcome surely yet to be decided.

To read Sands, twenty-five years after his death, to read the survivors of the prisons and the protests now in their oral and written histories, is to be struck, after all the rhetoric of counter-insurgency, by two things in particular: by how rare reference is to the whole apparatus of Celtic mythology and blood sacrifice and by how little, on their own confession, the young men who entered the H-Blocks even knew of the past of republicanism, even of the so-called tradition of hunger striking.

It is no less to be struck by how aware the prisoners were of the fact that they did not inhabit some mystified past of Celtic warriors, but what a British home secretary was pleased to call "the most modern prison facility in Europe". What they inhabited was the most sophisticated carceral system – as, indeed, what Northern Ireland as a whole experienced was the advent of the surveillance state – so that their experience was that of the hard face of coercive modernity. Its function was not to cure, but, as Thomas Clarke recorded of a prior prison regime, to "smash".

Sands rightly dubbed the Blocks "the breaker's yard". What we have yet to learn to the full from the instance of the political prisons in Ireland, and from Sands' and other prisoners' analyses of their experience, is not the therapeutic lesson of pathologising myths, but the ways in which resistance and recalcitrance to the imposed structures of the state, rather than to the "deep-structure of the past", emerge in and through the very architecture of modern institutions.

That architecture retains in its very form the memory of the past struggles from which it has itself emerged, from Clerkenwell to the Cages, and we would be ill-advised to forget the past it incorporates.

To remember the past is not to repeat it, but to recognise in it the complex set of encounters and interfaces out of which our present conjunctures have emerged, different from but informed by that past. The legacy of the prisons and of the hunger strikes has been slow to sediment and to clarify, but there is no doubt that it has placed us in a new and unanticipated situation, one which demands, not a backward look, but a continuing alertness to how the new emerges from the apparent cages of the present.

YOU'RE LUCKY YOU HAD THE CHOICE
(*Some Mother's Son*)
Terry George, film-maker

FOR BETTER OR WORSE, FEATURE FILMS HAVE BECOME THE WORLD'S history class. *Schindler's List* educated the world about the Holocaust. *The Killing Fields*, Roland Joffe's superb film of the Cambodian genocide, moved audiences in a way few history books could.

I have just spent four emotional years working on *Hotel Rwanda*. I am far too close to the film to make any critical judgment, but one thing I now know: millions of people who barely knew where Rwanda was came to learn about the 1994 Rwandan genocide because of the film. I hope it endures as a teaching tool and as a piece of humanist film-making. But the work I am proudest of, and hope has a long afterlife, is *Some Mother's Son*.

My family and I left Belfast in 1981 and fled to New York. Like most of Belfast, we were traumatised by what had happened during those momentous days. I spent years afterwards haunted by the events and the memories of the hunger-strike year. I felt I needed to write about it but wasn't sure how. In the mid-1980s, I became involved with a theatre group – the Irish Arts Center in New York. I wrote a play called *The Tunnel*, based on a tunnel escape from Long Kesh. Jim Sheridan, who was artistic director of the theatre, agreed to direct the play.

Around this time, I read David Beresford's masterpiece, *Ten Men Dead*. It captured the political intrigue and the sad pageantry of 1981. The players were giants: Adams, Thatcher, Cardinal Ó Fiaich, Sands, Hughes, the Pope. Beresford masterfully chronicled the misinformation, dis-information, deceits and downright lies.

But the most heartbreaking aspect of Beresford's book was his descriptions of the stoicism and ultimate impotence of the families, particularly the mothers. I can think of no greater pain than to have to sit and watch the child you brought into the world die in front of your eyes, and to be told all the while that you could save your child with the stroke of a pen.

In all my naïve arrogance, I decided I'd write a film script centred around the mothers. The only thing I had in my head was a title. It came from the words my grandmother, Alice Quinn, used to rebuke some of my friends when she overheard them laughing about a soldier who'd been shot outside her door in Cromac Square in the Markets. She said, "He's some mother's son!"

I'm not a big believer in things spiritual, but there have been two occasions in my career where the central integrity of a story and its need to be told seemed to hold it together despite massive obstacles. They were *Hotel Rwanda* and *Some Mother's Son*. The greatest obstacle in the case of *Some Mother's Son* was that I'd never written a film script. I had no reputation, no representation, no track record, none of the elements necessary to get a film made. I sat down and read every "How to write a script" book I could find.

I gleaned two important questions to ask myself from the pile of self-help books.

1. What is the film about? It would be about two mothers, both desperate to save their sons' lives. However, the only way they can do that is to betray the cause their sons are willing to die for.

2. Why will people go and see this film? Because it will be a universal drama about mothers and sons caught up in war. It will transcend its political and geographical location and speak to people everywhere.

I sat down and wrote the story of Kathleen Quigley, a widowed middle-class schoolteacher, and her son, Gerard, a university drop-out and, unbeknownst to his mother, an IRA volunteer; and

Annie Higgins, a traditional republican, and her IRA veteran son, Frankie Higgins. The story spans eighteen months, 1980 through 1981, from the arrests of Frankie and Gerard up to their last days on hunger strike. I tried to cram as much of the real-life political intrigue involving Sinn Féin, the Brits and the Catholic Church as I could, along with the sad pageantry of it all, while still keeping the mothers' story firmly in the foreground.

I didn't give much consideration to budget. First-time scriptwriters never do. My most optimistic scenario for the script was that I might find someone in the film industry to read it and they'd immediately snap it up and take it to a movie star. At that time (the late 1980s), there was much speculation about a hunger-strike film. The actor Mickey Rourke nurtured the idea and met with several of the families. There appeared to be a buzz around the topic. I would later learn that the buzz was generated by Mickey's good heart and intentions, and rumour. None of the major studios in Hollywood had the slightest interest in a "hunger strike" movie.

I did meet up with two independent film-makers, the documentarian Pam Yates and a lawyer/producer, Ed Burke, who were very passionate about my script and set about trying to find financing to make a low-budget film.

However, *Some Mother's Son*'s big break had nothing to do with 1981 or my script. Rather, it sprang from another monumental act of British stupidity.

In October 1989, the Guildford Four were freed from prison after a fifteen-year campaign to prove their innocence. Soon after his release, I met Gerry Conlon in New York. At the time, he was collaborating with Gabriel Byrne to make a film about his ordeal. Gabriel brought me on as the writer. I subsequently sent Jim Sheridan (who had just received six Oscar nominations for his film, *My Left Foot*) a synopsis for a script called *In the Name of the Father*.

Two years later, *In the Name of the Father* was a big critical and box office hit, and Sheridan and I had demonstrated to Hollywood that it was possible to make a hit movie about the Irish Troubles.

I wanted to leverage the success we had with *Father* to make *Some Mother's Son*. I asked Jim if he wanted to direct it, and if he didn't, then I'd direct it. He said he'd rather rewrite it with me and produce it. We set out to try to find the money to make it.

Mother was a much harder sell than *Father* which was viewed as a classic story of triumph over injustice. *Mother*, on the other hand, was about IRA "terrorists" and the questionable morality of their hunger strike, and I was a first-time director. Our biggest asset was that the great British actress, Helen Mirren, had agreed to play the lead role of the schoolteacher, Kathleen Quigley.

There are two ways to raise money for films in Hollywood. You can go with a project that appears to have a strong possibility of making a lot of money – a teenage comedy or any film starring Tom Cruise, for example. Or, you can go with a project that offers the possibility that Hollywood executives might get to put their tuxedos on in February and go to a lot of awards shows, which will then translate into (smaller) profits.

Some Mother's Son found funding from an adventurous production company called Castle Rock. The executives were willing to take risks, and they recognised that, in the right role, Helen Mirren is as good an Oscar gamble as you can get.

Castle Rock agreed to put up a budget of six million dollars for the film. It was a reasonable budget for a first-time director but not enough to deal with the aspirations of the script, which included recreating Bobby Sands' funeral. There was a provision that the budget would increase if I attached another star. Both Johnny Depp and Angelica Huston came in and fell out just as quickly.

In the spring of 1996, we set up shop in Dublin, in Sheridan's Hell's Kitchen company offices, to make the film. Until then, the idea of a "hunger strike" film had evolved from a fantasy in my head to a dream sketched out on paper. Now I had to face up to the fact that here I was in Ireland, about to attempt a fictionalised dramatisation of the single most important and certainly the most emotional event that had occurred on that island in fifty years. And I had written the script without consulting any of the families, politicians or principal players in the political events of 1981. This made me very uneasy, but I kept asking myself, "Who should I talk to?"

I knew there was no chance of coming to an agreement with all the hunger strikers' families about a movie that had at its heart their very disagreement. There was even less chance of any sort of formal agreement with the political forces involved both inside and outside the republican movement. I had a strong supporter, Jim Sheridan, and a singular vision of what the film should be about – mothers and sons. This was no time to become "inclusive".

Still, I was acutely aware that I was in the business of recreating pain, violence, triumph and despair, for entertainment. At the end of the day, that's what films are – entertainment. You want people to pay money to come and see the story you are telling. If you don't work on that basis, you shouldn't be, and probably won't be, in the film business long. I happen to believe, along with most of my fellow Irish directors, that people will pay to be inspired, outraged, moved and educated. I believe that cinema-going audiences have a much broader definition of entertainment than Hollywood, or even European, studios have. I believed that many of the people involved in the events of 1981 wanted a film made. I knew for sure that people who were then within the republican movement wanted a film made, because they told me so – they also told Sheridan and me that *Some Mother's Son* was not the film they wanted made. We were asked, very politely, at a meeting in a hotel in Dublin, by representatives of the movement, to step aside so that a film written by some H-Block prisoners could be made. We, equally politely, declined, pointing out that the more movies made about the events of 1981, the better.

By now, the wonderful Fionnula Flanagan had not so much joined as elbowed, her way onto the cast – after a transatlantic screaming match over the phone where she assured me that if I cast anyone else in the role of Annie Higgins, I'd regret it. Aidan Gillen was cast to play Helen's character's son, and David O'Hara to play Fionnula's character's son. We picked Skerries, just outside Dublin, as the location for our fictional North Antrim seaside village. We converted a derelict building into an RUC station and imported Danny Devanney to paint authentic hunger-striker murals all around the town.

The film was shot in forty days. We filmed British army raids, white-line pickets, police station riots and midnight vigils in Skerries. We built a replica of a H-Block in a warehouse on the Quays in Dublin. And we recreated the Bobby Sands funeral on a bright Dublin Sunday, using some three thousand people whom we recruited by offering donations to charitable organisations and trade union groups. Many people showed up just to be in a film; others showed up because they hadn't seen the real funeral and wanted to see what it was like or wanted at least to be counted as having attended something that commemorated Bobby's sacrifice.

The problem with using volunteer recruits as extras for a film is that there is no incentive for them to remain once they discover how boring it is to be an extra. By afternoon, our crowd had dwindled to a few hundred. But we'd got the big crowd shots we needed, and, with digital enhancement, we were able to recreate a little of the enormity of the day. However, the recreation of the funerals and the riots was secondary to the main focus of the film, and that was to capture the terrible dilemma faced by the families.

On that front, no director has been more nobly served. Helen Mirren and Fionnula Flanagan brought all their acting skills and spirit to the roles. The final scenes, where one mother saves her son and another lets her son continue until death, are heart-breakingly real. We wrapped the film just before Christmas 1995. There had been an IRA ceasefire in place throughout the film shoot, which gave the impression that we were all stepping back from a historical event and reflecting on it.

Three months later, we all gathered again in London to shoot a couple of extra scenes that we felt would help clarify the political machinations that went on toward the end of the hunger strike. But the atmosphere had changed. A few weeks earlier, the IRA had called off the ceasefire and planted a massive bomb in the docklands area of east London. The cast and crew were jittery and uncomfortable. Everyone was anxious to get our work done and get out of there before something else happened.

Some Mother's Son had its world premiere at the Cannes Film Festival, in a section called *Un Certain Regard*. I had a boisterous shouting match with the *London Standard* film critic, Alexander Walker, who had made attacking films about the Troubles his party piece. According to the official speak in Cannes, it was "well received". The press reviews were mixed: the Brit press generally denounced it as IRA propaganda; the Europeans seemed to like the film. The Americans didn't know what to make of it. We had two premieres in Ireland. In Dublin, I had another shouting match with the film critic from the *Irish Independent*. In Belfast, we arranged a screening in Andersonstown. Several relatives of hunger strikers and many ex-prisoners came along, and many of them appeared deeply moved by the film.

In America, the film distributor, Castle Rock, decided to open *Some Mother's Son* on Christmas Day. The date isn't as crazy as it sounds. The hope is to get Oscar nominations and attract critical and press attention to the film. All four of the serious films I've been involved in, *Father, Mother, Hotel Rwanda* and *The Boxer*, have opened during Christmas week. Twice, the strategy has worked; twice it hasn't.

Some Mother's Son never made it into more than thirty cinemas across the United States. It made less than $1 million at the box office and was gone by the end of January. The world-wide box office was slightly better. We did well in Ireland and in southern (Catholic) Europe. You can still buy the film on video. It has yet to come out on DVD. Castle Rock took a hit, but nothing like the $100 million hit they took soon after on Eddie Murphy's *Pluto Nash*, which basically sank the company.

I saw the film again recently at a Boston event honouring Fionnula Flanagan. I watched a good portion of it. I hadn't seen it in ten years, but on watching it again, I'm very proud of it. Some of the direction makes me cringe, but the lead actors, Helen, Fionnula, David and Aidan, control the screen, and the story will always tear me apart because, even though it's fictional, it contains a greater truth, a distillation, a small part of the pain felt by ordinary decent mothers as they watched their sons die.

I hope that, in one hundred years time, schoolchildren might be able to watch the film and feel that they are inside the world of Kathleen Quigley and Annie Higgins. I think it will help them understand what those ten families and the families who took their sons off the hunger strike, and the families across Ireland, North and South, went through in that momentous year.

Today, as I look back across an ocean and twenty-five years to Belfast in 1981, the final significant line of *Some Mother's Son*, spoken by Fionnula's character, Annie Higgins, after her son's death, sums up my feelings about that year and my ability to look back and reflect on it.

"Oh, Annie," says Kathleen Quigley. "I'm so sorry. I took Gerard off."

"Somebody had to do it," replies Annie Higgins. "*You're lucky you had the choice.*"

WRITING *TEN MEN DEAD*
David Beresford, journalist

"THERE IS NO NEED TO FASTEN A BELL TO A FOOL," GOES A DANISH
proverb. And, thinking back on it, I dropped enough clangers to
let them know I was coming.

It must have been in 1976 that I had my first taste of Ireland.
It was love at first sight. Like falling in love with a gypsy woman,
I suppose. I did not begin to understand her, but the passion
could not be denied. I was a South African foreign correspondent, working for what was then the biggest newspaper group in
the southern hemisphere (before Tony O'Reilly got his claws into
it). I'd flown to Dublin, planning to take a train ride north to
Belfast the next day.

But the next morning, I was told there was a bomb on the railway line and trains to Belfast were cancelled. Not to worry, I was
reassured, this often happened, and all I had to do was take a bus
to Derry, then I could catch a train from there to Belfast. So that
was what I did, finding Derry railway station looking like bombed-
out Berlin at the end of the war. But it seemed that life continued as normal there. And my train to Belfast would be departing
in about an hour, as scheduled.

Determined to play the foreign correspondent, without
further ado, I inquired of a gnarled old porter sweeping the platform as to where I could find the nearest working telephone.

"Who do you want to phone?" he asked.

"A taxi," I said.

"Where do you want to go to?"

I waved my hand in a vague sort of way, "Oh, around."

He led me to a phone booth and offered to make the call. I

thought that most gentlemanly and handed him some coins. After several calls and muttered conversations, he turned to me and said, "Sorry. Taxis are all taken."

"Here. Let me speak to them," I said, reaching for the phone which he reluctantly surrendered. Adopting a plummy, pommy accent, which white South Africans in those times used to mistake for the voice of authority, I made a short speech, declaring the need of the good people of Derry to get their public relations in order if they wanted the world to know the truth of their fair city.

"Hello," I said, assuming the silence was a tribute to my blarney.

"Wait outside. We'll pick you up in five minutes," said a voice.

"They're coming," I announced triumphantly to the big-eyed porter, placing the phone back on the cradle with proud aplomb.

As I waited outside, I pondered momentarily as to why taxi drivers in this part of the world used the collective pronoun. I didn't have to wait long. An unmarked sedan pulled up.

"Where d'ya want to go?" asked the driver.

"Derry?" I hazarded.

"The Bogside?"

"Is it near by?" I asked, envisaging a town some distance away and worried about my train.

"Right under the city wall," he assured me, cheerily.

As we drove around the Bogside, it quickly became apparent that my driver knew his way, giving a running commentary on who had been shot on that street corner last Thursday, who had been hit by a sniper up there on the wall on Friday and the wee young girl killed just there by a rubber bullet.

Warned by people in Dublin never to ask a man his religion in the North, I asked cunningly, "Do you feel safe around here?"

"Oh, aye. I live here," he said, waving nonchalantly to a group of men on a sidewalk. They waved back enthusiastically.

The car pulled up.

"See the soldier looking at you?" said the driver. I stared back in horror. It was the first time anyone had pointed a firearm at me! The soldier was obviously trying to identify me with his telescopic sight, but that seemed no excuse for the breach of bushveld lore drummed into me from childhood: "Don't point guns."

As we pulled up at the skeletal Derry railway station, I asked the driver how much I owed him.

"Nothing," he chuckled. "This isn't a taxi, you know."

"What do you mean?"

"We get a bit worried when a man with an English accent phones up and wants a tour of Derry." With a wave, he accelerated away.

A couple of years later I was back in Ireland, this time as the *Guardian*'s Belfast correspondent.

"What's a South African doing in Ulster?" asked the Ulster Unionist Euro MP, John Taylor, when I was introduced to him at a *Fortnight* party.

"Oh, I feel at home here."

"What do you mean?" he demanded.

"Well, you've got partition and we've got Bantustans."

It wasn't the way to make friends, particularly unionist friends, and to some it might seem oversimplistic, but "the joy" of the Irish conflict to me, as a writer, a reporter and a commentator, was that it was so simple, and the parallels with South Africa so obvious. The Irish border was a gerrymander in just the same way as the "historic" borders of the Bantustans. To me, both of them were nothing more than wishful thinking by politicians who had found themselves on the wrong side of history.

I could feel a twinge of sympathy for the unionists, fighting for their lost cause, just as I did for the Voortrekkers who had fled British imperialism and, when cornered, fought the British army to a standstill. But that feat of arms no more justified apartheid than Lambeg drums justified Protestant rule.

Some of the parallels were eye-openers even to me, when I discovered them.

In South Africa, for example, we (the liberal, opposition press) often used to cite the example of the unarmed British bobby as the epitome of civilised policing. It was startling to realise that the equivalent force in Northern Ireland, the RUC, was carrying out roadside executions (shoot-to-kill) comparable in their cynicism, if not in viciousness, to the political murders of the South African security services.

Such perspectives were, of course, anathema in the eyes of most British newspapers. But I was blessed in my employment by the *Guardian,* a newspaper which was, at times, quite prepared to run an editorial taking one position on Ireland and a piece by me, on the opposite page, arguing the contrary.

So, I felt I was well positioned when the major story of my Irish posting broke, with the hunger strikes. Again, we had to deal with some wishful thinking on the part of politicians, notably from Mrs Thatcher, such as her claims that the hunger strikers had been "ordered" to die and that there was an IRA plot to burn down the Short Strand in Belfast.

But, ludicrous though such claims might be, there were end-less, unanswered questions surrounding the hunger strike by the time it ended. And it was with eagerness that I waited for the emergence of a book answering them, a book that some Irish writer, assuredly, must be busy finishing. Somebody like Tim Pat Coogan, whose *On the Blanket,* an account of the run-up to the hunger strike, had been an Irish bestseller.

Eagerness changed to impatience. "Why can't I do it?" I asked myself as the months passed without sign of such a book. I had never written a book, but one has to start somewhere. Eventually I decided to go for it, making an approach to Sinn Féin, asking for help in getting co-operation from the IRA, which I assumed would be my main obstacle.

My pitch was a simple one: unless Thatcher was right and the IRA had ordered the hunger strikers to their death, which was clearly ludicrous, they had nothing to lose and lots to gain from such a book. I said I was prepared to submit the final manuscript to them, for checks on possible inaccuracies, and they could make representations to me as to any objections they had. But the final decisions were mine, and they would have no veto.

To my surprise, I was promptly given a go-ahead.

"If you're going to do a book on the hunger strike, you'll need the comms," Tom Hartley of Sinn Féin observed one day. I knew what a comm was – a message written by prisoners on a cigarette paper and smuggled out on visits – because one or two reports in the local papers had described how the prisoners used them to communicate with the external leadership. But I had not appreciated the extraordinary number of them, or that the IRA had kept them. So I duly sent a message asking for access to the comms.

I remember the day clearly. It was winter and freezing cold, with slushy snow and ice on the pavements. I had been told to wait in a West Belfast safe house. I had an Epson PX8 with me, one of the early laptop computers, with a screen of about twelve lines and a built-in mini-cassette recorder as a primitive hard drive.

There was a bustle at the front door, and in walked Danny Morrison from Sinn Féin, with shopping bags stuffed full of screwed-up comms. As I began unscrumpling them in an upstairs bedroom, I realised I had been given a writer's gold mine. I had assumed the comms would be little more than military-style reports and commands, but in fact they contained the writers' most private thoughts, confided to close comrades. Everything seemed to be there, down to a nightmare dreamed by Brendan

McFarlane, officer commanding IRA prisoners, the night before, as they waited helplessly for Bobby Sands to die.

I had been warned that I could have only a limited time with the material. I was then a fast touch typist, and my half-frozen fingers started flying over the little PX8 keyboard as I tried frantically to get it all down, verbatim.

As I read them, I realised there were a couple of holes. I had been told, quite frankly, that some comms would probably be kept from me, as being "just too sensitive". By placing what I did have in chronological order, I quickly found out where the sensitive areas lay: the collapse of the first hunger strike at the end of 1980, and the initiative of the (Catholic) Irish Commission for Justice and Peace during the second.

By the time the book was published, I had the details of the missing areas, showing that Mrs Thatcher had lied when she had made her often-repeated statement that her government "does not talk to terrorists".

My publisher was Grafton (a subsidiary of HarperCollins), which is now defunct. I had received only a nominal advance and now, inspired by my good fortune, I decided I needed some more money to cover costs. The *Guardian* had asked me to open a bureau in Johannesburg. South Africa was beginning to burn, and the posting was one I could not turn down. The editor, Peter Preston, had given me two months' paid leave to finish the book. Now, I just needed a couple of hundred pounds so I could buy a second-hand jalopy to rush around Northern Ireland in search of the interviews I would need.

Highly excited at my good fortune with the comms, I could hardly wait to boast of it to my young editor at Grafton. I phoned and made an appointment, little realising that my biggest problem with the book would be more with Grafton – the very people who would share my good fortune – than with the *Guardian* or, for that matter, the IRA.

My young editor did not turn up for the meeting. Instead, there were two senior editors, looking grave. After the introductions, I excitedly told them what I had got, showing them some of the transcripts. They just looked at me po-faced. I could not understand their lack of enthusiasm. After all, this was the "age of terrorism". The IRA was the oldest and most sophisticated "terrorist organisation" in the world. The book was not only the story of what was probably the most serious crisis in that organisation's history, but the comms, which stood no comparison in the annals of prison literature, gave an unprecedented insight into their thinking during that crisis. And here were these men looking at me po-faced!

The enthusiasm was lacking, but at least the money was not. I bought an old Peugeot and wrote the book, beginning it in London and finishing it in South Africa.

I was having a celebratory glass of champagne with my cousin, Robert Nugent, in the garden of his Johannesburg home, when the courier arrived to take the completed manuscript. Bob was a barrister (he is now a judge of appeal), and he had earlier cast a professional eye over my contract with Grafton, suggesting I include a clause by which if the book was ever put of print for more than three months, the copyright would revert to me.

Newspapers are, of course, part of the publishing industry. As a journalist and something of a long-time bookworm, I had strong opinions as to how a book should be marketed, at least in its packaging, and had conveyed those opinions both to my London agent and to Grafton. Most of it was self-evident. The biggest marketing problem we faced was that the Irish hunger strike had been given saturation coverage by the media at the time. The public was sure to be tired of the subject, even though publication of the book was coming five years after the event.

There should be nothing on the front or back covers to evoke press coverage of the hunger strike, I begged them. No text describing it as the story of the 1981 hunger strike. No clichéd press photographs as the cover design, no aerial shot of the prison, no picture of alienated youths tossing petrol bombs at army or police forts.

I spent hours crafting a short blurb for the back cover, stressing the unique nature of the comms. And *Ten Men Dead*, which I feared was reminiscent of the childhood rhyme, was a working title only, I stressed. I would come up with a better one.

No prizes for guessing what the published book looked like. "It's too late," came the answer when I offered a new title. *Dead Faces Laugh* was my choice, the last line from a Yeats play about a hunger strike.

The front cover was an aerial shot of the H-Blocks. Slashed across it was "The Story of the 1981 Hunger Strike". The blurb on the back might have been designed to persuade would-be buyers that they had read it all before.

Shortly before publication, I had been told the print run would be 10,000. I had protested strongly that the book would sell at least five times that.

"It's a question of warehouse space," said Grafton, reassuring me that a new run could be printed in a matter of days.

The *Guardian,* as ever, did me proud, taking out a full-page advert in the *Observer* to launch the book, and running a four-part serialisation, kicking off with the disclosure that Mrs Thatcher's government had engaged in negotiations with the IRA during both the 1980 and the 1981 hunger strikes.

The book leapt into the London and Irish bestseller lists and was sold out in three days. Grafton, it transpired, had printed only 5,000. It took several months for them to do a reprint. Subsequently, I was invited to a Grafton boardroom lunch so the publishing house could "apologise" to me. During the lunch, I challenged the managing director. I could forgive the title and everything else on the front cover, but I just could not understand why they had ignored my carefully wrought blurb for the back, in favour of the boring, platitudinous rubbish they had used.

"Ah yes, the blurb," he said. "It was written by a committee." He refused to say any more on the subject.

He did, however, make another remark which I was to recall years later.

"There are some books," he said, "which become underground classics and do unexpectedly well, continuing to sell for years after publication. This book could turn out to be one of them." He had got at least one thing right. Twenty-five years after the hunger strike, *Ten Men Dead* is still in print and selling strongly.

But my frustration in the early years of the book's life was intense, in the face of what I saw as the complete failure by Grafton to market the book. A hundred copies did make it to South Africa, but the marketing manager of the local distributors locked them away in his safe on the grounds that it was about the IRA and therefore "subversive".

Although I was by now based in South Africa, I used to spend as much of my spare time as I could in London, where my girl-friend, Ellen, and our baby son, Joris, lived in Fulham. Just around the corner, there was a local branch of WH Smith. The manager of the shop had tired of my persistent complaint that they did not stock *Ten Men Dead,* and one day he announced he was bringing in three copies, "just to see how it sells".

Every morning I would pop around to buy the *Guardian* and to check how the sales of my book were doing. The sales attendants insisted on placing them in the "history" section, on the bottom shelf. So I would replace them on the "bestselling" shelf at eye level, usually on top of the latest Jilly Cooper blockbuster, featuring a woman's backside, erotically clad in the tightest possible jodhpurs.

Two of the copies of *Ten Men Dead* had sold and they were

down to one when I walked into the shop one morning and did my usual job of rearranging before standing in the queue, clutching my copy of the morning newspaper. Suddenly, to my astonishment, I heard two hefty and dusty Irish navvies in vests, obviously from some nearby building site, ask the manager for a copy of *Ten Men Dead.*

"You're in luck we've got just one copy left," said the manager, reaching down to the history section. "Stuuuuh . . . I'm sorry, it looks like we're sold out."

"No, no," I cried. "There it is, there it is," pointing to where the book stood proudly in the bestseller section.

"That's it!" said one of them, grabbing it. As they paid and headed for the exit, my pride of authorship became too much for me.

"Do you like that book?" I asked. They looked at me as if I was bats. "You know, I wrote it," I said with a big smile. The two of them hurried out the door, throwing anxious looks over their shoulders as they went.

Watching through WH Smith's plate-glass window as they walked up the street, I thought: *Hell, it was worth it.*

I hesitate in my writing, recognising the ambiguity. Was what worth it?

I met Bobby Sands. He was the only one of the hunger strikers I did meet. I went in on a visit on the third day of his fast. Being a journalist and having an eye on an intro, my first question was, "Do you think you will die on this fast?" I had been asked to take in some cigarettes for him, and he was lighting one. He paused, said, "Yes, I think I will", and took a pull on his cigarette. I'm not sure who started it, but we both chuckled at the incongruity of the answer as the cigarette smoke spiralled upwards.

I did see him again, but then he was dead in his coffin at the house in Twinbrook Estate. As I looked at his waxen face, I was struck again by the incongruity.

I love Ireland, my memories of it, but I am not an Irishman, an Irish nationalist, or an Irish republican. I guess I just don't hold to man-made borders and division,s whether they are in Ireland or South Africa. So I cannot assess whether it was "worth it" in terms of the "five demands", or even constitutional change. Instead, I am driven to use the words of W.B. Yeats with which I concluded *Ten Men Dead*:

> When I and these are dead
> We should be carried to some windy hill
> To lie there with uncovered face a while
> That mankind and that leper there may know
> Dead faces laugh. King! King! Dead faces laugh.

THE YEAR '81
By Mícheál Mac Donncha, Writer, activist

I WENT TO PRIMARY SCHOOL AND SPENT MUCH OF MY CHILDHOOD AND youth in Howth, County Dublin, my father's home place. I walked that hill countless times and on clear days you can see all the way northwards over the Irish Sea where the Mountains of Mourne in County Down stand out on the horizon. Yet for many of us as young people in Dublin in the 1970s, the North was less a part of our island than a distant place of darkness and violence.

The term used in those days was 'men of violence', rather than 'terrorists'. I knew no-one from a northern nationalist or republican background and there were no family connections there. So we relied on radio, television and the newspapers for our scant knowledge of the euphemistically named Troubles, brought about, we were told, by 'men of violence'. For most people it was literally a turn-off. But for anyone, like myself, with an interest in Irish history, it raised many troubling questions, because, not far beneath the surface all around us were reminders of our republican past, including armed struggle.

A friend of my father whom we often visited was a Howth woman called Fanny Cooney. She was an Irish speaker and a veteran of Cumann na mBan who had been active throughout the 1916-22 period. She whetted my appetite for Irish history, though initially at least, my weak school Irish did not equip me to understand the conversations she tried to start with me. I read a lot of history and in 1979, the centenary of PH Pearse's birth, I read all his republished writings. Still, there seemed to be little connection with what was happening in the Six Counties. Then, in 1980 the first protest demonstration that I ever attended was one organised by Conradh na Gaeilge calling for more Irish language programmes on RTÉ television. I bought a Conradh magazine and inside was an article on the H-Blocks of Long Kesh. I had seen H-Block slogans on walls around Dublin but did not know what they meant.

Shortly after this the first H-Block hunger strike began. It was during the second strike that I first attended a H-Block protest and the very first issue of An Phoblacht /Republican News that I bought was the one that reported the death and funeral of Bobby Sands. In a few months I received the political education of a lifetime. The gap in history as taught to us in school, from the 'foundation of the State' in 1922 to the present was filled. I became aware for the first time that the television and radio news was censored under Section 31 of the Broadcasting Act and Sinn Féin and republican voices in general – even in the form of rebel songs – were banned from the airwaves.

What made the most impact, of course, was the heroism and sacrifice of Bobby Sands and his comrades. There in Bobby's writing was encapsulated both the republican tradition that had endured long after 1922 and the experience of nationalists in the Six Counties under the Orange state right up to the obscenity of the H-Blocks. How could anyone argue that the sacrifice of Terence Mac Swiney, IRA Volunteer, elected representative and martyred hunger striker in October 1920, was any different from that of Bobby Sands, IRA Volunteer, elected representative and martyred hunger striker in May 1981?

I had formed this view strongly, even though I was still at the edge of the crowd at H-Block protests and marches, including the one that ended in the British Embassy riot in August 1981. The succession of ten agonising deaths was appalling. The apathy among so many people in Dublin was infuriating. But the sense of solidarity among activists – none of whom I knew at that stage – was obvious even from the outside. In 1982 I joined Sinn Féin in UCD and soon I was meeting former prisoners who had known Bobby Sands and his nine comrades. After that, there was no turning back politically for me.

I tried a few times to write a song or poem about the hunger strike but strangely it was only when I was a good bit older than Bobby Sands was when he died that I finally finished this one. I think it was the sense that he was so young, something that only really hits you when you are older.

THE YEAR '81

(Air: *The May Morning Dew*)

How well I remember the year '81
The words that were spoken, the deeds that were done
From the depths of the prison, a voice clear and true
And we listened with wonder young Bobby to you.

Long years of torture, long years of pain
Then your portrait was carried through the streets in the rain
You wrote words of freedom, the lark in the blue
And we vowed to be faithful young Bobby to you.

The Tyrant for answer would only say 'No'
Blind to all reason while bitter tears flowed
You hungered for justice and what could we do
But march and keep vigil young Bobby for you.

Long was the silence of those who stood by
Loud were the voices who broadcast the Lie
But sweet was the music of hearts brave and true
Who sang through the darkness young Bobby for you.

The news of your passing that morning in May
Rang like a bell through the world in a day
You showed what a fighter for freedom could do
And we pledged to march onward young Bobby for you.

With your comrades your body lies cold in Milltown
With McCracken your spirit from the Cave Hill looks down
With the laughter of children this land we'll renew
In the nation we're building young Bobby for you.

DEICHNIÚR

Deasún Breatnach

Sinne a d'éalaigh ón gcarcair
trí gheataí an bhásocrais:
glinne ga ár solais
ná tóirsholas na Corónach;
buaine ár ndaonnacht
ná claoine ár gcuid naimhde,
is fágann muid agaibh san uacht anois
sciath an mhisnigh mar chosaint,
ocras na córa mar shéadchomhartha,
agus, mar ortha, deichniúr an phaidrín;
Roibeard Ó Sandair, Pronnsias Mag
Aoidh, Peatsí Ó hEara, Taimí Mac
Giolla Bhuí, Caoimhín Ó Loinnsigh,
Ciarán Ó Dochartaigh, Seóaí Mac
Domhnaill, Mícheál Ó Duibhinn,
Máirtín Mac Ursain agus Réamoinn Mac Raois.

TEN

Deasún Breatnach

We who escaped from jail
through the gates of the death fast:
Brighter our light say
than the searchlight of the Crown;
more lasting our humanity
than the perversion of our enemy,
and today we bequeath to you, in our will,
the blade of courage as defence,
the hunger for justice as monument,
and, as prayer, a decade of the rosary:
their unforgettable names:
Bobby Sands, Francis Hughes, Patsy O'Hara, Raymond
McCreesh, Joe McDonnell, Martin Hurson, Kevin Lynch,
Kieran Doherty, Thomas McElwee, and Micky Devine.

Robert Ballagh was born in Dublin. His artwork is represented in many important collections including the National Gallery of Ireland, the Irish Museum of Modern Art, the Crawford Municipal Gallery, Cork, the Hugh Lane Municipal Gallery Dublin, the Ulster Museum and the Albrecht Durer House, Nuremberg. He has produced book covers, posters, limited editions, over 70 stamps for the Irish postal service and the last Irish banknotes produced by the Central Bank of Ireland. He designed the imagery and set for 'Riverdance' and the staging for the opening ceremony of the Special Olympics in Croke Park, Dublin. He is a member of Aosdána. In 1991 he was elected chairperson of the national organising committee for the celebration of the 75th anniversary of the 1916 rising. He is also one of the founders of "Le Chéile – artists against racism in Ireland". His autobiography, *A Reluctant Memoir*, was published in 2018.

Tony Benn was born in London in 1925, the son, grandson and father of MPs. He was the longest serving Labour MP in the history of his party and served as a cabinet minister in two Labour governments. He was a long-time supporter of Irish unity. He retired from the House of Commons in May 2001, after fifty years in Parliament. His *Diaries* have been published in several volumes. He also wrote a number of books, including *Arguments for Socialism*. He was a leading figure in the British opposition to the war on Iraq. Tony Benn died in March 2014, a month before his 89th birthday.

Ronan Bennett is the author several novels, including *The Catastrophist* and *Havoc, in Its Third Year*, which won the Hughes & Hughes Irish Novel of the Year (2005). His screenplays include *Rebel Heart* (BBC, 2001) and *The Hamburg Cell* (2004), which was nominated for an International Emmy. He is a regular contributor to *The Guardian* and *The Observer*. His recent work includes the feature film *Gunpowder* (2017), television series *Top Boy* (2011) and *Undisclosed, Hidden* (2011), and the film *Public Enemies* (2009). He was in Long Kesh from 1974-76 and Brixton Prison 1978-79.

South African born **David Beresford** was a distinguished journalist who was the *Guardian's* Irish correspondent in the early 1980s. He was twice voted International Reporter of the Year. David Beresford moved on from Ireland to cover the townships' rebellion in South Africa, the release of Nelson Mandela and the political settlement which led to majority rule. *Ten Men Dead* was published in 1986 and is still in print. In 1991, while covering the Gulf War for the *Guardian*, David developed symptoms of what was to be diagnosed as Parkinson's disease. He was *The Observer's* correspondent in Johannesburg when he died in 2016.

Senator **Frances Black** is an Independent Senator and is currently a member of the Joint Committee on Justice and Equality, the Seanad Special Select Committee on the Withdrawal of the UK from the EU and the Committee on the Implementation of the Good Friday Agreement. She is also a singer and founder of the RISE Foundation, a charitable organisation working with people with a loved one in addiction. A strong advocate for social justice and equality, Frances was elected to the 25th Seanad in 2016, the first female Independent from the Seanad's panel system in the history of the state. Senator Black is passionate about being a voice for the vulnerable, and continues to work with organisations in the voluntary and charitable sectors alongside her work in Seanad Éireann.

Deasún Breatnach was born in Dublin in 1921. He was a former editor of *An Phoblacht* (1974-'79), author of ten books, spent his active life in journalism as freelance, reporter, sub-editor and contributor, at home and abroad. The poem published here is from his book of poetry, *Dánta Amadóra'*, in a translation by the author. Deasún died in Dublin in 2007.

Anne Cadwallader, has worked for BBC Belfast, RTÉ, *The Irish Press, Ireland on Sunday, The New York Times, The Irish Echo, Reuters* and *The Christian Science Monitor*. She wrote *Holy Cross - The Untold Story* and *Lethal Allies: British Collusion in Ireland* upon which the documentary film *Unquiet Graves: The Story of the Glenanne Gang* is based. She is an Advocacy Case Worker with The Pat Finucane Centre.

Owen Carron was born in Macken, County Fermanagh. He had been a schoolteacher at the time of the blanket protest and joined the National H-Block/Armagh Committee. In April 1981 he became Bobby Sands' election agent. After British PM Margaret Thatcher amended the Representation of the People Act, barring prisoners for standing for election, Owen stood in the by-election after Bobby's death and became MP for Fermanagh and South Tyrone. Owen was also elected to the Northern Ireland Assembly in October 1982. In 1986 he was arrested and charged with possession of a rifle in Fermanagh. He jumped bail and spent two years on the run before being arrested in the Republic of Ireland. He served two and a half years in prison before the Supreme Court ruled that the British extradition warrant served on him was for a political offence and he was released. Despite the Belfast Agreement and early prison releases the British government is still seeking to prosecute Carron (and Rita O'Hare). Owen returned to teaching but retired in 2014 due to health grounds. Currently a hobby farmer and part-time voluntary teacher of Gaeilge, Owen lives in County Leitrim with his wife Siobhán, dog Cheeky and cat Miawsalot. They have four grown up children and five grandchildren.

Sorj Chalandon is an award-winning French writer and journalist who from 1973 until 2007 worked as a journalist on *Libération*, covering events in Lebanon, Iran, Iraq, Somalia, Afghanistan and Ireland. His books include *Une promesse* (2006), *My Traitor* (2008) and *Return to Killybegs* (2011) which won the Grand Prix du roman de l'Académie française and was shortlisted for the Prix Goncourt.

Jude Collins is a retired university lecturer and well-known broadcaster and commentator. He has written two short story collections (*Booing the Bishop* and *Only Human*), two novels (*The Garden of Eden All Over Again* and *Leave of Absence*) *and* four interview collections (*Tales Out of School, Whose Past Is It Anyway?*; *Martin McGuinness; The Man I Knew*, and *Laying It On The Line: The Border and Brexit* (2019).

Shane Connaughton trained as an actor at Bristol Old Vic Theatre School. He is a playwright, screenwriter and novelist. He is the winner of the George Devine Award 1971; the Hennessy Award 1985; London *Irish Post* Community Award 1987. He appeared in Mike Leigh's film *Four Days in July,* set in Belfast, He wrote: *The Dollar Bottom* (Oscar best live action short, 1980); *My Left Foot,* nominated for an Academy Award, 1990; *The Playboys,* and *The Run of the Country.* His best-selling novel, *A Border Station* was short-listed for the GPA Award (1989). Other books: *The Run of the Country; A Border Diary; Married Quarters.* He has adapted for the screen novels by Patrick McGinley (*Bogmail*), Colm Tóibín (*The Blackwater Lightship*) and Maeve Binchy (*Tara Road*).

Mary Doyle lost remission as a result of her protest in Armagh Prison and had to serve an extra two years in jail. In Crumlin Road Prison in 1989 she married former IRA escapee and blanket man Terence (Cleaky) Clarke. When she was eight months pregnant with their first child, Marie, Terence had been arrested and held on remand for six months. Their second child, Seamus, was born when Terence was in jail again, serving six years. In the H-Blocks, Terence was diagnosed with cancer. He died in June 2000. From 2011 until 2019 Mary was a Belfast City councillor for Sinn Féin and currently works in the party's constituency office in north Belfast.

Frank Durkan was a partner in the law firm of O'Dwyer & Bernstien, LLP, which represented many persons who encountered difficulties with American law by virtue of their interest in the 'Northern Ireland Question'. Included among their clients have been the late Joe Cahill and Desmond Mackin, prominent member of Sinn Féin. Frank died in Greenwich, Connecticut, in 2006.

Biographies

Terry George, from the Short Strand area of Belfast, is an Irish screenwriter and director. He has been nominated twice for Academy Awards, for *In the Name of the Father* and *Hotel Rwanda.* He was named Young European Director of the Year in 1996 for *Some Mother's Son.* His film *The Shore* won the Academy Award for best Live Action Short Film in 2012. He also wrote and directed *The Promise*, set during the Armenian Genocide of 1915. Terry and his wife Rita Higgins spend their time between their homes in County Down and New York.

Michelle Gildernew served as Sinn Féin MP for Fermanagh and South Tyrone from 2001-2015, a position she again held after the 2017 Westminster election. She also served as Minister for Agriculture and Rural Development in the power-sharing northern executive. Her parents, grandmother and others highlighted the blatant sectarian discrimination in housing a squatting protest in Caledon in 1968, which culminated in their eviction, and added impetus to the embryonic Civil Rights Movement.

Roy Greenslade is a Visiting Honorary Professor at City, University of London, and a writer and broadcaster on media matters. In his fifty-five-year career as a journalist, he has worked for most of Britain's national newspapers, notably as editor of the *Daily Mirror* (1990–91) and as a columnist for the *Guardian* (1992–2019). He is the author of three books, including a best-selling biography of the late press tycoon Robert Maxwell. His most recent book is a history of British newspapers, *Press Gang: How Newspapers Make Profits from Propaganda.* He divides his year between Brighton and County Donegal.

Tom Hayden was an activist and prolific author who wrote about US society and politics, war, the environment, and was passionate about Ireland in his two works, *Irish Hunger* (1997) and *Irish on the Inside* (2001). As a former California state senator, he passed legislation incorporating the Great Hunger into the public school curriculum used by 500,000 students, and co-authored California's Mac Bride Principles. He was an advisor to the late US Commerce Secretary Charles Meissner during his economic mission to Ireland in 1997.

Tom's final book, *Hell No – The Forgotten Power of the Vietnam Peace Movement*, was published after his death at the age of 76, in 2016, following a lengthy illness, including a stroke.

David Lloyd, Professor of English at the University of Southern California, is the author of *Nationalism and Minor Literature* (1987); *Anomalous States* (1993); and *Ireland After History* (2000). He has co-published several other books, including *Culture and the State*, co-authored with Paul Thomas (1997); *The Politics of Culture in the Shadow of Capital* (1997), with Lisa Lowe; and *The Nature and Context of Minority Discourse* (1991), with Abdul Jan Mohamed. His *Irish Times: Temporalities of Modernity* was published in 2008.

Ken Loach was born in Nuneaton, England, in 1936. His directorial work for television from the early 1960s has included *Z Cars, Cathy Come Home* and a series of stylistically ambitious films for *The Wednesday Play*. His films include *Kes, Hidden Agenda* (about the RUC's shoot-to-kill policy), *Land and Freedom* (the Spanish Civil War), and *Carla's Song* (about Nicaragua). *The Wind That Shakes the Barley*, a historical drama set during the Tan War and Civil War, won the Palme d'Or at the 2006 Cannes Film Festival, as did his film, *I, Daniel Blake* in 2016.

Mícheál Mac Donncha is a former Ardmhéara/Lord Mayor of Dublin (2017-2018) and is a Dublin City Councillor for Sinn Féin. He is the author of a centenary history of Sinn Féin *A Century of Struggle* (2005), and of numerous articles on political and historical subjects in Irish and English in *An Phoblacht*, of which he was editor (1990-1996) and other journals.

Eugene McCabe was born in Glasgow in 1930 of Irish parents. He has written novels, short stories, stage plays and television drama. His trilogy of plays on the differing traditions in the conflict was titled *Victims* and was filmed by RTÉ. About it he said: "The overall theme is, of course, the futility of violence. It does also show that there is an underlying cause for violence but it proffers no solution and there is no message." *Cancer,* part of the trilogy, won the Writers Award in Prague, and *Heritage* the second prize in the Prix Italia. His 1992 novel, *Death and Nightingales* was critically acclaimed and was adapted for television as a historical drama, broadcasted in 2018. A member of Aosdána, he lives and farms in Monaghan.

John Montague was born in Brooklyn, New York, and reared on the family farm in County Tyrone. His major publications include *Death of a Chieftain* (stories); *The Rough Field*; *The Great Cloak*; *The Dead Kingdom* and *Mount Eagle*. *Collected Poems* appeared in 1995, the year he received the America Ireland Fund Literary Award. In 1998 he became the first Ireland Professor of Poetry. *Shadow* and *Sands* are from *Smashing the Piano*, Gallery Press, 1999. John died in Nice at the age of eighty-seven in 2016.

Marie Moore was a republican activist since her early teens. She joined the Civil Rights Movement in Belfast in the mid-sixties and Sinn Féin in the late sixties and was particularly close to Maire Drumm, the Vice-President of Sinn Féin who was assassinated in hospital in 1976. Maire herself was shot by a British army raiding party close to her home. In 1978 she, along with the Belfast executive of Sinn Féin and the editorial staff of *Republican News*, were remanded in custody on false charges which were eventually dropped the following year. Maire played a leading role in establishing and running a network of people who smuggled information and essential items into the prisoners on protest and hunger strike. From 2000-2001 she was the first Sinn Féin woman to be elected Deputy Mayor of Belfast City Council, on which she served as a councillor for thirteen years. Marie died in 2009 at the age of seventy-two.

During the 1981 hunger strikes **Danny Morrison,** Sinn Féin's then director of publicity, was a spokesperson for Bobby Sands. At Sinn Féin's annual conference (the ard fheis) in 1981 he called for the party to embrace electoral politics, coining the phrase which was to sum up the Republican Movement's dual strategy of progressing struggle with *"an Armalite in one hand and a ballot box in the other." A* former prisoner and member of the IRA he was elected to the Northern Assembly in 1982. He became a full-time writer in the late 1990s. His novels include: *West Belfast; On the Back of the Swallow; The Wrong Man*; and *Rudi*. He is also the author of three works of non-fiction, including, *Then The Walls Came Down*, based on his prison letters. He is secretary of the Bobby Sands Trust.

Edna O'Brien is an internationally acclaimed novelist. Born in County Clare, she moved to London in the 1950s. Her first book, *The Country Girls* (1960), led to instant fame and was banned in Ireland because of its sexual content. As well as writing over a dozen novels, she has also written short stories, plays and screenplays, and is a contributor to magazines such as the *New Yorker* and *Cosmopolitan*. She has received many awards, including that of the *Los Angeles Times;* Writers' Guild of Great Britain; European Literature Prize (1995); and the Italia Prima Cavour. In 2018 she was named as the winner of the PEN/Nabokov award for achievement in international literature. She is a member of Aosdána, and lives in London.

Timothy O'Grady was born in Chicago and has lived in Ireland, London, Spain and Poland. He is the author of four works of non-fiction and three novels. His novel *Motherland* won the David Higham award for the best first novel in 1989. His novel *I Could Read the Sky*, a collaboration with photographer Steve Pyke, won the Encore Award for best second novel of 1997. *I Could Read the Sky* was filmed and also travelled as a stage show. His most recent novel is *Light*, published in 2004. His non-fiction books are *Curious Journey: An Oral History of Ireland's Unfinished Revolution; On Golf* and *Divine Magnetic Lands*, an account of a return journey to the United States after thirty years of living in Europe, published in 2008. His book *Children of Las Vegas* was published in 2016.

Terry O'Sullivan is the General President of the Laborers' International Union of North America (LIUNA), a half-million-member trade union founded in 1903 by immigrants and other workers who rose up against abuse, exploitation, and discrimination. A proud descendant of Irish immigrants, O'Sullivan holds dual American and Irish citizenship, and works tirelessly to build bridges between the Irish and American labor movements. He is a vocal supporter of Sinn Féin, and serves as President of New York Friends of Ireland, and Chairman of DC Friends of Ireland.

Kevin Rafter is an Irish academic who has held senior editorial positions with the *Irish Times, Sunday Times* and *Magill* magazine. He is the author of numerous books on the media and politics, including biographies on *Martin Mansergh* (2002). His histories of Irish political parties include - *Clann na Poblachta* (1996); *Sinn Féin* (2005), *Democratic Left* (2010), and *Fine Gael* (2010).

Colm Scullion was imprisoned from 1976-82 for possession of explosives. When sent to the H-Blocks he immediately went on the blanket protest where he met Bobby Sands, the two men sharing a cell in H-3 for several months. It was his conversations with Colm that inspired Bobby to write the poem, *Rodaí Mac Corlaí*. Today, Colm lives in Ballyscullion, where he was born in 1958. A keen local historian and Gaeilgeoir, he regularly speaks to students of politics and history, academics and researchers, about the blanket protest and the hunger strike.

Anne Speed works with UNISON in Belfast. Anne has participated in political struggles as a feminist, a socialist and as a republican since the 1970s. A member of People's Democracy and Irish Women United in the 1970s and early 1980s she was active in campaigns to end the Twenty-Six-County ban on contraception and abortion, to promote workers and human rights and to oppose partition. Anne joined Sinn Féin in 1986 serving on the Sinn Féin Ard Comhairle and supporting the strategy which led to the Good Friday Agreement.

George Stagg's parents had strong connections to the IRA during the Tan War and the Civil War. George was the third youngest in a family of thirteen and was six years younger than Frank. In search of work he took the immigrant boat to England in 1966, working in various factories before qualifying as an electrical engineer and returning to Ireland. In England he was very close to Frank, socialising together and playing for the same football club in Coventry. Now retired, he remains a committed republican and activist, and faithful to his brother's memory.

Ann Zell was born in Idaho, USA, and eventually settled in West Belfast. She was a member of the Word of Mouth Poetry Collective and her work has been included in *The Word of Mouth Anthology* (Blackstaff Press, 1995); *The White Page* (Salmon, 2000); and the *Field Day Anthology Vol. V* (CUP 2003). *Anniversary March* is from *Weathering*, her first collection, published by Salmon Press, 1998. Ann died in Belfast in 2016.

Trisha Ziff lived in Derry between 1981-1986 establishing Derry Camerawork, returning to London as director of Network Photographers. She has curated many international exhibitions and edited books on photography. In 2008 she directed her first documentary, *Chevolution*. Others films, *The Mexican Suitcase* (2011), *The Man Who Saw Too Much* (2015), *Witkin & Witkin* (2017). She has an Ariel (Mexican Academy Award) for best documentary. In 2019 she became a Sundance recipient and is a member of Film Fatales, (women directors). She is developing a feature documentary about Gerry Adams for 2020. She lives in Mexico City and has a son, Julio.